Building democracy

Building democracy

*COMMUNITY ARCHITECTURE
IN THE INNER CITIES*

Graham Towers

UCL
PRESS

First published in 1995 by UCL Press.

UCL Press Limited
University College London
Gower Street
London WC1E 6BT

The name of University College London (UCL) is a registered trade mark
used by UCL Press with the consent of the owner.

ISBNs: 1-85728-088-1 HB
        1-85728-089-X PB

British Library Cataloguing in Publication Data
A catalogue record for this book is available from the British Library.

Typeset in Bembo and Gill Sans.
Printed and bound by
Biddles Ltd, King's Lynn and Guildford, England.

CONTENTS

FOREWORD
Rod Hackney

Graham Towers has great faith in community architecture. This personal testament is his story of how a few architects, sometimes forgotten, sometimes alone, are struggling to provide a worthwhile service to the thousands of people entrapped by a system that cares little for community and even less for architecture.

Although Towers is new to publishing, with this work he has filled a niche that needed to be filled, between the distorted figures provided by quangos and government of how well statistically Britain is faring in the provision of housing numbers, and the stark reality of the growing need for caring professionals in the building world to provide an affordable service for those in desperate environmental need.

He sees through the so-called glamour of the headline grabbers, including developers who see much mileage in calling their (otherwise speculative) schemes community architecture, a term that will guarantee them a better hearing in front of the planning committees.

He dispels the overt credits given to a movement heralded by monarchy and fêted by sycophants. Community architecture is a daunting task, yet inevitably satisfying, having often achieved remarkable results.

Community architecture is hard work. The majority of those who practice it do so without much recognition, and yet those who persist and succeed trigger a tremendous rich vein of enthusiasm that gets things done. Towers credits many through the fine case study analyses at the end of most chapters.

Why is it money and power cannot solve these inner-city problems? Why do people destroy their community centres and damage the very property they live in? Perhaps they are fed up with the sham and hypocrisy that surrounds them. Towers hints at other reasons. He concludes rightly that nothing can be done until the community gears itself up to the task.

Towers has survived his own inner doubts about the community architecture movement. He has seen the real benefits of the movement and comes solidly down in favour of this simple way of working as a real opportunity to give ordinary people something worthwhile. Community architecture is about raising the spirit. Reading this fine work should raise the spirit of the reader.

PREFACE

During the late 1960s, as a newly qualified architect, I worked on some of the large-scale public projects which were so characteristic of that era. First on a new hospital, then on the development of an urban motorway. That experience convinced me that elevated roads offered no solution to urban transport problems and were highly destructive to boot. It was with more positive anticipation that I moved on to work on a large new housing development. The designers were socially committed and they set high environmental aspirations. The work was technically demanding and it created interesting design problems, but it was wholly a drawing-board exercise and it seemed entirely divorced from reality. It was taken for granted that the existing houses and the people who lived in them would simply be swept away. In two years I never once met a representative of the Council that commissioned the scheme, let alone any of the people who might eventually live in it. My tentative suggestions that users might participate in the design of buildings they were to occupy were dismissed with incredulity by my, otherwise enlightened, employers.

It was a time of radical protest, and by the early 1970s community action was beginning to generate direct intervention in urban environmental issues. Planners, architects and other designers were beginning to get involved in supporting these protests. In 1972 I went to work for an inner-city community organization campaigning for better local facilities and, in particular, for more sensitive housing redevelopment. Over the following few years I worked with several small community groups who were developing their own housing or social buildings. By the late 1970s, I and others who had been doing similar work for years were somewhat bemused to find our activities redefined as "community architecture". The new interpretation generated a wide-ranging debate about the nature of community architecture and the direction it should take. For myself I was convinced that local government could be reformed to provide a genuine service to the community.

In the early 1980s I went to work for a local authority. There was a constant struggle against entrenched attitudes, but I believe we did succeed in developing effective user participation in social housing improvements and other community projects. Meanwhile, the cause of community architecture was attracting increasing attention, although it was attention of a peculiarly narrow and distorted kind. The focus of the trade press was on a few individuals and a handful of projects. There was little understanding of the development of community technical aid. There was still less interest in the work of local authorities. However innovative their approach, they were all tarred with the brush of insensitive bureaucracy. My attempts to publicize our work with tenants in modernizing run-down estates met with luke-warm responses. It became evident that the architectural establishment in general, and the professional press in particular, were beset by exclusive pre-occupations. First was the pre-occupation with innovative design and the visually eye-catching. Such bias left little room for recognition of the social value of design ideas and processes. Second was the presumption that innovation was invariably the work of the creative individuals. This put private practice in the forefront of press attention and gave little recognition to the co-operative mores of the voluntary sector or the collective approach of the public sector. These preconceptions meant that, where community architecture was publicized at all, it was almost exclusively as the work of individual private practitioners working with self-help groups.

The purpose of this book is to try to correct this imbalance: to counterbalance the pre-occupation with design with a better understanding of the process and practice of community architecture, to place alongside the work of well known individual practitioners the achievements of co-operatives and the impact of the work of local government. In doing so I hope to give credit to some of the many people who have helped to produce successful community projects. By no means all of them conform to the traditional image of the architect. The story behind the cover illustration demonstrates that, to succeed in community architecture, you don't need to be a middle-class man – you don't even need to be an architect. Jo Thwaites worked for years in a variety of administrative jobs. At the age of 30, finding herself to be a single parent, she decided to re-train as a building surveyor. After serving her apprenticeship, she undertook the conversion of a disused basement into a nursery. She had no training in design but worked closely with the user group and had the support of a co-operative technical group with a collective approach to design work. The completed Walnut Tree Nursery is an attractive scheme, highly valued by its users. In the cover photograph, Jo's daughter sizes up the finished product.

Many people have contributed to the creation of this book. Special thanks are due to John Bussy, Pauline Nee and Suzy Nelson who have shown dedication and perseverance in reading the text as it progressed. Their commentary, based on their own expertise in this field, has informed and helped to shape the contents. Thanks also to the following who have, at various times, provided advice, support, information and material drawn from their own experience and archives: Norman Beddington, Judith Blakeman, Alison Clark, Keith Cook, Sheila Field, Liz George, Jo Thwaites, Stelios Voutsadakis and Gill Watson.

Published and textual sources of information are acknowledged at the end of each chapter. In addition, thanks are due to the following, who have provided information on their own work and organizations (in contents order):

Rod Hackney; Mike Daligan; The Walter Segal Self-Build Trust; Members of Collective Building and Design; Rod Yeoman, Co-operative Development Services, Liverpool; Steve Fisher, Pollard Thomas Edwards; John Bussy, Support; Suzy Nelson, Paula Williams, Ann de Graft-Johnson of Matrix; Lesley Klein, CLAWS; Michael Parkes, Kings Cross Railway Lands Group; Stephen Kirby, COMTECHSA; Miles Sibley, Association of Community Technical Aid Centres; Ian Finlay, Maureen Reid of the RIBA Community Architecture Group; Rita Begum, Jagonari; Bill Reed, former Birmingham City Architect; Sandy Pearce, Bethnal Green Neighbourhood, Tower Hamlets; John Murray, former Haringey Borough Architect; James Geoghegan, Islington Estate Action/Tufnell Park Estate; Tom Woolley; Pauline Nee, Besant Court; Robin Nicholson, Edward Cullinan Architects; John Birchall, Lambeth Community Care Centre; George Nicola, leader, Broadwater Farm Area Team.

Graham Towers   October 1994

ACKNOWLEDGEMENTS

Page

5: photograph by permission of Birmingham City Library

11: illustration by permission of The British Library

29: photograph by Norman Beddington

30: both photographs by permission of Leeds City Council

35, 36, 39, 41, 42, 48, 50: photographs by permission of *The Architects' Journal*

38: upper photograph by permission of Birmingham City Library

57: drawings by Louis Hellman

60: illustration by permission of the Greater London Record Office

68, 69, 92, 105: drawings by permission of *The Architects' Journal*

68: photograph by permission of the *Kensington & Chelsea Post*

98: drawings by permission of Pollard Thomas & Edwards, Architects

113: proposals map by permission of the Kings Cross Railway Lands Group

115: perspective drawing by COMTECHSA

116: isometric drawing by Support Community Building Design

126, 127: drawings and photograph by Matrix Feminist Architectural Co-operative
Ltd

134: map taken from *Community areas policy – a record of achievement* (Greater London
Council 1985)

136-7: upper drawing by the Richard Rogers Partnership

136: perspective drawing by the Association of Waterloo Groups

164: rough model by Matrix Feminist Architectural Co-operative Ltd

165: computer model by Maureen Diffley

180 and front cover photograph: by Jo Thwaites

199, 200: drawings by Edward Cullinan Ltd, Architects

202: both photographs by Martin Charles

221, 222: drawings by permission of the London Borough of Haringey.

All other photographs and drawings are by the author.

for Pamela

INTRODUCTION

Homelessness, poverty, declining educational and moral standards, increasing crime and lawlessness, sporadic violent unrest, derelict land and crumbling buildings: any or all of these phenomena blight much of urban Britain in the mid-1990s. The problems are serious, perhaps approaching crisis proportions. Some see their origin in the social and economic policies of 1980s. Certainly, economic decline and reductions in social spending have made matters much worse, but many of the problems were already there. Others look further back, to the large-scale redevelopment of the 1960s. Then, large parts of the old cities were destroyed and replaced with huge new estates. High-rise housing proved decidedly unpopular. Those who could choose, opted not to live there. The estates quickly degenerated into ghettos of the deprived and have become breeding grounds for deep-seated social problems. The redevelopments of 30 years ago have undoubtedly visited their legacy on the present day, but it would be wrong to see in them the origin of the urban predicament. The housing drive of the 1960s was, itself, an almost desperate attempt to solve a problem that had already been at the top of the public agenda for more than a hundred years.

The roots of the urban question go back to the beginning of the industrial revolution. During the early nineteenth century the co-incidence of new industrial technology and large numbers of people displaced from the land combined to generate rapid urbanization. As a result of the unprecedented speed with which the new industrial cities grew, they were unplanned and poorly built. Within a short time they became polluted, overcrowded, insanitary and disease-infested. Living conditions for much of the urban population were appalling. Social reformers and philanthropists sought to address the worst of the evils, but their efforts bore little fruit until the last quarter of the nineteenth century. Then, public health was improved by better sanitation and regulation to control new construction. More positively the efforts of philanthropic institutions and the public authorities were directed to the construction of new types of buildings, buildings that were purpose-designed to improve conditions for the urban working class – blocks of flats to provide better-quality and healthier housing; centres for recreation and personal development; spacious schools for the education of the children; public baths, libraries and other facilities for the improvement of the body and the mind. In these buildings the skills of architects – hitherto the preserve of rich patrons – were exercised for the benefit of the mass of ordinary people. It was the beginning of a new field of building design: social architecture.

From the 1840s, conditions in the industrial cities aroused increasing public concern. Despite the efforts of reformers, early progress was so slow as to be indiscernible. The squalor intensified and in the process the very notion of the city was besmirched. Radicals of the time, almost universally, detested the urban nightmare around them. They sought a future free from the industrial city, a future that lay in small self-contained settlements set in the countryside where even the poorest could live close to nature. The new ideal became the Garden City – combining the best of town and country – and the urge to escape the industrial city was to become a major force in shaping the urban development of the twentieth century. As the State began to take more and more responsibility for social provision, local authorities were given new powers to tackle the problems of the cities. New and more spacious standards were adopted for the design of new housing for the working classes. Decentralization became the key objective. Estates of social housing were built on the urban fringes to relieve overcrowding in the cities. Meanwhile, the middle classes were busily rehousing themselves in the suburbs that speculative builders were throwing up around the major cities.

By the 1930s, it was evident that this strategy was not working. Generally, it was the better paid workers who moved to the peripheral estates and, with the increasing flight of the middle classes, the old cities became concentrations of the poor and disadvantaged. Physically, they were as bad as ever: concentrations of poorly built overcrowded houses lacking adequate sanitary amenities; or of larger houses, which several families were forced to share together. Decentralization alone had not solved the urban problem, it had exacerbated it. It was evident that the cities had to be rebuilt and, because of the severe congestion, blocks of flats were increasingly seen as the most appropriate housing for the urban poor. After the Second World War, these trends were accelerated. Decentralization continued, both as public policy and individual choice. More and more effort was put into urban redevelopment in an attempt to solve, once and for all, the persistent problem of the slums.

The urban local authorities were given unprecedented powers and capital funding to achieve this historic task. Social architecture approached its zenith. Many designers were inspired by the ideals of the modern movement in architecture. Like the Victorian idealists, the modernists despised the industrial city. Unlike them they did not look towards an extra-urban Utopia but resolved to sweep away the old cities and replace them with a new ideal: cities of multi-storey flats, bathed in light and air, set in generous parkland and served by spacious highways. Released from the slums, housed in their bright new flats, the workers would become healthy and contented. All this could be achieved quickly and efficiently by exploiting the benefits of industrial mass-production. Here, at last, was a model to replace the discredited image of industrial urbanity. The model, the means and the historical imperative came together to set the stage for a determined approach to urban renewal that accelerated throughout the 1950s and culminated in the massive redevelopment drive of the 1960s.

That period had a major impact in shaping the cities of today. It is manifest, not just in the multi-storey housing estates, but in the legacy of elevated urban motorways, commercial office blocks and shopping centres. But the more redevelopment took place, the more evident it became that the reality of the modern city fell very far short of the ideals of its protagonists. It was not just the inadequacy of the new developments that excited controversy, it was the sheer destructive power of the process. During the late 1960s and early 1970s, widespread protest movements swept through Britain's inner cities. Community action (as it became known) was in part a protest against the destruction of familiar environments and the break-up of urban communities. It was opposed to the unbridled power of the large urban authorities and, equally, to the commercial forces that were seeking to capitalize on urban redevelopment. More positively, it sought to draw attention to the real needs of deprived urban areas and to create new structures through which urban communities could take part in determining their own future.

Community action generated a wide range of new ideas and revived quite few old ones. It created new movements that were to have a significant impact on urban life.

Among these was a new approach to building design and development that became known as community architecture. Community architecture began with the architects, planners and others with technical expertise who entered community action to support local groups in their resistance to redevelopment plans, and in their efforts generated urban development that reflected their own needs. Initially, the work of all these activists was disparate and unco-ordinated. By the late 1970s they had assembled under the community architecture umbrella, and some basic principles had emerged. There was extensive debate, though, about the way forwards. Three broad schools of thought emerged, each of which claimed the true path to enlightenment. One was based around the support provided by sympathetic architects to a broad range of community groups who were organizing their own developments through "self-help" initiatives. A second sought to bring specialist help to locally based campaigns for urban improvement by setting up "community technical aid centres". The third aimed to reform and break down the large technical departments in local government, making them truly responsive to community need.

Although these schools of thought contended with some hostility, they shared many basic principles and objectives. Chief among them was the belief that the users of building developments should play a key role in the design of the environments in which they were to live and work, or the facilities that were intended for their benefit. With user participation as the key principle, other things flowed from it. The involvement of technically untutored users could be achieved only through co-operation. Aloof professionalism, intent on protecting its role and expertise, was inimical to the process. Co-operative principles had emerged strongly from community action and they were to come to characterize the practice of community architecture. Once users were allotted a leading role, comprehensive redevelopment was largely ruled out. Preserving communities commonly meant preserving existing buildings, adapting and improving them for modern use. Where new building was essential, it should be small scale or piecemeal, presenting minimal disruption to the community structure and respecting the existing built environment. Above all, buildings should be designed to reflect the needs and demands of their users, rather than the concerns of their designers or developers.

In the development of its principles and practice, the term "community architecture" has become something of a misnomer. In the first place, it is by no means the preserve of architects. It embraces all aspects of building design in the broadest sense – planning, architecture, surveying, landscape, interiors, graphic design – and seeks an integration of these skills, which have become increasingly disconnected. It requires the development of new skills to assist inexperienced user groups in the initiation, development and funding of their projects. Its successful practice requires understanding well beyond the conventional concerns of building design; understanding of the social organization of communities and the historical context of urban environments; understanding of the political context and the tactical realities of campaigning, which can make or break a community project.

In its motivation, community architecture has the same objective as the social architecture that went before. It seeks to improve the lot of the poorer members of society. Not, though, by paternalistically imposing preconceived solutions that are supposedly for their benefit. Rather, it seeks to empower those who have least opportunity to control their own environment and who could not normally afford to employ architects – tenants, community groups, ethnic minorities – the disadvantaged. Over more than 20 years it has built up a solid body of practice. This practice has been widely influential. Rehabilitation has become more common than comprehensive redevelopment. There has been a more sensitive approach to the planning and design of new developments. "Consultation" has become widespread in the development process. The full implementation of democratic building design has, however, been relatively limited. Given wider understanding and commitment, it could yet make a major contribution to the lasting resolution of Britain's seemingly perpetual urban problems.

This account is divided into three parts. The first reviews the historical developments that led to the emergence of community architecture. Chapter 1 deals with the nineteenth century. It outlines the development of the industrial cities and the various responses to industrialization. In these responses lay the seeds of many ideas that were to influence later urban development and organization and which still have considerable relevance to the present day. Chapter 2 traces the impact of decentralization in creating the social divisions that have exacerbated the problems of the inner cities. It also traces the origin of the urban "ideal" that resulted in the misguided large-scale developments of the 1960s. The third chapter deals with community action and its impact in generating a new approach to urban development.

Part Two covers the practice of community architecture. Each of the three broad strands is given a separate chapter. That on self-help covers community self-build, new types of producer organizations, and the development of housing co-operatives, all within the context of a re-invigoration of co-operative principles. Chapter 5 covers the development of community technical aid and the growth of the new voluntary organizations that formed the basis of their work. Chapter 6 deals with the response of local government: policy changes in response to community action, the decentralization of services, and the development of participation in addressing the problems of housing estates. The final chapter in Part Two discusses the principles of participation and outlines the range of techniques that have been developed through which people can be effectively involved in building design.

Part Three takes up some of the theoretical aspects of community architecture. Chapter 8 discusses the implications for design. It focuses primarily on the conventional process of architectural design. Architects have no monopoly on the design of building developments, but the perspective generated by architectural education, and the attitudes that it engenders, govern the prevalent approach to most building design. If the architectural establishment were to take on board the lessons of community architecture, far-reaching changes would be both desirable and necessary. Chapter 9 reviews the political implications. The political basis of the community movement stand outside conventional perceptions. In part, at least, it represents a third way that is characteristically different from either the "free market" or the organization of provision through the State. As such, it has suffered in the conflict between the predominant ideologies. The final chapter examines the three main facets of community architecture – social awareness, environmental sensitivity, democratic participation – and the implications that these might have for a new approach to addressing the problems of the inner cities.

The chapters are interspersed with a series of case studies. These explore seven participatory projects in some detail. Most relate directly to the issues set out in the preceding chapter. Although they are not integral to the main text, they help to amplify it. All the case studies are projects developed in Inner London over a period of 20 years. Community architecture developed in many British cities. London, though, has by far the largest inner urban area, which has been the focus of enormous problems both historically and more recently. As a result, both the number and the variety of participatory projects has been greater in inner London than anywhere else. The case studies offer a flavour of the range of social background to community architecture and the often dramatic protest movements that led to new approaches in urban development. They describe and illustrate the building projects that emerged, projects quite different from what would have happened otherwise. Taken together, the case studies illustrate a new approach to the design of developments in the inner cities, which provides both appropriate and sustainable urban renewal.

Community architecture is a broad movement with many areas of interest. Focusing on its urban roots – and its potential role in the regeneration of the inner cities of Britain – means that other areas are not fully covered. One of these is ecological design. "Green architecture" sprang from similar political roots and many of those involved in community architecture are also interested in this field of design. It relies primarily, however, not on participation, but on the commitment of designers to seeking alternative technical solutions. Such solutions seek to create buildings and lifestyles that are in sustainable balance with the environment. They seek to conserve the world's natural resources through energy efficiency and the recycling of materials and waste products. A major concern of urban community architecture has been conservation and the re-use of old buildings. Although this is part of the Green agenda it does not fully reflect the range of "alternative" design. Not does it encompass the moral commitment to world conservation with its emphasis the use of renewable and environmentally friendly materials.

A concern with global issues is also reflected in the potential, which many see in community architecture, in the Third World. Communal co-operation has very strong traditions in many Third World countries. In rural housing, community self-build often plays a major role and has considerable potential in the cities of the Third World. Particular interest focused on the 1960s work of the British architect, John F. C. Turner, in the squatter communities of Lima, Peru. This lead has since been followed in other parts of Latin America. More recently, Yousef Mangunwijaya worked with a squatter community in Yogyakarta, Indonesia. The architecture of Kampong Kai Cho-de was a distinguished achievement that has been recognized by the Aga Khan Award for Architecture. Similar community projects have taken place in Sri Lanka, Botswana, Kenya and elsewhere, often assisted by technical aid charities such as Intermediate Technology. Through such projects, participation and co-operation could play a significant role in world development.

In the First World there have been a wide range of participatory projects. Developments in America and Europe have been given some coverage where they exerted a direct influence on community architecture in Britain. But there have been many other interesting projects, which it has not been possible to include. In the Kreuzberg district of Berlin, campaigns by squatters groups led to the regeneration of the area. The architectural group Stern renovated old housing with the participation of residents and, in one area, introduced a range of experimental ecological solutions. In Cahors, France, workers in a co-operative bank participated in the development of an innovative design for their new building. In West Germany, Austria and Denmark,

xvii

co-operative housing developed with the participation of users has produced novel and distinctive designs. These, and many other projects, offer considerable scope for further exploration of the benefits of participation in design.

In Britain itself, community architecture has not been an entirely urban phenomenon. Its ideas and its principles have spread into rural areas. In some projects they have been used in the regeneration of communities in economic decline, particularly those affected by the collapse of rural industries such as mining. Many of the practices of community action have also been adopted by wealthier communities in defence of their environment or in the promotion of new facilities. These various spheres of interest, at home and abroad, all deserve fuller investigation and coverage. Some are already written up elsewhere, but there may well be scope for other publications. This book concentrates on urban Britain, the forces that gave rise to and nurtured community architecture, and the considerable contribution it could still make to the regeneration of the inner cities.

PART ONE

The historical background

CHAPTER 1

The legacy of the nineteenth century

THE RISE OF SOCIAL ARCHITECTURE

The nineteenth century, when Britain came to rule half the world. was a time of massive industrialization and urbanization. The growth of empire abroad and of great cities at home brought with it wealth for the few. For much of the population it brought exploitation, poverty, overcrowding and squalor. Gross inequality and harsh treatment were the hallmarks of Victorian Britain. But the misfortune of the many also brought forth the seeds of social movements that attempted to improve the lives of industrial workers and the urban poor – initiatives that were to bear their fullest fruits in the twentieth century. Among these movements, attention was given for the first time to the application of architecture – of good design and construction – to social purposes.

The history of architecture has traditionally been seen solely in the legacy of important buildings – temples and cathedrals. palaces and mansions, civic buildings and cultural institutions – the icons that spelt out the development of the great styles of Western architecture. Although historians analyzed these landmarks in painstaking detail, only rarely did they lower their gaze to the mass of everyday buildings that surrounded them – the homes and workplaces of ordinary mortals; these were, quite simply, not architecture. This was partly disdain for the humble and vernacular, partly a reflection of historical fact: design was largely the prerogative of the rich. The holders of wealth – princes and merchants, the institutions of Church and State – were the patrons of the arts. The artists and architects served the wealthy. Slowly, during the nineteenth century, this situation began to change. Once the sole preserve of the rich and powerful, architectural skills began to be used for the benefit of poorer members of society.

The pioneer

Perhaps the earliest example of social architecture was the work of Robert Owen (1771–1858) at New Lanark in Scotland (Fig. 1.1). In a narrow valley of the fast-flowing upper reaches of the river Clyde, New Lanark was founded in 1784 by banker and industrialist David Dale. Dale brought to his newly built cotton mills orphans from workhouses, and destitutes displaced from the land. By 1796 Dale employed 1,340 workers, more than half of them children as young as six, who worked in the mills for 13 hours a day. Today, such conditions truly evoke the "Dark Satanic Mills" immortalized by William Blake. Yet by the standards of the time Dale was one of the more enlightened employers.

Figure 1.1

New Lanark, the Scottish industrial settlement where
Robert Owen conducted his pioneering experiment in
enlightened social provision and co-operation.

Robert Owen, a Welshman who had made his fortune in Manchester, bought New Lanark from Dale in 1800 and set about building a model community. In the mills he established a regime that was firm but fair, and set up a pension fund, levied on wages, for the sick and old. He built a school for the children, taking them out of the mills and into full-time education from the age of 5 to 10. He built the Institute for the Formation of Character, where workers attended morning exercise classes and evening lectures. He built a co-operative grocery store, a bakery, slaughterhouse and

3

vegetable market. He organized refuse collection and a communal wash-house. He improved the existing houses and built new housing to standards well ahead of the time, with large rooms, well lit and solidly constructed. The houses were a mixture of two-storey cottages and four and five-storey tenements (even then, multi-storey flats were a common form of housing in Scottish cities). Housing was built in a plain style from locally hewn grey stone. The public buildings were a little more elaborate, designed in a pared down classical style.

New Lanark was an experiment in social progress, although it was by no means a democratic exercise. Owen was noted for autocratically imposing on his workers his own ideas for their self-improvement. He sought to prove that a good environment could mould a healthy individual with stronger character; that a well treated work-force was a productive one. And his experiment was an economic success, showing steady profits and increasing value. The many thousands of visitors who flocked to New Lanark during Owen's 25 years in charge came not just to see the social facilities but, no doubt, to learn what enlightenment could do for their own self-interest. What Owen practiced, he preached at length. Later in his life, in his writings and speeches, Owen formulated many of the ideas that were to form the basis of the co-operative and trade union movements.[1]

Although Owen's ideas became widely influential, his foundation could not provide a physical model for what was to follow. New Lanark was a small community, never larger than 2,500 people. The mills of the early industrial revolution were dependent on water power and many were sited in steep and inaccessible valleys, with strict limits on their potential for expansion. Early in the nineteenth century, the development of steam power freed industries from the valleys. Long before Owen left New Lanark, the stage was set for the most massive upheaval in social geography.

Urbanization

Between 1800 and 1850 the population of England and Wales more than doubled and the number of households increased by 135 per cent. At the turn of the century 80 per cent of people still lived in the countryside or in small settlements. By 1851 over half were living in cities and 25 per cent of the population was packed into ten urban areas with a population of 100,000 or more. Much of this development took place around London, but growth was most rapid in the industrial cities of the north. During this period Glasgow's population more than tripled. In a single decade between 1811 and 1821 Manchester grew by more than 40 per cent. In the decade from 1821 Liverpool and Leeds grew at a similarly rapid rate.[2] The development of the railways from the 1830s only served to accelerate urban growth.

The urbanization of Britain has no parallel in terms of its scale and speed, and the effect on housing standards was disastrous. By the time Engels and Chadwick conducted their influential surveys in the early 1840s, much of the urban population was living in the most appalling conditions. A great deal of urban working-class housing was provided by the now notorious "back-to-backs". "An immense number of small houses occupied by the poorer classes in the suburbs of Manchester are of the most superficial character" reported Chadwick, "The walls are only half brick thick . . . and the whole of the materials are slight and unfit for the purpose . . . They are built back-

Figure 1.2
A back-to-back court in Birmingham, photographed at the turn of the century.

to-back; without ventilation or drainage; and, like a honeycomb, every particle of space is occupied. Double rows of these houses form courts, with, perhaps, a pump at one end and a privy at the other common to the occupants of about twenty houses".[3] Thousands of these back-to-backs were built throughout the cities of northern England. Mostly they were two rooms about 12ft×10ft built, "one-up, one-down" in two-storey terraces. Some also had a third storey, some a cellar beneath (Fig. 1.2).

Bad as they were, at least the back-to-backs provided families with the privacy of self-containment. Many lived in much worse conditions. Much urban housing was adapted. "Tenementing" was common – larger houses built for better-off families were divided up, let and sublet. Whole families lived in one room sharing such toilet and cooking facilities as there were. Many older houses became common lodging houses where letting was by the bed rather than by the room. Six or seven strangers might share a single room, with no furniture other than bare mattresses, Men were mixed with women, couples and families with single people. Often the beds themselves were shared, their users taking turns to sleep in shifts. Tenements and lodging houses could be found in all cities, but were most numerous in London where the slums they created reached into the heart of the metropolis. Soho, Westminster and Covent Garden contained areas of lodging houses – or "rookeries" as they were then called – as well as more outlying areas.

Worst of all were the cellar dwellings. Poorly ventilated, poorly lit – sometimes without windows at all – cellars were always damp. Many were just bare earth or partly paved, and poor drainage often caused them to flood. Insanitary and often grossly overcrowded, cellars offered the barest form of shelter to the most destitute of the urban poor and were often a breeding ground for infectious diseases such as typhus.

5

Throughout the older industrial towns thousands of families lived in cellar dwelling, but they were most prevalent in Manchester and Liverpool. Engels estimated that, in 1844, 40,000–50,000 people lived in cellars in greater Manchester, while in Liverpool 45,000 subsisted in cellar dwellings – more than 20 per cent of the city's population.[4]

Small wonder that such conditions led Engels and Marx to prepare their revolutionary treatise. In the Communist *Manifesto*, first published in 1848,[5] they declared "The bourgeoisie has subjected the country to the rule of the towns. It has created enormous cities, has greatly increased the urban population as compared with the rural and has thus rescued a considerable part of the population from the idiocy of rural life" and proposed a "Combination of agriculture with manufacturing industries; gradual abolition of the distinction between town and country, by a more equable distribution of the population over the country." But Marxism had no immediate impact and was never to have significant influence in urbanized industrial countries. More immediately two strains of reform started to develop during the 1840s. In the cities the emergence of the philanthropic movement and the beginnings of legislative control slowly began to try to improve life. On the other hand, many rejected the evils of the city altogether and proposed a return to the idyll of rural life.

Flight from the cities

The earliest practical attempt to rescue working people from the evils of the city was the Land Company founded by the Chartist leader Feargus O'Connor. The Chartists were mainly concerned with pressing for electoral reform and, in particular, the abolition of the property qualification for the franchise. Very few workers owned their homes at that time and the vast majority were thus deprived of the right to representation. As a working-class organization the Chartists were also concerned at the dire working and living conditions of their supporters.

In 1843 O'Connor attacked the evils brought by machinery and sought independence for the victims of the industrial revolution from employer and landlord. He proposed life on the land as a way out of the new industrial society. He planned to build 40 "estates" providing 5,000 families with a cottage and a smallholding from which they could earn a living and, in pursuit of Chartist aims, the entitlement to vote. Each estate would have its own community centre, school and hospital. In 1845 he formed the Chartist Co-operative Land Society to carry out the plan. O'Connor sought the support of Marx and Engels, but they disapproved of all forms of private property and saw in this a diversion from their revolutionary aims.

But it did catch the imagination of a large section of the urban working class. By 1847 the Land Company had 60,000 members with 600 branches in England, Scotland and Wales, mostly drawn from the skilled section of the working class. Each member held 2 or 3 shares at £2 10s. Like an early version of the football pools, these shares would entitle them to enter a lottery for a smallholding and an escape from urban life. The first estate was started at Heronsgate (or O'Connorsville) near Rickmansworth. In 1845 the Company completed 35 cottages built in semi-detached pairs, each in its own smallholding of 2, 3 or 4 acres. 1,487 members had sufficient shares to qualify for a homestead, and a ballot was drawn for the winners. Over the next three years a further five estates were started in Worcestershire, Gloucestershire and Oxfordshire. 250 houses were built, as well as schools and community buildings. The houses were designed by O'Connor himself, often as homes and farm buildings combined (Fig. 1.3). They were built from O'Connor's sketches by small builders, some of whom were members of the Land Company. And they were very well built. The great majority survived, suitable modernized, as twentieth century commuter homes.

O'Connor's project attracted national attention at the time, but its economic concept – of supporting a family on a smallholding and making enough to repay a debt – was always dubious and repeatedly attacked. Worse, the Land Company fell foul of the law and was never properly registered as a legal entity. In 1851 the Company collapsed amid allegations of disorganization and corruption. The project had largely failed, but it had raised the dream of escape from the cities.[6]

Figure 1.3
Cottage cum small-holding at Minster Lovell in Oxfordshire, one of several settlements built by the Chartist Land Company to provide working people with an escape route from the industrial city

The Arts and Crafts movement

That dream was shared by leading intellectuals of the day. The prolific critic of art, architecture and politics, Oxford academic John Ruskin, similarly despised machinery and modern urbanity. Ruskin emphasized the importance of craft work as an antidote to drudgery and the poor quality of machine production, and supported a somewhat authoritarian version of socialism. But it was his pupil William Morris, rather than the esoteric Ruskin, who was to popularize these ideas.

William Morris (1834–96) earned his living as an interior designer to the rich, but he was a polymath in the arts and politics and a major figure in the latter half of the century. Through his activities, Morris brought together the Pre-Raphaelite painters and poets and the Arts and Crafts architects. Through his membership of the Social Democratic Federation and as editor of *The Commonweal*, he propounded an idealistic view of socialism. Morris had strong views on the environment. He regarded the timeless domestic architecture of England as a model for future development – an architecture of simplicity that owed little to the historical styles. He believed in repair and conservation, and set up the Society for the Protection of Ancient Buildings.[7]

Towards the end of his life, Morris set down the beliefs that had guided his work in the utopian novel *News from nowhere*. In it the narrator goes to sleep in a suburb of the hated industrial London and wakes up in an idealized socialist society in the twenty-first century, full of healthy, happy people living a co-operative life. He is taken on a journey into central London and he witnesses Morris's vision of the urban future.

> We turned away from the river at once and were soon on the main road that runs through Hammersmith. But I should have had no guess as to where I was if I had not started from the waterside; for King Street was gone and the highway ran through wide sunny meadows and garden-like tillage. . . . There were houses about, some on the roads, some amongst the fields with pleasant lanes leading down to them, and each surrounded by a teeming garden. They were all pretty in design, and solid as might be, but countrified in appearance. like yeoman's dwellings; some of them of red brick like those by the river, but more of timber and plaster, which were by the necessity of their construction so like medieval houses of the same materials that I fairly felt as if I were alive in the fourteenth century; . . . On the north side of the road was a range of building and courts, low but very handsomely built and ornamented, and in that way forming a great contrast to the unpretentiousness of the houses round about; while above this lower building rose the steep lead-covered roof and the buttresses and higher part of a great hall, of a splendid and exuberant style of architecture, of which one can say little more than that it seemed to me to embrace the best qualities of the Gothic of northern Europe with those of the Saracenic and Byzantine, although there was no copying of any one of these styles.[8]

Morris's vision took as its model an idealization of the vanished medieval lifestyle and the replacement of the Victorian city by a dispersed agrarian craft economy. It has often been dismissed as backward-looking and romantic, but it was an ideal many were to come to share. In many ways *News from nowhere* was a retrospective manifesto for the Arts and Crafts movement in architecture. Morris worked only briefly as an architect, as a pupil of G. E. Street in 1856, but he undoubtedly had an influence on the house that Philip Webb designed for him in 1859. The Red House, with its steep pitched roof and traditional materials and details; its simple and informal approach to design is normally seen as the key influence that started the Arts and Crafts movement.

The movement did look backwards and it revived such traditional features as expressed pitched roofs, bay windows, casement windows, tile-hung walls and expressed timber beams – all of which had been obliterated by the classically inspired Georgian and Recency urban housing. It was to take these features, and a traditional approach to detailing and use of materials, forward into a new synthesis of British vernacular architecture in which new buildings respected the environment and were designed to fit in with their surroundings. For the first time, humble buildings provided the inspiration for architects – not the Great Styles of historical monuments. Not that the leading lights of the movement exhibited any practical social commitment. Webb, Lethaby, Norman Shaw and Voysey all earned their living from prestige buildings for wealthy clients – mostly large houses set in the beloved countryside. Only Ashbee was to form a direct relationship with the urban poor. Nevertheless, they created an architecture that was more democratic in its origins and that was highly influential and very popular.

Model towns

From mid-century onwards a handful of employers became concerned about the living conditions of their workers. Whether from philanthropic motives or from self-interest, the idea, pioneered by Robert Owen, of building good housing for a company workforce, began to take physical shape in new settlements. First was the Halifax worsted manufacturer Edward Akroyd. He built two model villages at Copley (1849) and Akroydon (1859) on virgin land in the Yorkshire Dales. Akroydon was designed in domestic Gothic by the noted architect George Gilbert Scott.[9] In 1853 Titus Salt, a Bradford alpaca manufacturer, started the more famous model town, Saltaire, designed by local architects Lockwood and Mawson in a simplified Georgian style. In 1888 the soap manufacturer W. H. Lever founded Port Sunlight near Birkenhead (Fig. 1.4). The model village he built for his workers was designed by several architects and drew on a mixture of styles. Predominantly, though, it is a romantic and evocative revival of domestic Gothic, authentically replicating the design and construction of Tudor housing. A little later came the chocolate towns: Cadbury's Bournville near Birmingham (1893) and Rowntree's New Earswick near York (1901). In all these model foundations working conditions were good and high quality housing, public buildings and facilities were provided all on Owenite lines.[10]

In many ways the model towns were the embodiment of Morris's vision and the later ones in particular were strongly influenced by Arts and Crafts architecture.

Figure 1.4
Port Sunlight, most picturesque of the model industrial towns which generated a new ideal as an alternative to the industrial city.

9

Bournville owed much to domestic Gothic and the revival of English vernacular. New Earswick was designed in cottage vernacular by the architects Parker and Unwin, who provided a strong link between the Arts and Crafts Movement and the new campaign for Garden Cities. Raymond Unwin was a committed socialist and contributor to Morris's *Commonweal*. As a collaborator he was, undoubtedly, familiar with the ideas of Morris and his friends. Garden cities were promulgated by Ebenezer Howard in his book *Tomorrow: a peaceful road to reform* (1898) and had been given impetus by the Garden City Conference at Bournville in 1901. Unwin was active in this movement and, with his partner Barry Parker, went on to design the first Garden City at Letchworth in 1903.[11]

The Model Towns and the Garden Cities movement were to form an important influence on twentieth-century planning. But all these models, praiseworthy as they were, contributed not one wit to the improvement of the lot of the urban slum dwellers. All the models attempted to solve urban problems by running away from them and starting afresh on greenfield sites. While the nineteenth-century socialists and enlightened employers turned their backs on the cities, it was left to the conscience of the establishment to instigate urban reforms

The urban philanthropists

Conditions in the slums had given rise to increasing concern among the establishment. This was not just distress at the appalling living conditions of the poor, but concern at effects on the rest of society of crime, vice and, in particular, disease. Repeated outbreaks of cholera, typhoid and other infectious diseases were a major threat to public health. Attempts to reform urban housing began in the early 1840s with the formation of two societies. In 1841 the Metropolitan Association for Improving the Dwellings of the Industrious Classes (MAIDIC) was founded by the Rector of Spittalfields. In 1844 came the more high-powered Society for Improving the Condition of the Labouring Classes (SICLC). The Prince Consort, Prince Albert, was its President, and its many vice-presidents included such luminaries as the Archbishop of Canterbury and several Peers of the realm. It also attracted the support of the celebrated reformer Lord Shaftsbury.[12] SICLC's Honorary Architect was Henry Roberts, who carried out several model schemes on its behalf.

Roberts's first scheme was a double row of two-storey houses in Clerkenwell, but more important was his Model Homes for Families, built in Streatham Street, Bloomsbury in 1849 (Fig. 1.5). This was a five-storey block of flats with basement workshops. The flats were of a standard unheard of at the time. Each was self-contained with a living room, two bedrooms and a kitchen. Off the kitchen a separate compartment was provided for a WC and refuse storage. The flats were approached on each floor by the access galleries in the open air, an innovation that Roberts suggested would "Obviate the evils to be apprehended from internal staircases common to several families".[13]

SICLC also sought to establish new standards for lodging houses. It acquired and improved lodging houses in Charles Street, Drury Lane – described by Roberts as "one of the worst areas of London" – and built new model lodging houses in George street, Bloomsbury. SICLC's role was to exemplify and campaign for improved housing

Figure 1.5
Henry Roberts's
drawings for his
influential model flats in
Bloomsbury. The block
still provides good hous-
ing and is now owned by
the Peabody Trust.

rather than to provide it on any significant scale. Roberts travelled widely in Britain and Europe, investigating housing conditions and visiting new schemes for workers' housing, including employers housing, in Mulhouse, Berlin and St Petersburg. As a national society it sought to influence standards and intervened to criticize new tenement housing in Birkenhead, Glasgow, Huddersfield and Edinburgh.[14]

SICLC's preferred solution was "philanthropic" housing. Developer Societies would be formed which would limit their profits to 5 per cent per annum. For investing capitalists their "philanthropy" would be to forgo the higher rate of interest they might receive elsewhere. MAIDIC was the first of such societies. Its earliest scheme in Old Pancras Road, Clerkenwell, in 1848 housed 110 families in a multi-storey block. Again the flats were self-contained, but unlike Roberts's scheme they were approached by an enclosed access staircase that incorporated the novel feature of a refuse chute More philanthropic societies were founded from the early 1860s; the Improved Industrial Dwellings Company, founded in 1863 by Sidney Waterlow, was followed by 25 similar organization over the next 20 years.[15] These innovations were accompanied by new approaches to the management of workers' housing pioneered by Octavia Hill. She started her work in 1865 as manager of a block of tenemented housing in Marylebone, purchased for improvement by John Ruskin, and over the years established principles of good standards of occupancy, hygiene and repair, accompanied by an authoritarian strictness with tenants who could not match her high ideals.[16]

The activities of the more commercial philanthropic societies was put in the shade by an American merchant. In 1862 George Peabody gave £150,000 to found a Trust dedicated to providing working-class housing. Unlike its rivals, the Peabody Trust was non-profit making and was able to use all its resources to developing housing, and within 25 years the Trust had built more than 5,000 dwellings. Its early developments, however, fell far short of the standards set by Henry Roberts. Most were of a type called "associated dwellings", in which tenants shared sculleries and toilets.[17] Nonetheless the fully philanthropic Trust proved more successful than the 5 per cent societies. It was to become the model for the future. The Peabody Trust was soon followed by others, such as the Guinness and Samuel Lewis Trusts, which were to provide the forerunners for modern Housing Associations. Many of the early philanthropic developments were undistinguished repetitive barrack-like buildings, although in some of the later developments considerably more effort was put into the designs.

The contribution of philanthropic housing was considerable, but it fell far short of a decisive impact. By the time of the 1885 Royal Commission on the Housing of the Working Classes, philanthropic societies in London housed 147,000 people – just 4 per cent of the population of the capital.[15] They were also socially divisive: most of those they housed were the families of the better-off skilled workers. Partly this was because their rents were relatively high, partly because they were highly selective in their choice of tenants, preferring those who would conform with their strict rules of cleanliness and behaviour and would not create problems for their managers and rent collectors.[18] Philanthropy created a new class of housing, below that of the growing middle class but above that of the slums which remained as pressing a problem as ever.

The settlements

While some of the philanthropic Victorian upper and middle classes were doing good works in the field of housing, others were dedicating themselves to the educational and social welfare needs of the poor. The settlements were a peculiarly Victorian manifestation of voluntary service. They were a combination of hostels and community centres where volunteers from the wealthy classes would live among the poor and minister to them with activities for their education and self-improvement. They can best be understood as a latter-day version of Voluntary Service Overseas or the Peace Corps. The slums were not in a foreign country but, given the intense class divisions of the time, they might as well have been. Rich and poor truly lived in different worlds.

Starting in the 1880s, institutions such as public schools and universities, as well as individual philanthropists, set up settlement buildings in working-class areas where young middle-class professionals would live. During the day they carried on their normal occupations, but during their leisure they spent their time with local people who could join the settlements and use them as social centres. Meetings, lectures, sports activities and entertainments took place there and classes were organized in domestic skills and crafts. As well as providing valuable facilities for the poor, the interchange that took place in settlements helped to educate the visiting professionals in the need for social reforms to benefit deprived urban areas.

One of the grandest settlement buildings was the Mary Ward Settlement (Fig. 1.6), built in an area – Tavistock Place, Bloomsbury – that was famous in the 1920s for its literary circle and where, today, commerce has largely taken over from housing. In the late nineteenth century it was, evidently, a poor residential area. In 1890 Mary Ward set up her settlement in temporary buildings. A benefactor was found in the newspaper proprietor Passmore Edwards, who provided funds for a new building. A design competition was won by two young architects – Dunbar Smith and Cecil Brewer – who were former residents of the settlement. Smith and Brewer were disciples of Webb and Lethaby, and their building, designed in 1895, is one of the finest examples of urban Arts and Crafts Architecture. The buildings contained a large hall and several smaller meeting rooms, a library and a gymnasium, as well as residential accommodation for about 30 visitors, a warden and permanent servants.[19]

If Mary Ward created the best building, the most socially successful settlement was probably Toynbee Hall, founded in 1884 in Whitechapel, east London. This was a good deal more remote from wealthy residential areas and it undertook a variety of initiatives for the benefit of the poor. It was here, in 1886, the young C. R. Ashbee set up craft classes for local people and in 1888 established the Guild of Handicrafts. He discussed his ideas with William Morris who dismissed them, preferring a campaign for political change to the direct approach Ashbee was proposing. Nevertheless the Guild of Handicrafts established a successful craft centre combining a school and a co-operative workshop making and selling woodwork and metalwork. In 1891 the Guild moved to new premises in Mile End Road. In 1902, after a democratic vote, Ashbee moved the Guild to rural Chipping Camden in Gloucestershire, taking 150 men, women and children from the East End with him. Once again the idealist sought to escape the city, but the Guild was not to maintain the success it had in London, and it collapsed five years later.[20]

Settlements became widespread and by 1914 there were 27 in various parts of London and there were similar foundations in provincial cities such as Bristol, Birmingham and Edinburgh. They have long since ceased to be residential, but more than a dozen of the early settlements continue to operate as centres of social action providing a range of education, training and community facilities.[21] Many, though, have lost their original purpose and have converted to a variety of social functions. The Mary Ward building

Figure 1.6
*Mary Ward Settlement.
One of many philan-
thropic institutions
established in deprived
urban areas to provide
community education
and recreation.*

now houses the National Institute for Social Work, while The Harrow Club, in west
London, functions as the Notting Dale Urban Studies centre, a learning resource for
local schools. The settlements were a form peculiar to their time, but they did lay the
basis both for modern community centres and for vocational and adult education.

Enter the State

For much of the nineteenth century, voluntary action and philanthropic reform were
the only sources of addressing the burgeoning urban problems. Urbanization had
exposed the weakness of a State primarily geared to defence and foreign relations and
ill equipped to improve conditions for its own people. In 1830 the 656 members of
the House of Commons represented just 465,000 people – 2 per cent of the adult population. Major cities such as Manchester, Leeds and Sheffield were entirely unrepresented, while Members were returned for "rotten boroughs" with no population at
all. The Reform Act of 1832 partly redressed the situation but, by the maintenance of
the property qualification, still restricted the electorate to barely 4 per cent.[22] Rising

14

public concern over housing conditions did produce one legal reform – the Common Lodging Houses Act sponsored by Lord Shaftsbury in 1852 – but, other than that, there was no significant State intervention until the 1870s.

The Reform Act of 1867 doubled the electorate. Suffrage was still far from universal – it was not until 1884 that the vote was extended to all adult males. But the wider representation produced by the 1867 Act gave a new stimulus to action. Before the 1860s, local authorities had very limited powers to control building standards. Gradually, bylaws had been introduced, but it was the 1875 Public Health Act that gave local authorities powers to make building bylaws and introduce much more stringent controls on the layout of developments, the construction of buildings and their sanitary provision.[23] This Act was permissive rather than mandatory, but its progressive adoption was to change the face of urban Britain. A new type of terraced housing became predominant. The "tunnel-backs" (sometimes called "bylaw housing") gave each house a front and back with through-ventilation and a private yard or garden at the rear, reached by a narrow alley. Dustbins and privies were now confined to the back tunnel, greatly improving health and sanitation. The new type became the normal standard for working-class housing, In the new cities it gradually replaced the back-to-backs, although these were not finally outlawed until 1909. In the older cities urban housing had predominantly been multi-storey terraces which were often tenemented. The tunnel backs were mostly two-storey and provided better-quality self-contained accommodation. They also looked different – smaller in scale and influenced in design by the Gothic and vernacular revival. They generally had bay windows, expressed pitched roofs and decorative brickwork or window dressings.[24]

Also in 1875 came the first legislation to start clearing the slums. The Artisans and Labourers Dwellings Improvement Act gave urban authorities powers to clear "unhealthy areas" by compulsorily purchasing the buildings, evicting the occupants and demolishing. Once cleared, however, local authorities had no powers to redevelop and the sites had to be sold to one of the philanthropic societies or trusts.[25] The State fought shy, for the time being, of direct involvement in providing housing. In fact, the first large-scale State intervention in social provision was not in housing but in education.

The Board schools

Until late in the nineteenth century, education for the poor was left to philanthropic institutions – generally the Church – and attendance at school was entirely voluntary. Through economic necessity, many sent their children out to work as soon as they were able. But the plight of children had long since attracted the attentions of reformers and in 1870 the Elementary Education Act set up a 10-year programme for the introduction of universal education. A network of School Boards was set up with the objective of providing compulsory education for all 5–10 year-olds by 1880. It was in the direct elections for these Boards that women were, for the first time, given the vote.[26]

London was to lead the way in this provision and the London School Board began its work in 1871, appointing E. R. Robson as its architect. Over the next 30 years the Board built over 500 schools – a programme directed by Robson until 1884 and then by his deputy T. J. Bailey. In outer areas the Board schools were single-storey developments spread over generous sites. In the dense inner areas, though, sites were much more restricted and the design of the school buildings was approached with deliberate social objectives. As Robson wrote in 1881, "We have seen how abject are the homes of countless thousands. If we can make the homes of these poor persons brighter, more interesting, nobler, by so treating the necessary Board Schools planted in their midst as to make each building undertake a sort of leavening influence, we have set on foot a permanent and ever active good . . .".[27]

These schools were tall buildings as high as six domestic storeys (Fig. 1.7). While offices and ancillary spaces were normal scale, the teaching areas were double-height rooms with large windows and heated by open fires. Infants would be on the ground floor, with schools for older boys and girls on the upper floors reached by separate entrances. Large tarmac playgrounds were provided, similarly segregated. The schools provided for the children an environment they were unlikely to experience in their homes or at work – well heated rooms, well ventilated and with good natural lighting, and outside clean safe areas for sport and play. The sheer scale of these buildings made them prominent, but in their design and construction a distinctive style was developed. Strongly influenced by the vernacular revival, these already lofty buildings were topped with steep tiled roofs, tall chimneys and expressed gables. Simply but very

Figure 1.7
Camden Institute, 1874, one of the earliest of the London Board schools which made a distinctive social and environmental improvement to the Victorian city

16

carefully designed and strongly constructed, these early schools made a major contribution to the Victorian urban environment and the wellbeing of the poor.

With the raising of the school leaving age to 11 in 1893 and 12 in 1899, schools had to accommodate more and more pupils, and the later schools were even larger in scale and designed in a more elaborate manner. The School Boards were set up to provide a service which had not previously existed. The children they educated would not otherwise have gone to school, and all of them were from the poorer sections of society. With large numbers of children to accommodate, a great many buildings were produced by the Boards, many of them in the distinctive style pioneered by Edward Robson. A very few – such as the Scotland Street School in Glasgow, designed by Charles Rennie Macintosh[28] – have made their way into architectural history. But the system produced many fine buildings that still stand as lasting monuments to the entry of the State into the provision of social architecture

Municipal housing

Where education led the way, social housing was soon to follow. The earliest example of local authority housing dates from 1869 when Liverpool City Council built St Marlin's cottages, a small tenement block. At that time, though, local government had no specific powers to provide housing. Some authorities became involved in a small way with house-building or improvement, but it was to require legislation before local government would make a significant impact. The Royal Commission on the Housing of the Working Classes had identified the urban problems of the metropolis as the most serious. Once again London was to be given the lead.

The Housing of the Working Classes Act of 1890 empowered the metropolitan authorities to buy land for improvement schemes with the obligation to rehouse at least half those displaced. These powers were not to be extended to the rest of the country until 1900, and the initiative given to London was seized by the London County Council. Founded only a year before the 1990 Act, the LCC was controlled by the Progressive Party – an alliance of radical Liberals, Fabians and Socialists – which had been elected on a programme of housing initiatives.[29] The LCC set up an architects department, under the direction of Thomas Blashil, committed to social improvement. Many of its younger members were disciples of Arts and Crafts leaders Webb and Lethaby, and were in touch with them and William Morris through membership of the Society for the Protection of Ancient Buildings.

The LCC inherited about 15 cleared sites from its predecessor, the Metropolitan Board of Works, and in its first few years acquired two dozen or more slum clearance areas. Its first development was Beachcroft Buildings in Brook Street, Limehouse (now demolished). But the most significant of its early schemes was the Boundary Street Estate in Bethnal Green (Fig. 1.8). Here "Old Nichol", a maze of narrow streets covering 15 acres, was demolished and replaced with a comprehensive new development. A new radial pattern of wide tree-lined streets was laid out focused on a raised open space at the centre. Housing for 5,000 people was built in five-storey blocks of flats. There was a deliberate attempt to raise standards and the flats provided considerably better accommodation than the philanthropic housing developments of the time. The LCC was also keen to ensure that what was provided was not just housing but included other necessary facilities: open spaces, shops on the ground floor of some blocks, and two schools built by the London School Board.[30]

17

Figure 1.8
Boundary Street Estate,
Bethnal Green. Built by
the London County
Council in 1895, one of
the earliest local authority
slum clearance schemes.

Similar tenement developments followed, notably the Millbank Estate behind the Tate Gallery, but from 1902 the LCC adopted a policy of rehousing all those displaced by its developments. This meant that not everyone could be accommodated on urban sites, and a series of cottage developments took place on the less densely populated fringes of the county. This began with the Totterdown Fields Estate in Tooting, and further cottage estates were developed in Norbury, Tottenham and at the Old Oak Estate, Hammersmith. Old Oak, built in 1911, is the most celebrated of the early LCC cottage estates. Built to a relatively high density but without high buildings, great attention was given to the visual quality of the estate and its amenity.[30] It was as if William Morris's disciples had returned to the site of *News from nowhere* and realized his dream (Fig. 1.9).

The legacy

At the close of the nineteenth century, Britain was more urbanized that at any time before or since. The rapid urbanization in the first half of the century, which had created such enormous problems, was continued in the second half. In 1851, 54 per cent of the 18 million people of England and Wales lived in cities. By 1911 this had risen to 79 per cent of 36 million.[31] Over the century as a whole the urban population which, in 1801, had stood at 1.7 million had increased to 28.5 million. The massive amount of development required to house these millions was almost entirely unplanned. Almost all of it took place around existing roads and settlements, carried out by speculative builders and developers. They laid out new estates and provided such roads and public services as there were.

Figure 1.9
The LCC's early cottage estate at Old Oak Common, Hammersmith, forerunner of many peripheral council estates.

For most of the century the State stood back unable or unwilling to intervene. Nowhere, even in London, was there exerted the State control of planning and development that lends such distinction to continental cities such as Paris and Berlin. Only in the last quarter of the century did the State become active and even then its intervention in housing was mainly through the negative sanction of legislative controls. By the end of the nineteenth century, new development, at least, was under better control – produced to better standards with much better services. The influence of the philanthropic movements and the intervention of the State had begun to improve conditions for the teeming millions in the cities. But they had barely scratched the surface of the problems created by the first waves of urbanization. In London the philanthropic movement had completed just 40,000 new homes by 1905, while the combined efforts of the London local authorities produced just 13,000 by 1914.[26]

In the provision of social services the positive intervention of the authorities in the late nineteenth century was more effective. Free education was been provided for all – rich and poor alike – in the fine new buildings produced by the school boards. The educational potential of the population as a whole was fostered by the construction of public libraries. Local councils had intervened to improve health and sanitation with the installation of piped drinking water and public sewers and public baths had been constructed in most urban areas (Fig. 1.10). Nevertheless, for the vast majority of people, late Victorian cities were extremely unpleasant places in which to live – grossly overcrowded, notoriously polluted and riddled with vice, crime and disease.

In spite of slow and limited progress in social improvement, the fledgling field of social architecture yielded a positive legacy. The pioneering work of Henry Roberts had established the forerunners of improved urban housing for the poor, although very few architects were involved in such work until the last quarter of the century. The key influences had come from non-architects – Robert Owen and William Morris. Owen had shown by example the benefits of enlightened employment practices, education, health and a good environment. His model had been emulated in the new industrial towns which had led to the formation of the Garden City movement. Morris had helped create a new architecture based on humble traditions, and his idealism had inspired both the builders of new communities in the country and the architects

Figure 1.10
*St Pancras Public Baths,
1900. One of the many
distinguished social buildings put up by local
authorities in the late nineteenth century. Architect
T. W. Aldwinkle
unknown and unsung.*

engaged in improving conditions in the cities. By the end of the century a new generation of architects led by such as Robson, Blashill and their staff were committed to
using their skills for social purposes. They sought to demonstrate that the city environment could, after all, be made pleasant for the mass of ordinary people.

But the ideals of urban reformers were only one half of the coin. Many early socialists and radical intellectuals rejected, altogether, urban industrialization and all its
works. They sought a new pattern, where industry would be contained in smaller-
scale settlements and where people could live in closer proximity to, and in harmony
with, the countryside. Already, those who could afford to had begun to forsake the
overcrowded cities for the relative tranquillity of the new satellites and suburbs which
had sprung up along the railways. These two trends were to form the pattern of developments for more than half a century – the flight from the cities and the continuing
problem of humanizing the degraded urban conditions which were the main legacy
of the Victorian era.

References

1. Colin & Rose Bell, *City Fathers – the early history of town planning in Britain,* (London: Penguin, 1972), 240 ff.; and *David Dale, Robert Owen and the story of New Lanark* (2nd edn) (Edinburgh: Moubray House Press, 1989).

2. John Burnett, *A social history of housing 1815–1985* (2nd edn) [first edition 1978] (London: Routledge, 1986), 4 ff.

3. Edwin Chadwick, *Report on the sanitary condition of the labouring population of Gt Britain (1842)* (Edinburgh: Edinburgh University Press, 1965), 343–4.

4. Friedrich Engels, *The condition of the working class in England in 1844* (translated and edited by W. D. Henderson & W. H. Chaloner) (Oxford: Basil Blackwell, 1958), 43, 78.

5. Karl Marx & Friedrich Engels, *Manifesto of the Communist Party.* (London,1848).

6. Alice Mary Hadfield, *The Chartist Land Company* (Newton Abbot: David & Charles, 1970).

7. Peter Davey, *Architecture of the arts and crafts movement – the search for Earthly Paradise* (London: Architectural Press, 1980).

8. William Morris, *News from nowhere* (1890) (London: Routledge & Kegan Paul, 1970).

9. John Burnett, op. cit., 180.

10. Colin & Rose Bell, op. cit., 253 ff.

11. Peter Davey, op. cit., Chapter 13.

12. John Burnett, op. cit., 85.

13. Henry Roberts, *The dwellings of the labouring classes – their arrangement and construction* (London, 1850).

14. Henry Roberts, *The essentials of a healthy dwelling – and the extension of its benefits to the labouring population* (London, 1862).

15. John Burnett, op. cit., 178.

16. David Clapham, "A woman of her time", in *Built to last? Reflections on British housing policy*, Carol Grant (ed.), p. 15 (London: ROOF magazine, Shelter 1992).

17. Hugh Clout, *The Times London history atlas*, p. 100 (London: Times Books, 1991).

18. Jerry White, "Business out of charity", in Carol Grant (ed.) op. cit., p. 1

19. Adrian Forty, "The Mary Ward Settlement" *The Architects' Journal* (2 August 1989), 28

20. Peter Davey, op. cit.

21. Bassac 1993 Directory (British Association of Settlements and Social Action Centres)

22. Robert McKenzie, *British political parties* (London: Heinemann, 1963), 4–6.

23. John Burnett, op. cit., 156 ff.

24. Stefan Muthesius, *The English terraced house* (New Haven, Connecticut: Yale University Press, 1982).

25. Carol Grant, op. cit., 5.

26. Brian Simon, *Does education matter?* (London: Lawrence & Wishart, 1985), 35.

27. Greater London Council Historic Buildings Board, 27 September 1972 Report of the Architect: *The Schools of the London School Board (1972–1904);* and the London County Council Education Department (1904–1910): "Investigation for preservation", quotation from Robson in *Art Journal of 1881.*

28. Jackie Cooper (ed.), *Mackintosh architecture* (London: Academy Edition, 1978).

29. John Burnett, op. cit., 183–7.

30. Susan Beattie, *A revolution in London housing – LCC Housing Architects and their work 1893–1914* (London: Greater London Council/The Architectural Press, 1980); and Peter Davey, op. cit., Chapter 12

31. John Burnett, op. cit., 140.

CHAPTER 2

The Welfare State

THE MAKING OF A JUGGERNAUT

The hallmarks of the modern Welfare State – full employment, universal welfare benefits for the poor, an egalitarian system of free education, access to social housing, a free health service – are generally associated with the political consensus that lasted for about 30 years after the Second World War. But the comprehensive welfare system created after 1945 did not emerge from nowhere. Its roots lay much deeper. It could not be claimed that the Victorian era created the Welfare State, but it did provide the seeds from which it developed. The creation of the new, more powerful, local authorities in the late nineteenth century had a significant impact on education and public health. Although these new councils didn't begin to solve the housing problem, the achievements of the LCC provided a model of what could be done for the degraded cities by enlightened public intervention.

Victorian concepts of social housing and town planning were slowly developed during the first half of the twentieth century. Central and local government became more and more involved in the housing problem without really being able to make a significant impact on the persistent problem of slums and urban squalor. Only after the Second World War was the comprehensive planning and development machinery put in place which had the power to resolve these problems once and for all. But it went too far. The State machine became over mighty. It swept away the good with the bad. The idealism which had set out to renew the industrial cities and rescue people from bad housing ended by treating the exercise as a mere numbers game, destroying communities, and consigning those it sought to serve to soul-less and unmanageable estates – a process in which the people affected had virtually no power and precious little choice. The first significant steps on this long road were taken after the First World War.

The making of the suburbs

Great wars almost always bring great changes. In Russia the First World War brought about the Bolshevik revolution. The defeat of Germany led to the Spartacist rising. In the British establishment there was considerable fear that the poison of social unrest would bring about their downfall. During 1918 there were police strikes and army mutinies. In January 1919 the Clydeside strike for shorter working hours was reported to the Cabinet by the Secretary of State for Scotland as a "Bolshevist rising". In February London Underground workers went on strike, followed, later in the year, by railway workers nationwide. Strikes were threatened in the mines and the docks.[1] Faced with this turmoil, the coalition government led by Lloyd George decided on social reforms.

In a belated concession to the long-running movement for women's suffrage, the right to vote in parliamentary elections was given to women over 30, although it was to take a further 10 years to achieve universal suffrage.[2] A new Education Act raised the school leaving age to 14 and required education authorities to provide separate classes for children over 11 – the beginnings of secondary education.[3] In the world of work, protection was given against unemployment, working hours were reduced, and new rights were given to trade unions. But at the heart of these reforms was the promise of a great housing campaign. During the war, house-building had virtually ceased and the housing shortage was exacerbated by war-time rent controls. The slums were as bad as ever and the government was very much aware of the likely reaction of troops returning from the trenches to housing condition worse than those they had left.

Under the slogan "Homes fit for heroes", the government promised to build half a million new houses. The 1919 Housing and Town Planning Act – introduced by Dr Christopher Addison, President of the Local Government Board – required local authorities to establish the need for new houses in their areas and to prepare plans for their provision. Almost all the costs were to be born by the Treasury – for the first time the State took responsibility for the provision of social housing. Lloyd George believed the promise of better housing would restore the people's faith in the status quo and, even if not everyone could benefit, the sight of new housing being built would work wonders in restoring morale. Waldorf Astor, Parliamentary Secretary to the Local Government Board, reported in 1919, "The money we are going to spend on housing is an insurance against Bolshevism and Revolution".[4] So great was the fear of social turmoil that even the monarchy was brought into the act. Addressing representatives of the local authorities at Buckingham Palace in April 1919, King George V said ". . . the housing of the working classes has always been a question of the greatest social importance . . . if unrest is to be converted into contentment, the provision of good houses may prove one of the most potent agents in that conversion".[5]

The council house

The intention of the Addison Act was to relieve urban housing conditions by building new estates on the urban periphery on garden city lines. This policy had its origins during the war. In 1914 Raymond Unwin, the architect of Letchworth, was appointed Town Planning inspector to the Local Government Board. The Board's wartime role was to build housing for munitions workers and in all about 10,000 new houses were built in various parts of the country. One of the earliest of the developments was the Well Hall Estate, built in 1915 to house the workers of the Woolwich Arsenal. Designed by Frank Baimes, a pupil of C. R. Ashbee, Well Hall was a development of picturesque cottages in best Arts and Crafts tradition. But it was a design that stirred a controversy.

In 1913 Patrick Abercrombie had attacked Letchworth's architecture as a "bucolic fantasy". Unwin himself recognized that it was elaborate and costly and, for mass housing, favoured a simplification of the garden city architecture. Stanley Adshead, Professor of Town Planning at University College London, went much further, pro-

23

posing a standardized approach that would provide, at low cost, an egalitarian uniformity in new working-class housing. His firm – Adshead Baddon & Ramsey – designed the munitions housing at Dormanstown, York in 1917. Dormanstown was a formal layout of houses in a severe, pared down, classical style with sash windows, cornices and pediments, but with expressed pitched roofs.

These arguments exercised the Tudor Walters Committee in 1918, of which Unwin was an influential member. Their report produced a range of model cottages and set new standards of space and layout. Particular exception was taken to the monotony of long, parallel rows of narrow-fronted terraced housing – the tunnel-backs which had been the predominant form of new urban housing before the war. Instead, wider frontages were preferred, which would allow more light and air. Houses should be built in semi-detached pairs or in short terraces of four to six, with blocks placed a minimum of 70 feet apart to allow adequate sunlight. Layouts should be more informal and the value of the cul-de-sac was stressed for economy and privacy. The wartime controversy on design produced a simplified approach. The argument as to whether a house was to be pared down Arts and Crafts or simplified classical with a pitched roof made little practical difference. The result would be plain, unadorned, repetitive and uninspiring. In short, the "council house" was born, of which a million were to be built between the wars (Fig. 2.1).

In fact, Lloyd George's "homes fit for heroes" campaign quickly petered out when his government lost power and the economic crisis of 1921 forced Treasury cuts. Of the 500,000 houses proposed, only 176,000 were actually completed, although most local authorities had prepared plans for new housing. Many used outside architects to prepare their schemes. Some entrusted them to the Borough Engineer. A few had in-house architects departments. The LCC Department was, by now, well established, and it prepared plans, using standardized house types, for 29,000 houses. Among these was the gigantic Becontree Estate near Dagenham. Sited on Essex farmland and designed to relieve overcrowding in the East End, Becontree was to comprise 24,000 houses –

Figure 2.1
Typical "council houses" – legacy of Tudor Walters – anodyne mixture of classical and vernacular elements.

the size of a fair-sized country town – and became the largest council estate in the world. In the event only 4,000 houses, were completed at Becontree by 1921, under the Addison Act, and it was not fully complete until 1934.[6]

The economic crisis caused a hiatus in council house-building. It was to be three years before the powers of local authorities as house providers were restored in a new Act of 1924 by the first Labour Government – The Wheatley Housing Act – which remained in force until 1933. Where the Addison Act provided a general exchequer subsidy for approved plans, the Wheatley subsidy was a fixed sum per house. This encouraged new housing on greenfield sites, rather than in the more difficult and costly urban areas. The general drive of relief of the slums through decentralization was continued and more than 500,000 houses were built under the Wheatley subsidies, intensifying the growth of new council estates on the urban fringe.

Middle-class migration

While the local authorities were building their estates of unadorned council houses during the 1920s, the private sector built three times as many new houses in suburban developments for the growing middle classes. Those who could afford to buy wanted something more distinctive for their money. In early suburbs, wealthy patrons had commissioned houses from Arts and Crafts architects such as Lethaby and Voysey in considerable numbers. Smaller prototypes had been produced in the model towns such as Bournville and New Earswick. Letchworth also provided a rich source of inspiration. In particular M. H. Baillie Scott produced for Welwyn Garden City a range of simple cottages and semi-detached houses that provided an ideal model for the modest suburban house. Speculative builders were able to take elements of these designs – steep pitched roofs, bay windows, half-timbered gables, tile hanging, rendered brickwork – and mix and match them in new developments. Although these houses were all basically the same three-bedroom "semi", the juggling of design elements gave them a superficial aura of individuality and distinction. This new mass housing might properly be regarded as a degenerate dilution of the Arts and Crafts tradition, rather than as a continuation of the movement. Nonetheless it proved immensely popular with the swelling ranks of the middle classes (Fig. 2.2).

At the outbreak of the First World War only 10–15 per cent of households in Britain owned their own homes. The remainder rented, the great majority from private landlords. During the 1920s and 1930s a million families had the chance to rent from councils in the new cottage estates. Three million more had the chance to buy their own suburban house. Often the middle-class estates were built close to the plain and socially inferior "council houses". This led to a certain amount of conflict, at its most extreme in the north Oxford suburb of Cutteslowe. In 1934 a private housing scheme was built on land purchased from the City Council. The council itself built housing on the adjoining land. Originally the two estates were linked by a pair of roads, but there were soon disputes. Owner-occupiers complained of graffiti and "children and dogs everywhere" in the council housing. Claiming that the council estate lowered the value of their investment, the developers of the private housing built walls. seven feet high with iron spikes on top, across the roads linking the two developments. Despite protests and threats from the council, the "Cutteslowe walls" remained in place for 25 years.[7]

Such conflicts were petty – and ironic – for it was the suburbs themselves that rep-

Figure 2.2
Superior 1920s semis in north London strongly influenced by the architecture of the Arts and Crafts movement.

resented the real social division. It was only the better off who could afford to move to the new suburbs. Those who could afford to buy did so, but even in the council housing the rents were high so that only better paid workers could afford them. The four million houses built between the wars were housing development on a massive scale. Even in the 1980s these houses comprised about a fifth of the total housing stock. In the process of development, great areas of suburban sprawl were thrown around the Victorian cities including a suburban belt around London 4 to 5 miles wide. The old cities were cut off from their rural hinterland and their inhabitants denied easy access to the countryside. Worse still, while those who could afford to had escaped the evils of the city, those that were left were increasingly the poorest and least capable.

These developments gave rise to growing concern amongst urban professionals. Writing in 1940, town planner Thomas Sharp drew attention to the high cost of transport and public services associated with suburban growth, the socially divisive effects of commuting, and the separation of work and home. He attacked suburbia as ". . . socially sterile, it is wasteful and uneconomic . . . eating up great areas of valuable agricultural land and [causing] the banishment of the countryside. Suburbia is essentially selfish and antisocial in this respect. Every person who goes to the suburbs seeking the edge of the countryside pushes the countryside away from somebody else." With some sympathy he expressed concern at what might happen if there was not a new approach to urban development:

> If we let things take their course . . . the much desired rehousing of the vast, dreary Victorian quarters of our towns will take place in new suburbs beyond the recent suburbs and then in new suburbs beyond those again. There is no doubt that the English tendency today is "all suburban pseudo-cottage". And it is basically understandable why it is so. Men are sick of the wretched towns they have been given to live in.[8]

The Arts and Crafts movement, which had sought to replace the evils of the industrial city with new settlements based on a traditional rural architecture, had run into the sand. So had its offspring, the Garden City movement – for the moment. Clearly, a new inspiration was needed that would address the still festering problems of industrial urbanity with greater physical and social success.

Attack on the slums

During the 1920s house-building by local authorities concentrated almost entirely on new suburban cottage estates. A very small amount of new tenement housing was built to replace the urban slums, notably in London where about 25 per cent of new housing built by the LCC and the London Boroughs was slum clearance. Generally these were small developments, up to 100 flats in four- or five-storey blocks. Liverpool also built some blocks of flats – about 8 per cent of its new housing during the 1920s.[9] Generally, though, reliance was placed on decentralization to relieve housing conditions in the dense inner areas. It didn't happen – the problem of the slums remained as intractable as ever. George Orwell, travelling in the north of England in 1936, described conditions:

> As you walk through the industrial towns you lose yourself in labyrinths of little brick houses blackened by smoke, festering in plan-less chaos round miry alleys and little cindered yards where there are stinking dustbins and lines of grimy washing and half-ruinous WCs. The interiors of these houses are always very much the same, although the number of rooms varies between two and five . . . At the back there is the yard, or part of a yard shared by a number of houses, just big enough for the dustbin and a the WC.[10]

Orwell described the interiors of houses such as this one in Barnsley:

> House in Wortley Street. Two up, one down. Living room 12ft by 10ft. Sink and copper in living room, coal hole under stairs. Sink worn almost flat and constantly overflowing. Walls not too sound. Penny in slot gaslight. House very dark . . . Upstairs rooms are really one large room partitioned into two. Walls very bad – wall of back room cracked right through. Window frames coming to pieces and have to be stuffed with wood. Rain comes through in several places. Sewer runs under house and smells in summer . . . Six people in house, two adults and four children, the eldest aged fifteen. Youngest but one attending hospital – tuberculosis suspected. House infested by bugs.[11]

By the end of the 1920s the authorities finally decided on a concerted attack on such conditions. National concern was aroused by newspaper reports, broadcasts, appeals by the Church of England and speeches by the Prince of Wales. The National Housing and Town Planning Council in 1928 concluded that the slum problem had not improved since 1918 and that there were at least a million unfit and two million overcrowded houses.[12] In 1930, the second Labour Government introduced a new Housing Act – the Greenwood Act – which gave new impetus to slum clearance. A specific subsidy was provided on the number of people rehoused from slum clearances rather than on the number of houses provided. For the first time, councils had the powers to tackle the slums. The question was how to do it.

For more that 80 years the slum problem had caused national concern. Relief through decentralization had not been very effective and had created its own problems. In any case, the building of the suburbs was taking place more rapidly in the southern half of England than the economically depressed North, where the private house-builders found many fewer buyers. It seemed evident that the slum areas could not be rebuilt as cottage estates – there were, simply, too many people, too densely packed. The home-grown solution offered by the Victorian tenements had not proved popular, being seen as barrack-like, grim and hard. Perhaps fresh inspiration could be gathered abroad.

The Viennese model

During the early 1930s, delegations from the LCC, Birmingham, Liverpool, Yorkshire and Leeds were dispatched to Europe to seek inspiration for their impending urban redevelopment. Elizabeth Denby, a young housing specialist on a travelling scholarship, visited social housing projects in several countries in Europe. Among their various travels in Germany, France, Czechoslovakia and Scandinavia, it was the achievements of the post-war socialist Municipality of Vienna that impressed these tourists most. Vienna, a great city, capital of the defeated and dismembered Austrian Empire, faced huge problems after the First World War. Serious housing problems in the dense tenements of the inner city were exacerbated by an influx of refugees. From 1923, over a ten-year period, the City Council carried out a crash programme of more than 60,000 new homes.

Elizabeth Denby described the Vienna she saw in 1934:

> . . . the structure of the town is clearly defined, with its hard inner core of narrow streets and high blocks of grim tenements, dank, dark, squalid – a disreputable memorial to the ideals of the nineteenth century. This is surrounded by an area of great beauty and gaiety, containing the Ring, trees, flowers, cafés, great public buildings, the Opera House – with trams radiating to the new estates in the suburbs. And here in these post-war estates, although the people are still housed in high tenements, there is a very different spirit informing their plan; and within and behind the estates are trees, grass, courtyards, flowers. Beyond these tenements comes an area of small houses with their own gardens, which are also "municipal estates" containing their own shops, laundries, meeting rooms and kindergartens. Farther out still are experimental groups of co-operative "garden city" colonies, and finally are the allotment estates for the unemployed.[13]

These allotment estates, interestingly, were similar to the smallholding settlements pioneered by the Chartists. Known as the Gesiba scheme, unemployed families were given allotments each of 5/8th acre, which was considered sufficient to yield produce equal to unemployment benefit. Under a self-build scheme, the settlers built small brick semi-detached houses. Co-operatives were set up to organize training, common use of equipment and marketing.

But it was the new blocks of flats that were to influence the municipal visitors most: Karl Marx Hof – six storeys containing 1,380 flats in a continuous development more than a kilometre long – designed in 1927 by Karl Ehn, a pupil of Otto Wagner; George Washington Hof – a four-storey courtyard development of 1,085 flats –

Figure 2.3
George Washington Hof, Vienna. One of the many social housing develop- ments of the 1920s which so inspired visitors from Britain

designed by Robert Derley, also in 1927, in a vernacular style (Fig. 2.3); Engelsplatz; Winarsky Hof, and others.[14] What impressed them was not the style, the construction or the standards of the flats – which were poor in British terms. Here was a new social concept. It was recognized here that housing did not just mean shelter. Unlike the Victorian tenements, these blocks provided not just homes but all the social and rec- reational faculties necessary fur a full and happy life: extensive green spaces, well designed and cared for; safe places for children to play, and nurseries for their care and education; communal laundries and public baths: community centres for spare-time recreation. Here, then, was model to be emulated

The modern flat

The rebuilt slums could be new blocks of multi-storey housing with generous social facilities. But, unlike the Viennese prototype and home-grown tenements, the new blocks would contain modern flats with generous space standards and facilities. Such flats were then being built for the prosperous middle classes in Maida Vale, Finchley, Hendon and other parts of London, as well as in the well heeled coastal resorts such as Bournemouth and Brighton. It was this vision that inspired the most adventurous British urban development of the 1930s: the Quarry Hill Estate in Leeds.

Leeds had some of the worst housing problems of the industrial North. There were 75,000 of the back-to-back hovels described by Orwell and they were still being built during the 1930s.[15] In 1933 the Labour Party, led by Rev. Charles Jenkinson, came to power with a promise to build 30,000 new homes. The architect R. A. H. Livett was appointed to direct the new housing initiative. Livett had recently designed Ken- net House in Manchester – a long block of 181 flats with flat roofs stepping down in terraces – and was an enthusiast for the modern flat. He and Jenkinson were amongst the pilgrims to Europe. They conceived a model development which would contain the best of all the ideas they could muster.

29

Figure 2.4
Above: the back-to-backs of Quarry hill, Leeds before redevelopment: Coketown personified. Below: part of the huge 1930s estate designed as a model development of high standard modern flats with generous social facilities

Quarry Hill was a notorious area of semi-derelict back-to backs less than a mile from Leeds Town Hall, Using the statutory clearance powers under the Greenwood Act, Livett planned a new development of long blocks, mostly six to eight storeys high containing 938 flats covering 29 acres (Fig. 2.4) . The estate was planned with communal green spaces, 20 shops, communal laundry and restaurant, and a social centre. The social inspiration came from Vienna, but the new flats were to have space standards higher than any previous council flats, with generous bathrooms and fitted kitchens. The multi-storey blocks were also to have lifts – the first, and only, pre-war council estate to do so. There were to be important technical innovations inspired by a new development at Drancy la Muette outside Paris. There, blocks had been built up to 15 storeys high, incorporating a mechanized refuse disposal system – the Garchy system. Most significantly they had been built using a novel method of construction.

Livett was aware of the urgency of the council's programme. He was also concerned about the cost. Normal housing subsidy would cover the cost of the flats, but it would not provide for the social facilities he considered essential to the scheme. He hoped to solve both these problems by adopting the Mopin system used at Drancy. This used a light steel framework erected first. To the steelwork were attached lightweight concrete panels forming walls, floors and roofs. The voids around the steelwork was then filled up with poured concrete. The panels were fabricated in a site factory, and the whole building was erected without the need for expensive scaffolding. By adopting this system Livett expected the construction to be quick and significantly cheaper than conventional construction. He reckoned without English builders. Notoriously traditional, contractors were reluctant to tender low against an unknown system and in the event could not cope with the technical problems. The development, begun in April 1935, which was planned to be quick and cheap, took more than four years to complete. Escalating costs led to the omission of some of the intended communal facilities.[16]

Flawed it may have been, but Quarry Hill was much admired at the time, mainly for the new levels for which it had raised the standards of the council flat. By 1939 Leeds had plans for a further 2,000–2,500 flats on the same lines. In London the building of flats in small estates had continued and by 1936 the authorities were building more new flats than houses.[17] Liverpool had completed 5,000 flats in new estates, and Manchester no less than 9,000. Both cities had plans for more new estates on the drawing board.[9] Overall, though, little progress had been made in clearing the slums when the Second World War intervened. The blitz was to devastate almost half a million houses and raise the housing crisis to new levels.

The post-war settlement

Hardly before the war had begun, the Churchill Government – a grand coalition embracing Conservative and Labour Ministers – started to prepare for eventual victory and reconstruction. The Barlow Commission, appointed to examine geographical distribution of industry in response to disproportionate unemployment in the North, was published in 1940 and was to form the basis of a new approach to regional planning. In 1941 three new Commissions were appointed
  • Uthwatt, which was to lay the basis of post war planning legislation
  • Scott to examine rural planning, and

- the Beveridge Committee on Social Insurance which was to lay the foundations for universal welfare benefits.[18]

In 1944 the Education Act established universal secondary education and raised the school leaving age to 15.[3]

After the war it was to fall to the new Labour Government to implement and oversee these reforms. They added measures from their own programme which were greatly to increase the power of the State – the nationalization of the great public utilities – gas, water, electricity – together with the railways, the mines and the steel industry; and their most enduring reform – the establishment of the National Health Service in 1947 – which was to add a new and major element to the field of social architecture. The greatest impact on the cities, however, was made by the new approach to urban planning and the greatly increased powers of local government.

The new urban plans

During and immediately after the war a series of plans were prepared for British cities, particularly those most affected by the bombing: Donald Gibson's plan for Coventry, which set the prototype for the pedestrianized town centre; Thomas Sharp's plan for Exeter (1946); Lutyens and Abercrombie's plan for Hull (1945). But the plans which were to have the most far-reaching impact were those prepared by Professor Patrick Abercrombie for Greater London (1944) and Glasgow (1946). These plans were not primarily to deal with war damage, but to address, once again, the continuing problem of overcrowded slum housing in the Victorian areas of the great cities.

Abercrombie proposed a two-pronged attack: redevelopment of the inner areas and new approach to decentralization. He set out acceptable densities for new housing in the cities in a hierarchy, highest in the centre and decreasing towards to the urban fringe. For Glasgow there were three zones: housing at 120 people per acre (ppa) at the centre, 90 ppa in the intermediate zone, and 60 ppa in outer areas. In both London and Glasgow existing population densities were so high that these new levels could be achieved only if many people were rehoused elsewhere. In Glasgow it was estimated that 500,000 would need rehousing. Half of these could be accommodated in the rebuilt urban areas, but the remaining 250,000 would be displaced.[19]

Some could be decentralized to new cottage estates, but concern about urban sprawl had long since exercised planners and politicians, and an Act to impose "green belts" around major cities had been placed on the statute book in 1938. Abercrombie proposed green belts around London and Glasgow, and beyond the green belts new settlements built as complete towns. Eight new towns were proposed around London and four for Glasgow. A corset was placed around the ever-spreading suburban sprawl, and Ebenezer Howard's garden city dream was about to be realized on a new and impressive scale, for the early new towns owed almost everything to the Garden City tradition and were developed as low-density estates in an updated version of cottage vernacular.

For the urban redevelopment new and unprecedented power and finance was accorded to the local authorities. Some had begun to establish bureaucracies before the war, but all the major authorities now did so: planning departments to implement the new legislation, architects departments to build, housing departments to manage their new housing estates, education departments to plan and oversee the new schools. The scope for public architecture was now enormous and many architects embarked on

32

their new social mission with enthusiasm and considerable optimism. They brought with them a fresh architectural ideology that was rapidly gaining influence

The Modern movement

Throughout the 1920s and 1930s, leading architects of the modernist school had been building individual projects, mostly in continental Europe, and publishing manifestos that had considerable influence on *avant garde* architects. Most influential of these was Le Corbusier's book of 1923 (English edition 1927), *Towards a new architecture*,[20] in which he extolled the aesthetic virtues of factories, ships, aeroplanes and machines and the purity of classical forms. He espoused an urban future – La Ville Radieuse – of a city of massive tower blocks set in parkland and linked by a grid of urban motorways. He closed with a challenge – "Architecture or Revolution" – which might have inspired Lloyd George. Either the people must be given new, modern homes based on the aesthetics and mass-production techniques of the machine age, or there would be insurrection.

The leading modernists, including Le Corbusier, Walter Gropius, Alvar Aalto, Richard Neutra, Marcel Beuer and Erno Goldfinger, banded together in the International Congress for Modern Architecture (CIAM) which held a series of conferences around Europe. The 1932 Congress produced the Athens Charter, which condemned urban sprawl and proposed a new approach to urban development based on multi-storey buildings. All this had little influence in Britain between the wars, where only a handful of modernist projects had been built. A few wealthy clients had commissioned modernists for their private houses. Towards the end of the period, Bethold Lubetkin's group, Tecton, produced some influential projects, and Maxwell Fry completed a public housing project in modernist style – Kensal House (Fig. 2.5).

Modernism did not really come to Britain until after the war when the Modern

Figure 2.5
Kensal House, 1938. Influential early modernist council housing designed by Maxwell Fry.

Architecture Research Group (MARs, the British arm of CIAM) organized its sixth Congress in Bridgewater, Somerset in 1947.[21] It promptly proceeded to rewrite history. A leading member of MARs, J. M. Richards, editor of the *Architectural Review*, published his highly influential *An introduction to modern architecture*. Early in the book Richards dismisses with a grandiloquent gesture an entire century of architectural history: "The best architects of the nineteenth century were . . . men of remarkable ability and enthusiasm who in other circumstances would have been producing fine architecture. They had all the talent necessary. It was the time that had gone wrong".[22] In promoting the achievements of the modernists he effectively dismisses most of the first part of the 20th century as well. The achievements of the Arts and Crafts movement are only accorded recognition where selected exemplars can be interpreted as stylistic antecedents to modernism.

In fact, the principles of the Arts and Crafts and modernist movements were diametrically opposed. The one despised machinery, the other applauded the machine age of factory production. Whereas the Arts and Crafts movement rejected the industrial city and all its works, the modernists embraced the urban concept and proposed a new urban form based on high-rise buildings using advanced techniques. Where Arts and Crafts architects respected the environment and the buildings of earlier ages, the modernists wanted to sweep away the existing environment and replace it with their own vision. Above all, in place of a reverence for traditional construction and techniques, the modernists produced an international style of flat roofs, exposed concrete and flat white facades, which took no account of the prevailing environment. The British prevailing environment is rain – and its traditional architecture was designed to cope with it. The modernists ignored it at their peril.

Cities of towers

Nonetheless, modernism became a growing influence in post-war urban redevelopment. Most influential, and perhaps the high point of Modern movement housing was the Alton West Estate in Roehampton, a west London suburb (Fig. 2.6). Alton West was a mixed development, of towers, slabs, family maisonettes and bungalows for the elderly, set in mature parkland. Designed in 1951 by the LCC Architects Department, it was not completed until 1960. In 1964 *The Architects' Journal* waxed lyrically on:

> . . . the great charm and fascination exerted by this project on the minds of so many architects, progressive and reactionary alike, in so many different countries. The fascination of Roehampton is generated by a force that is more subtle and powerful than could ever arise from considerations of technology. Behind the built form there is an ideal – the image of the park city of Le Corbusier, born in the mind of a poet and carrying the force of a poet's vision.[23]

Without doubt, Roehampton was an outstandingly good scheme of its type. But so much cannot be said of most the new housing inspired by modernism. Throughout the 1950s, multi-storey housing was increasingly seen as the appropriate solution to slum clearance. Target densities had been laid down and these had to be reached or the rehousing programme would not be achieved. Building high was seen as the answer. During the 1950s, high flats – five storeys or more – were a relatively small proportion of new housing in Britain, barely 7 per cent, But, of the flats that were built, more than a quarter of these blocks were in towers 15 storeys high or more.[24]

34

Figure 2.6
The LCC's Alton West Estate, Roehampton, gave credibility to modernist high-rise housing, but its mature landscape set a standard that proved unattainable elsewhere.

Unlike Roehampton, most of these towers were set in a bleak urban wasteland of concrete and tarmac – a world away from the park city of the poet's vision.

Until 1960, then, the modernist influence on housing design had been limited. Most new housing was traditional houses and gardens. Even in the inner cities, where flats were built in large numbers, most were small blocks of relatively traditional design which owed more to the Viennese model than to the modernist tower blocks. Where the modernist principles were vigorously pursued to their logical conclusion was in the programme of new school building.

Prefabricated schools

The wartime Education Act necessitated a thorough reorganization of school buildings. On top of that the post-war bulge in population – the baby boom – meant an escalating demand for primary schools. These demands were universal, but in the County of Hertfordshire, on the northern rim of London, there were added pressures. Three of the designated new towns were in Hertfordshire and it was home to two large LCC "out county" estates at Borehamwood and South Oxley, as well as a large amount of ill serviced private development. The pressure to provide new schools, the responsibility of the County Council, was immense.

During the war many young architects and architects–to–be worked as technical

35

designers in munitions industries and in the services. War required a regimen quite unlike the traditional world of the architect immersed in the individual creativity of one-off projects. It required them to work as part of a team, to use a scientific approach to design, and to conform to programmes for large-scale production from prefabricated parts. Admiration for the efficiency of industrial mass-production and its aura of progress was a key element of the Modern movement's philosophy, and it was not surprising that the post-war generation of architects embraced it with such enthusiasm.

In 1945 Sirrat Johnson-Marshall, destined to become LCC schools architect and a later head a major private practice, joined Hertfordshire County Council direct from his wartime job fabricating decoys in the military camouflage team. Under his leadership a rolling programme was established for school building. A means of construction was to be developed that would be simple, fast and economic, yet flexible enough to allow variation and regular revision in response to changing needs. The solution was a sort of "Meccano" system. Lightweight lattice beams and columns would be assembled, on simple point foundations, in frameworks based on a regular grid. To the framework were attached lightweight infill panels – prefabricated timber frames containing ready fixed doors and windows. Lightweight floor and roof panels completed the construction.

When Johnson-Marshall moved to the LCC, the system was adopted for their new schools. It was to be developed further when, in 1955, Donald Gibson left Coventry to become Nottinghamshire County Architect. Nottinghamshire was a mining area that suffered considerably from subsidence. Gibson concluded that an adaptation of the Hertfordshire schools system – with flexible joints – would successfully resist the uneven forces produced by mine tunnels collapsing below. Adaptations to the design allowed the exteriors of the schools to be finished in concrete cladding panels or more attractive, and homely, tile hanging (Fig. 2.7).

Figure 2.7
West Bridgford Grammar School designed by Nottingham County Architects Department. A typical product of the CLASP system.

The resulting system produced pleasing, open, airy buildings that were quick and cheap to construct. A number of other authorities joined with Nottingham to form the Consortium of Local Authorities Schools Programme – CLASP. Over the next few years hundreds of CLASP schools were built all over the country. Their success was to form a key element in the next leap forward in urban development.[25]

The final solution

The influence of the Modern movement came to full fruition in the 1960s. The movement's urge for urban redevelopment gripped public and private sector alike throughout the country. It was the era of town centre redevelopment. Birmingham led the field in the early 1960s when it ripped out the smoke-blackened and devalued Victorian buildings at its heart, destroyed the traditional street pattern, and replaced most of its city centre with a mass of modern buildings – offices, shops, a new railway station and pioneering new indoor shopping centre – surrounded by a ring of new urban motorways (Fig. 2.8).

The Buchanan Report, *Traffic in towns* (1963), demonstrated only too clearly what would happen if cities sought to accommodate unlimited motor traffic. Its case study of Bloomsbury showed the whole area flattened and rebuilt with multi-level motorways and multi-storey buildings in order to satisfy the demands of the motor car. Other studies of Leeds. Newbury and Norwich demonstrated the damage motorway building would do to smaller cities. Nonetheless. in breathtaking flight in the face of its own evidence, the report recommended new urban motorways and concluded:

> To accommodate large numbers of motor vehicles in towns and cities is bound to involve substantial physical changes. . . . It is necessary to secure the comprehensive redevelopment of large areas. . . . Recreating the urban environment in a vigorous and lively way could do more than anything to make [Britain] the most exciting country in the world.[26]

Following the lead of Birmingham, and spurred on by Buchanan's conclusions most major cities in Britain embarked, over the following few years, on ambitious town centre redevelopment. New urban motorways, pedestrianized shopping centres, and the ubiquitous glass-clad modern office blocks appeared all over the country. Few cities emulated the massive scale of redevelopment carried out in Birmingham but overall much of what remained of the nineteenth-century heritage in the old city centres was destroyed. Those cities which had escaped the war now embarked on a peacetime blitz of the bulldozer.

Most of this building was carried out by private developers who were content to use the Modern movement's urge for rebuilding and the cheapness offered by modernist design to make large gains in floor-space and profits. But the public sector had willed it. Councils, particularly in the poorer cities of the North saw commercial redevelopment as an essential component in generating prosperity in their areas. It was often the Planning Departments that had laid the foundations for the redevelopment process, even if they were not always happy with the results. Although the local authorities were only partial players in the town centre schemes, they had a leading role in the other great building boom of the 1960s – the drive for new housing.

Figure 2.8
Two views of Birmingham Bull Ring, both looking northwards. Above, the traditional public meeting place and market. Right, after the redevelopments of the 1960s: the market thrust beneath a motorway; the Victorian streets replaced by a jumble of modern offices.

The housing boom

Housing had become a central concern of the post-war consensus. The Labour Government's housing programme of the 1940s had been continued by the Conservative Government through the 1950s. The Conservatives had come to power with a promise to build 300,000 houses a year, a target that was achieved by 1953. Nevertheless, in 1954 the local authorities estimated there were still 850,000 slum houses. House-building continued under the leadership of Harold Macmillan, first as Housing Minister, then as Prime Minister. By 1964 a record output of 374,000 new houses was achieved, 40 per cent built by local authorities. In the General Election of that year the Conservatives promised 400,000 houses a year. But the victorious Labour Party topped this with a promise of 500,000.[27] The only question that this massive programme raised at the time was how to achieve the targets. The design professions and the building industry were already stretched by the amount of city centre building work. The answer seemed to be industrialization. The apparent success of the schools programme had led the Ministry of Housing, in the early 1960s, to develop a similar system for low-rise housing – the 5M system – using a steel and timber frame and prefabricated infill panels (Fig. 2.9).[28]

Lightweight systems were later developed for constructing high-rise buildings. More immediately available were the heavy panel systems that had been developed in Europe. These used precast concrete panels joined together at the edges so that they formed a series of rigid boxes that would stand up without an independent structural frame. The panels could be manufactured off site or in a site factory and erected quickly by crane, saving considerably on expensive onsite construction work. One of the earliest heavy panel schemes was the West Kentish Town estate in London, where construction began in 1960 using the Reema system (Fig. 2.10). But several large construction companies developed heavy panel systems and by the mid-1960s they were in widespread use.

What seems surprising, in retrospect, is that there was so little awareness, at the time, of the problems affecting the first estate constructed in Britain using industrial-

Figure 2.9
Prototype houses built in Sheffield using the 5M system, a method of lightweight prefabricated construction developed from the principles of CLASP.

Figure 2.10
West Kentish Town estate, north London, one of the first housing developments built using heavy panel prefabricated systems.

ized building: Quarry Hill. By 1953 the estate was already stigmatized as a slum and locally there were reports of crime, vandalism and infestation by vermin. More importantly, in the early 1960s serious technical problems were discovered. Panels had worked loose as a result of inadequate expansion joints allowing water to penetrate. The concrete casing to the steelwork had not been poured properly, leaving voids. Penetrating water then caused the structural steelwork to rust. Major repairs were carried out in 1963, but these could not save Quarry Hill in the long run and it was demolished in 1978.[16] Those who were aware chose to wish these problems away, given the commitment to the housing programme and the considerable investment in new system building. After all, the system used at Quarry Hill was 30 years out of date. The new systems had been tried and tested abroad. It couldn't happen again – or could it?

The protests

The other thing that no one seemed to notice was that by this time almost all the slum buildings had actually gone. By the end of the 1950s practically all the back-to-backs had been cleared and what were now being demolished to make way for new housing were the late nineteenth-century tunnel-backs built under the improved sanitary regime of the building bylaws. By now, questions were being raised about the social

40

effects of redevelopment. Orwell had first raised such questions in 1937: "A whole section of the town is condemned *en bloc*" he wrote "presently the houses are pulled down and the people are transferred to some housing estate miles away" The loss of the local shops, pubs and clubs "is a serious blow to communal life".[29]

No doubt these problems were dismissed as a necessary evil, since no-one doubted that the slums had to be cleared. But by the late 1950s these questions were being raised again, notably in Wilmot & Young's seminal study *Family and kinship in East London.*[30] Here, parallel sociological studies were carried out in Bethnal Green and a new estate 20 miles away to which many local people had been transferred. The complex and neighbourly social and family networks of the east London terraced streets contrasted sharply with the alienation and sense of isolation experienced by those in the new estate. In America, Jane Jacobs published her similarly influential study of the effects of redevelopment, arguing a strong case for the variety, spontaneity and communal values of the traditional urban street pattern.[31]

If these protests were heeded at all, they were taken as criticism of the form of redevelopment, not the process itself. There had by now been sufficient concern raised about the isolating effects of high-rise flats. The bleak stairs and internal corridors of tower and slab blocks were recognized as a barrier to the social interaction and neighbourliness engendered by the traditional street. In response, what was now offered was a new form of street: streets in the sky. The new concept made possible a different form of high-density housing – lower blocks linked together with open walkways. The first major realization of this concept was the Park Hill scheme in Sheffield, completed in 1960, a massive development of almost 1,000 maisonettes up to 16 storeys high on a hilly city centre site (Fig. 2.11). Taking advantage of the site, the flats were reached by wide open-access decks coming off the hillside at various levels. These "streets" were designed to carry small vehicles such as milk floats and were said to provide a meeting place for residents. Park Hill was widely acclaimed at the time. In 1964 Maxwell Fry, doyen of the British modern movement, described it as "One of the

Figure 2.11 (right and overleaf) The massive Park Hill development in Sheffield. The first large-scale realization of multi-storey housing reached by high-level open access decks – so-called "streets in the sky".

most interesting architectural works I can think of . . . extraordinary forms arising from the conception of the elevated street . . . it offers, as few modern works do, the subject matter for a painter . . .".[32]

Culmination and fall

Armed with industrialized building and the new concept of high-density, low-rise urban housing, the architects, planners and housing officials pressed on with the massive building programme – the final solution to the problems of bad housing. The years 1965–9 produced 1.8 million houses.[33] About half of them were multi-storey flats, including many thousands built using industrialized systems.[24] The target of half a million houses a year was finally reached in 1968. That same year saw an event that has now become notorious in sounding the death knell for industrialized building and high-rise housing – the collapse of Ronan Point.

Ronan Point was a 23-storey tower block, part of an estate in the East London Borough of Newham. The estate had been built using a heavy-panel industrialized system. Early one spring morning an explosion in a corner flat blew out one of the panels, causing the corner of the block to collapse, killing five people and injuring many more. The accident shattered the confidence of tenants in high-rise buildings all over the country and triggered a major investigation of system-built blocks. Many were revealed to have serious construction faults with improperly made joints that leaked and caused water penetration: Quarry Hill *déja vu*. Remedial works costing millions were required and system building bit the dust.

The corporate State

The building boom of the 1960s left behind radical alterations to the central and inner areas of the industrial cities. The modern commercial buildings of the urban centres did not capture the admiration or affection of the public. Still less did the new council estates that surrounded them. Technical problems were abundant. The environment they provided was stark and forbidding. Most seriously, the open access systems that had promised to recreate the city street were to provide open season for a wide variety of crime and abuse.

Contemporary critics tend to blame all this on the Modern movement; arguably it was a debasement of the movement's ideals. Were they to return from the dead, it is no more likely that Le Corbusier would recognize his legacy in a system-built estate than that Philip Webb would recognize his in the average suburban semi. Nonetheless, the ideas did originate with the Modern movement architects. They propagandized for redevelopment, high-rise buildings and machine production. In many ways, more influential that the vision of modernism was its blindness. By dismissing and denigrating the urban heritage, they helped to generate a distaste for the old and for Victorian buildings in particular. Once they were seen as monstrosities few protested when they were swept away.

The debasement of the modernist vision really began when it was taken up as the loadstone of the corporate State. The government machinery set in place after the Second World War had mushroomed into a huge bureaucracy. Central government had played an active and leading role in urban change and the development departments of local government had grown enormously. By 1967 40 per cent of the 21,225 architects were employed by local or central government and many of the rest worked in private practices employed on public sector projects.[34] For the designers who had set out in the early years with such commitment and high ideals, it was a soul destroying experience. They had become part of a machine which thought solely in terms of numbers. Programmes were the order of the day, designed to achieve "targets" of "housing units". The designers on the drawing boards hardly ever saw a "client" – and when they did it was an official of the housing department or a senior councillor. There was no contact whatsoever with those who were supposed to be the beneficiaries of their efforts. No input and no feedback. Social architecture had become a sterile technical exercise. And the numbers game went on. Working to new standards, a Ministry survey of 1967 showed there were still 1.8 million unfit dwellings.[33] For all the efforts of the corporate State, it had still not solved the problems of the cities. The Garden City movement had drowned in a sea of semis. The Modern movement had degenerated into an insensitive leviathan. It was time for a fresh approach.

References

1. Henry Pelling, *A history of British trade unionism* (London: Penguin, 1963), ch. 8.
2. Sheila Rowbotham, *Hidden from history* (London: Pluto Press, 1973), 182.
3. Paul Sharp & John Dunford, *The education system in England and Wales* (Harlow: Longman, 1990), 16.
4. Mark Swenarton, *Homes fit for heroes – the politics and architecture of early State housing in Britain* (London: Hutchinson, 1981), 79.
5. Quoted in John Burnett, *A social history of housing 1815–1985,* 2nd edn (London: Routledge, 1986), 220.
6. John Burnett, op. cit., 234.
7. Paul Oliver, Ian Davis, Ian Bentley, *Dunroamin – the suburban semi and its enemies* (London: Barrie & Jenkins, 1981), 120.
8. Thomas Sharp, *Town planning* (London: Penguin, 1940), 52–3.
9. Alison Ravetz, "From working class tenement to modern flat – local authorities and multi-storey housing between the wars" in *Multi-storey living – the British working class experience,* Anthony Sutcliffe (ed.) (London: Croom Helm, 1974), ch. 5.
10. George Orwell, *The road to Wigan Pier* (London: Victor Gollanz, 1937; Penguin, 1989), 46.
11. George Orwell, op. cit., 49.
12. John Burnett, op. cit., 243.
13. Elizabeth Denby, *Europe re-housed* (London: George Allen & Unwin, 1938), 150.
14. Elizabeth Denby, op. cit., 160–61; and Norman Beddington, "Viennese waltz ahead with urban renewal", *Planning 800* (6 January 1989).
15. Alison Ravetz, Chapter 5 in Sutcliffe, op. cit.; and John Burnet, op. cit., 173.
16. Peter Mitchell, *Memento Mori – the flats at Quarry Hill, Leeds* (Otley, West Yorkshire: Smith Settle, 1990); and Alison Ravetz, *Model estate* (London: Croom Helm, 1974).
17. John Burnett, op. cit., 247.
18. J. B. Cullingworth, *Town and country planning in Britain*, 11th edn (London: Routledge, 1994).
19. Roger Smith, "Multi-dwelling building in Scotland 1750–1970", in Sutcliffe, op. cit., ch 7.
20. Le Corbusier, *Towards a new architecture* (Paris: Editions Crès, 1923; London: John Rodker, 1927; The Architectural Press, 1946).
21. Sigfried Giedion, *Space, time and architecture,* 5th edn (Oxford: Oxford University Press 1941, 1967), 696–706.
22. J. M. Richards, *An introduction to modern architecture* (London: Penguin, 1940, 1962), 11.
23. "Housing at Alton Estate, Roehampton", *The Architects' Journal* (15 January 1964), 132.
24. E. W. Cooney, "High flats in local authority housing in England and Wales since 1945", in Sutcliffe, op. cit., ch. 6.

25. Andrew Saint, *Towards a social architecture – the role of school building in post-war England* (New Haven, Connecticut: Yale University Press, 1987).

26. *Traffic in towns* [the specially shortened edition of the Buchanan Report] (London: Penguin/ HMSO 1964), 236, 247, 248.

27. John Burnett, op. cit., 286–7.

28. "5M housing at Sheffield", *The Architects' Journal* (12 May 1965), 1135.

29. George Orwell, op. cit., 66.

30. Michael Young & Peter Wilmot, *Family and kinship in East London* (London: Routledge & Kegan Paul, 1957; Penguin, 1962).

31. Jane Jacobs, *The death and life of great American cities* (New York: Random House, 1961; London: Jonathan Cape, 1962; Penguin, 1965).

32. "Housing at Park Hill Sheffield", *The Architects' Journal* (15 January 1964), 147–9.

33. John Burnett, op. cit., 288.

34. Sam Webb, "Architecture, alienation and the omnipotent adminman", *The Architects' Journal* (19 October 1977), 751.

CHAPTER 3

Communities fight back

THE BIRTH OF A NEW ARCHITECTURE

The late 1960s was a remarkable time. In Eastern Europe, the Prague Spring attempted to reshape communism "with a human face". In Western Europe students staged take-overs of university campuses most famously in the events in Paris in May 1968. In the USA young people rioted against the war in Vietnam. This collective revolt by the young followed 20 years of stability during which the consensus of the post-war settlement had ossified into an entrenched paternalism. The immediate pretexts for these rebellions were many and various, but at root lay a rejection of repressive regulation and remote management, and a plea for more involvement and responsibility in decision-making. Once challenged, the tenets of the establishment were subjected to wide-ranging critical examination – a brainstorming of political and organizational ideas. Many of these ideas fell by the wayside, but many others were to form the seeds of social movements that were to become increasingly influential in the years that followed.

This period of intellectual upheaval saw the birth of the community action movement in Britain. During the late 1960s and early 1970s, community groups sprang up everywhere. Sometimes they were funded by charities, occasionally by local authorities. Most often they were entirely voluntary organizations relying on the goodwill of their members and supporters. Planners, architects and other building designers were among these supporters from the start. Sometimes they acted as advisers, providing the technical background for campaigns to fight the effects of development proposals; sometimes as enablers, providing their professional skills to help a group to control their own housing or bid for a community centre or playground. Over the following few years the social commitment of a fresh generation of professionals was gradually refined into a new approach to building design and development. An approach that became known as "community architecture".

Fresh ideas, new models

The intellectual upheaval of the late 1960s brought with it new demands for political rights and wide-ranging interest in alternative ideas of political economy. In 1970 William Morris's *News from nowhere* was republished, as were the writings of Robert Owen[1] in response to a revival of interests in the ideals of co-operation and egalitarianism. Coincidentally, the period saw a new challenge to the cosy presumption of never-ending growth and development. The new science of futurology was born.

Computer predictions showed that, if prevailing trends went unchecked, non-renewable resources would be largely exhausted by the end of the century.[2] The new millennium would dawn with an expanding world population increasingly short of food and industrial goods, and suffering a world massively polluted by twentieth century materialism. In response to these apocalyptic prophesies, *The Ecologist* magazine produced a comprehensive alternative for a low-energy society based on small communities, self-sufficient in industry and agriculture.[3] The ideals of nineteenth-century radicalism were revived in a new era of environmental consciousness.

Meanwhile, there was increasing concern at what was happening to the cities. In an atmosphere charged with new ideas and a challenge to the old order, the younger generation of urban designers began to question both the results and the process of rebuilding the cities. Was it right that people should be consigned to massive housing estates in which their individuality was submerged in a monotony of identical units? Wasn't more humane housing possible in which people could express their identity and their own taste? Could they not be given some choice, some involvement in shaping their own environment? Most basic of all, was it right to disperse communities and destroy the old urban fabric to make way for motorways, office blocks and gigantic barracks of mass housing? New models began to emerge which presaged an alternative urban future.

Model 1: rationalized tradition

In 1961 John Darbourne, then a student at Harvard Landscape School, won an open competition for a new estate for 2,000 people in Westminster. Although initiated in the early 1960s, the first phase of Lillington Gardens was not complete until 1968. It marked a new departure in mass housing. The facilities of the new estate were a distant echo of the Viennese model: not just housing, but shops, pubs, a library, a home for the elderly. There was a new emphasis on the quality of outdoor space – attractive landscaped courts, high-level walkways softened by shrubs and small trees, generous private balconies. Visually there was a new synthesis of vernacular traditions. In place of the flat, repetitive facades of the Modern movement, the planning of the units was articulated to create variety, interest and a semblance of individuality. In place of concrete facing and metal windows was the warmth of stained timber and traditional red brick (Fig. 3.1).[4]

Although it offered no more choice or involvement to those who would eventually live there, Lillington Gardens and the later projects of Darbourne and Darke, offered a new model of humane and attractive urban housing. Based on the vernacular approach that had largely been suppressed during the 1950s and 1960s, rationalized traditional architecture – or "ratrad" for short – became a major force in housing design in the 1970s. It not only influenced urban housing, it also generated a new approach to low-density housing based on the traditional architecture of small towns – an approach given impetus by the publication of the Essex Design Guide in 1973[5] and similar guidelines by other local authorities.

Figure 3.1
Lillington Gardens initiated a more organic approach to housing design, creating variety and interest, and heralded a revival of traditional materials and design.

Model 2: self-expression

In 1961 John Habraken published, in Holland, a critique that derided the paternalism of mass housing – of providing homes in which the occupants had no means of shaping their own environment or expressing their own preferences. Habraken proposed separating the structure and services – "supports" – and the enclosures forming the dwellings – "infill". Urban support structures could be built providing multi-storey serviced decks. People could rent or buy space on these decks and have their own homes built into them. A variety of manufacturers would be able to offer the infill components for a new home, custom planned using prefabricated elements. Having selected a supplier, customers could:

> . . . visit the showrooms of the manufacturer of their choice. With the help of a representative of the firm an effective arrangement of dwelling is decided upon . . . The representative invites [the] customers to return in a fortnight. The dwelling will be ready for inspection in the showrooms. At the appointed time they see a full-scale model of their dwelling. They walk about it, test doors and windows, visit kitchen and bathroom, try the usefulness of rooms and cupboards. After suggesting a few alterations they decide to buy. The manufacturer transports the parts to the support structure where the dwelling is finally assembled in a short time.[6]

This was the stuff of dreams, perhaps, but it contained important aspirations. People should have the right to plan their own homes and to choose what they looked like. The result would be satisfied customers and an urban environment enriched by the variety produced by individual self-expression. Habraken developed his ideas by setting up the Foundation for Architectural Research (SAR) at the University of Eindhoven. SAR was influential in several projects in Europe in the 1970s and its ideas were taken up in Britain by the Greater London Council.[7] But it was to achieve its most celebrated realization in the *zone sociale* of the medical school of the University of Louvain in Belgium (Fig. 3.2).

In 1968 the university decided to set up, in Brussels, a large hospital, medical school and residential facilities. Being 1968, the students rejected the plans of the university and demanded that the local residents be involved. The university demurred but allowed the students to propose the architect for the scheme. Lucien Kroll was appointed and he set about a dialogue with the students through a series of meetings. Through participation, the function, form and appearance of the proposed building was discussed at length, revealing a variety of aspirations and contradictions. To resolve these, Kroll settled on the SAR principle of a support structure based on a tartan grid. This would allow variation and adaptability in the planning of the rooms, apartments and social facilities. The infill to the facades could be completed with a variety of materials. "We sought to utilize materials which suggest popular culture" wrote Kroll, "slates of common cement asbestos, window frames out of the catalogue, exposed concrete, ordinary bricks and block, standard glazing on the balconies, some plastic, and so forth."[8]

The result is a strong visual framework provided by the main structure enlivened by the apparent randomness of the rich variety of infill materials. To some it was anarchy. To others an abnegation of design responsibility – although the apparent disorder was controlled and partly contrived by the architect. To most it was startling – including the university authorities who conspired to sack Kroll while the students were on holiday. What it did show was that participation and self-expression by users could result in residential buildings that, in function and appearance, were quite different from those produced by the systematic approach of the state machine.

Figure 3.2
The medical faculty, Louvain. Dramatic realization of the principle that, within a unifying framework, the licence of choice could be allowed to create diversity and variety.

Model 3: participation

In 1968 Newcastle upon Tyne City Council appointed Ralph Erskine to undertake a planning study of its redevelopment at Byker, a community of 12,000 people. Erskine, British born and trained, had spent his working life in Sweden. There he had shown a strong commitment to social architecture and, for several years, it had been his prac-

50

tice to consult users in the design of his schemes. Erskine formed a partnership with UK-based architect Vernon Gracie and they set up an office, in a disused undertaker's shop, in Byker. Gracie agreed to live on site and for several years lived over the shop and later in one of the maisonettes he had designed. The office became a focus for communication with local people who would drop in to seek help, to inspect the work in progress, or to pass the time of day.

Byker's most famous feature is the "Wall": a continuous multi-storey block almost a mile long, enclosing the northern edge of the site (Fig. 3.3). The wall had been included in the brief from the City Council and its main justification was to baffle noise from the projected Shields Road motorway. In fact, most of the planned motorway was never built and the wall stands as a redundant example of the "vigorous and lively" architecture that was to soften the impact of the motor car on cities. Although it lost its original purpose, the Wall became a key element in the scheme. It helped to

Figure 3.3
Byker. Housing redevelopment that pioneered the participation of users in design and development decisions. Still one of Britain's most successful social housing projects.

provide protection against the cold winds from the North Sea. But its main role was to create enough new housing to allow clearance to proceed on a phased basis, so that most people could be rehoused on the site. Preserving the community became a key to the development of the project. To reinforce this the housing department were persuaded to pre-allocate homes six months before completion, so that near-neighbours could be housed together.

Erskine had developed a clear idea of the separate interests of the "user client" and the "sponsor client". He sought to involve the people of Byker as user clients in the planning of their new homes. In addition to the onsite office, and its "open door" policy, there was also a liaison committee chaired by residents in rotation. The committee had an open membership and no formal structure, and participation seems to have been an *ad hoc* process of communication and discussion rather than a formal decision-making procedure. Nevertheless, it clearly influenced the scheme. Early on, Erskine had considered rehabilitation of the old houses. There were serious technical problems, but a key influence was a survey of the residents that showed that 80 per cent wanted new houses. Significantly, though, they didn't want flats, and the bulk of the scheme is family houses with gardens. The only flats are in the Wall and this contains family maisonettes at ground-level with flats for the elderly above. The first planning proposals involved wholesale demolition and rebuilding on the original street pattern. This was rejected by residents who wanted a more open layout but wanted to keep their corner shops, pubs, laundries and the public baths. The final scheme preserved and rehabilitated most of the public buildings. The scheme started with a pilot project on a cleared site, Janet Square. Comments on this, many of them adverse, influenced the design of the houses that followed.

Preserving the community, the onsite office, the dialogue with local people – these were important innovations in urban renewal. Critics have commented that, despite participation, the design is still recognizably Ralph Erskine's. It is true that the users did not have control over the design process. Vernon Gracie concedes "Participation, in this context, is . . . an aspect of urban management, rather than giving people a decisive voice in their areas." What participation did achieve was satisfaction and a positive response to the new housing. Gardens and flower boxes were planted and looked after. The relatively fragile timber balconies and cladding flew in the face of conventional wisdom that only rough hard surfaces were proof against vandalism. Yet vandalism has not wrecked the scheme, thanks to the residents' belief in and commitment to it.[9]

Model 3: rehabilitation

By the late 1960s, concern about wholesale clearance and the destruction of communities had finally impressed itself on the government. In 1968 the Home Office set up Urban Aid and some urban initiatives around the country. But of more immediate impact was the 1969 Housing Act, which established the concept of General Improvement Areas (GIAs). These could be declared in areas of run-down housing, and enhanced Improvement Grants would be made available for rehabilitation rather than demolition. In the wake of the Act, local authorities in London, Glasgow, Coventry, Birmingham and Leeds prepared proposals for improving areas of old housing.[10]

Most significantly, in Liverpool the City Council invited the national housing charity Shelter to investigate and promote rehabilitation of part of the Granby area of

Figure 3.4
Shelter's Neighbourhood Action Project in Toxteth, Liverpool – the first to attempt the rehabilitation of urban housing in partnership with tenants and residents.

Toxteth. The designated area contained 740 two-storey terraced cottages with narrow back alleys. Only 17 per cent were owner-occupied, with the remainder owned by private landlords. Many of the houses were let in multiple occupation. It was the sort of area that might previously have been demolished indiscriminately. Now the residents had a chance to stay in their homes and improve them. In June 1969, Shelter set up its Neighbourhood Action Project (SNAP) in a converted house in the area. Led by Des McGonaghy, a team of architects moved in together with a housing manager and a sociologist. Their brief was to articulate the needs of the residents and present them to the Corporation, and also to provide a free technical advice service.

It was no easy task. From the start the team encountered hostility form local councillors and soon fell foul of the local government bureaucracy. Organizing improvements became a nightmare of red tape: the team identified 71 separate procedures required to obtain a grant, and carrying out even a simple improvement could take up to two years. For the core of owner-occupiers, improvement was difficult enough, but many of the absentee landlords were unwilling or unable to improve their properties. Some were persuaded to sell, others were forced to by the application of individual Compulsory Purchase Orders. The availability of local authority mortgages allowed owner-occupation to increase by 33 per cent, while 58 of the larger houses were bought and converted by local housing associations. By the end of the three-year project over half the houses had been improved and a nascent housing co-operative had been formed. SNAP's work achieved a great deal, even although it was not a wholesale success. Its significance was that, for the first time, it had provided technical aid directly to low-income families to help them improve their own homes and, in doing so, had exposed the formidable obstacles involved.[11]

53

The impact of community action

What was significant about these new models was that they originated largely from enlightened professionals and authorities. What was offered to the residents of Byker and Toxteth, other communities had to fight for. During the early 1970s, community-based campaigns sprang up in the inner areas of several British cities. In the St Ann's area of Nottingham, in 1970, residents were fighting redevelopment proposals with a campaign for rehabilitation and selective renewal, a fight they ultimately lost.[12] More successfully, in 1971, the architectural aid group Assist was beginning its work in Glasgow to help tenants rehabilitate their tenement housing. By 1972 Rod Hackney had started his fight with Macclesfield Council to save Black Road. These battles marked the spread of the community movement throughout the country. But the earliest, and the most bitterly fought, of these community campaigns took place in Inner London.

The struggle for North Kensington

Kensington, with its Palace, its museums and its fine terraces, is generally thought of as one of London's most select and wealthy areas. But although the rich and famous made their homes in South Kensington, it was a different world in the north of the borough. North Kensington was developed during the nineteenth century as a series of speculative estates These were large terraced houses of four and five storeys built for the wealthy middle classes with servants quarters top and bottom. The process reached its peak during the building boom of the 1860s. But the boom had outstripped the market, and by the time these houses were finished, many could not be sold to their intended occupiers and were tenemented or let as rooming houses. By the turn of the century a large part of the area had degenerated into a grossly overcrowded slum. During the suburbanization of the 1920s and 1930s, wealthier residents were deserting the inner areas in droves and their flight from North Kensington was, no doubt, hastened by the blight of multiple occupation. Gradually, most of the fine houses, which had once boasted the carriage at the door and housemaids in the attic, were subdivided and let off. By the 1950s most of the area had become low-income accommodation.

The decentralization drive continued to encourage people to leave the inner urban areas. This tended to drain these communities of their younger members with saleable skills.[13] Increasingly, their places were taken by migrants, from the poorer regions of Britain and from overseas, who were willing to undertake the more arduous and unskilled work for low wages no longer acceptable to the home population, and to occupy poor-quality housing regarded as inadequate by those who had moved out. Housing conditions in North Kensington gave rise to increasing concern. By 1965 it was identified as one of the worst areas of overcrowded, multiple-occupied, furnished lettings in the capital and one of the few areas where there was strong evidence of increasing housing stress.[14] All this was exacerbated by the inactivity of the local council, which had provided only a small amount of council housing on the fringes of the area. The intervention of the Greater London Council only served to make matters worse. By the late 1960s the area was being cut in two by the construction of the M40 extension, a six-lane elevated urban motorway, while the GLC's solution to the shortage of good housing was to commission Erno Goldfinger, scion of the Modern movement, to construct one of the tallest housing blocks in London – the 36-storey Trellick Tower (Fig. 3.5).

Figure 3.5
*Golborne, deprived and run-
down area of North Kensington. From 1971, dominated by
Trellick Tower, symbolic of the
1960s concept of urban housing
renewal.*

Community organizations began to function from the early 1960s after serious
racial conflict in 1958/9 and in response to the activities of slum landlords. Following
rent de-control, landlords such as Peter Rachman – who became notorious through
the Profumo scandal – began evicting low-income tenants by vicious harassment in
order to re-let or sell for profit. At first, community action took relatively conventional routes: the formation of tenants and residents associations, setting up the Notting Hill Social Council, and the establishment of the Notting Hill Housing Trust. In
the late 1960s, more open campaigning organizations were formed with the setting up
of the Community Workshop and the People's Association. These two groups organized the 1967 Summer Project. In July of that year, young volunteers arrived in North
Kensington to start work on three key projects dealing with housing, play facilities,
and legal and social advice – projects that were to grow in importance over the years
that followed. The legal campaign resulted in the establishment of the first Neighbourhood Law Centre in 1970.

By that time, partly as a result of internal disputes, the housing and play projects
had evolved into three separate campaigns that were to have a significant impact on
planning and development in the area. Although united by similar problems of housing deprivation and lack of amenities, the two areas of North Kensington that were
the focus of activity were of quite different character. Golborne, to the north, was a
typical urban working-class community. Its housing was in poor physical condition

and was generally considered to be beyond repair. The Colville/Tavistock area, to the south, had a more colourful character. Although predominantly a community of low-income tenants, it had become a focus of the alternative "hippy" culture of the late 1960s and was a haunt of radical artists. writers and musicians. Its housing was grander, more sturdy, and attractive to speculators for conversion to higher-income self-contained flats. The two areas were now physically divided by the swathe of open land on which the Westway motorway was being constructed.

The housing campaign in Golborne was spearheaded by the Social Rights Committee, set up by George Clark, and it quickly bore fruit, at least in physical terms. By 1970 the Borough Council had agreed to organize two redevelopment areas, but there was increasing concern to safeguard the rehousing rights of those living in the area. It was evident that, if the community was to have an effective input into rebuilding the area, it needed a stronger voice. A working party was set up to establish a democratic forum to act as a bridge between the community and the local authorities. In 1971 it organized the election of Britain's first Neighbourhood Council, an urban version of the parish councils that still flourished in rural areas. From the start, the Golborne Neighbourhood Council was riven with personality disputes and these were to bring about its downfall within two years. But its short life saw a number of achievements. It helped residents of the recently built Kensal New Town Estate to raise funds to build their own community centre; it set up an adventure playground and organized summer holidays for children; and it ran events for pensioners and delivered food parcels at Christmas. Most significantly, after a tough campaign, it persuaded the GLC to undertake a pioneering redevelopment scheme in the Swinbrook area, aimed at preserving and rehousing the existing community.

The housing campaign in Colville/Tavistock continued under the aegis of the People's Association led by John and Jan O'Malley. It faced a more diffuse and difficult battle. There were some minor victories resulting in the compulsory purchase of individual houses, and small-scale redevelopment. But, essentially, the council was not interested in large-scale intervention in an area that it believed could be improved by private developers. In 1969 it declared a GIA in part of the area, which only succeeded in channelling funds to landlords who improved their buildings largely for the benefit of outsiders. To the campaigners this was a denial of natural justice. They wanted good housing at low rents for the existing low-income tenants. The campaign continued, culminating in the Colville "lock in" of May 1973 when 22 councillors and council officials were held prisoner overnight in a church hall by a meeting of 400 people demanding large-scale compulsory purchase, community rehousing rights, and the formation of tenant co-operatives. Eventually a Housing Action Area was declared under the 1974 Housing Act. Belatedly the Notting Hill Housing Trust was given powers to improve much of the area for social housing. But by then, much of the original community had been forced out by the pressures of private developers.

Meanwhile, the play campaign had succeeded in getting the use of a part of the land on which the motorway was being built. At that time the GLC had no real idea what to do with the space under its new elevated road and it had a vague idea that it might be used for car parking. The North Kensington Playspace Group realized the potential of the land and, in 1968 under the leadership of local photographer Adam Ritchie, turned itself into the Motorway Development Trust. With the help of architect Louis Helman, now better know as a satirical cartoonist, the MDT put together plans and drawings proposing a range of community uses for the land under the motorway (Fig. 3.6). The Borough Council gave its support, but there was a long period of negotiation on the form of the organization. Eventually, a partnership arrangement was made between the council and a consortium of community groups. A lease was negotiated with the GLC and, in 1971, the North Kensington Amenity Trust was formed with a brief to develop the land for the benefit of the community.[15]

Coincidentally, unconnected with these central campaigns, another issue was brewing on the edge of North Kensington that was later to lead to a key community initiative. When the GLC completed Trellick Tower and the surrounding blocks in 1971 they left a large part of the site undeveloped: a strip of land alongside the Grand Union Canal. It was supposed to provide open green space for the new housing. But there was a problem. Whereas the housing was in Kensington, the vacant land was in the neighbouring Borough of Westminster. Unsurprisingly, Westminster has little interest in developing an amenity for the benefit of another borough. While the authorities wrangled, the land stood empty and derelict for years until, in 1976, a young sculptor, Jamie McCullough, saw its potential. He begged and borrowed materials and equipment, persuaded a government agency to fund 13 unemployed people for a year, and scraped together a fund of £22,000 from more than 20 different statutory, voluntary and commercial sources, Over the next few years, with a huge

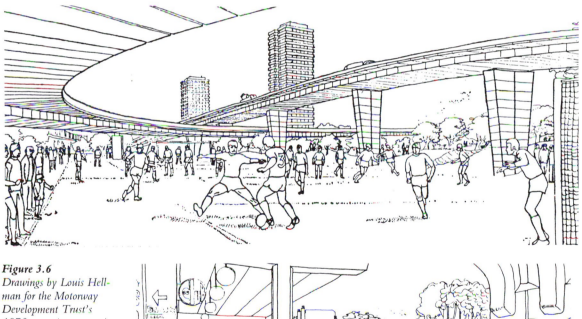

Figure 3.6
Drawings by Louis Hellman for the Motorway Development Trust's 1970 campaign, proposing community uses for the land under Westway.

Figure 3.7
Meanwhile Gardens. Built on derelict land for a shoestring budget largely by volunteers. Originally a temporary use it has now become a permanent and valuable community resource.

voluntary input, a community park was built, with a skateboard track, theatre, fish pond, and a scented garden for the benefit of a nearby hostel for the blind. Although it was originally conceived as temporary, Meanwhile Gardens has matured into a valuable local resource (Fig. 3.7).[16]

The community campaign in North Kensington exposed major threats to inner urban communities. It had suffered the after-effects of the twin symbols of the 1960s approach to urban development: the motorway and the tower block. Both had left behind a wasteland that others were left to clear up. It had confronted the threat of insensitive redevelopment with its power to break up and disperse communities. It had exposed the threat of the unfettered housing market that could inhumanely displace low-income tenants and commandeer their homes for the wealthier middle classes, a process that became known as "gentrification". But elsewhere there was another powerful threat: the pressure for commercial development.

Confrontation in the Garden

While North Kensington was an extreme case, it was fairly typical of conditions in Inner London in the 1960s. Covent Garden was a very special case. The area had a very long and rich history. From the twelfth century there had been a convent that started market providing fresh produce to the City of London. In the early seventeenth century the Earl of Bedford built the piazza and the celebrated church of St Pauls, designed by Inigo Jones. By the eighteenth century it was a bohemian area with a concentration of theatres, coffee houses frequented by famous writers, a mix of the fine houses of the rich, and the narrow courts and alleys of those who did the work.

58

All this was dominated by the market where Nell Gwynne bought the oranges that made her famous. By the mid-nineteenth century, Covent Garden had degenerated, and in St Giles, Seven Dials and Drury Lane were to be found some of the worst slums in London. Gradually, these had been eliminated by a mixture of philanthropic housing and commercial development.

In the 1960s a decision was made to remove the fruit and vegetable market to a less congested site and this was the signal to consider comprehensive development of an area where many of the buildings were run down and in poor repair. By this time the residential population was much reduced, although still substantial. Many of those who lived there worked in the market, the theatres and the wide variety of small-scale manufacturing and craft industries. A high proportion had deep roots in the area. But the planning team, set up in 1965 by a consortium of local authorities, was not much interested in the local community. It was primarily concerned with the potential of a prime chunk of Central London, ripe for development. In 1968 they produced a draft plan that proposed demolition of 80 per cent of the existing housing, and redevelopment of 60 per cent of the area, with a mixture of high-rise offices, hotels, new housing and a conference centre. To service this massive commercial development, parking would be increased from 600 to 4,300 spaces, and surrounding roads such as Charing Cross Road and Shaftesbury Avenue would be widened to motorway proportions.

The plan was a major concession to the pressures for commercial development and the massive profits it would bring. But the blow was softened by the inclusion of a substantial amount of housing and the designation at the centre of the area of a "line of character" that would preserve the old market halls and the surrounding buildings. Initially these concessions seemed sufficient to stifle criticism. The draft was put on exhibition for public comments, but the final plan emerged in 1971 little changed (Fig. 3.8). Meanwhile, one member of the planning team had become increasingly concerned at the lack of effective public consultation. Brian Anson decided to make covert contact with leading figures in the community and when this was discovered, by accident, he was carpeted by the planning hierarchy and removed from the Covent Garden team. He promptly resigned to lead the opposition.

Anson joined forces with Jim Monaham, a student at the Architectural Association, who had analyzed the plans with a group of fellow students, and Rev. Austen Williams, vicar of St. Martins in the Fields. Jointly, they called a public meeting on 1 April 1971 that attracted 500 people and agreed to set up of the Covent Garden Community Association. The Association organized committees by streets and blocks of flats, and prepared to put up a fight at the public inquiry into the plans. The Inquiry process lasted more than 18 months and, despite the opposition, the GLC's plan emerged virtually unscathed. But in the meantime the campaign had attracted widespread publicity and public debate that impacted on the political process. When the Labour Party gained control of the GLC, in April 1973, they scrapped the plan and set a new brief – no skyscrapers, no new offices, no new roads. Instead, more rented housing, a focus on entertainment, and a greater emphasis on conservation.

The Community Association now resolved to set up a more representative body to take part in the re-planning. George Clark appeared in the area, fresh from his experience in North Kensington (where the Golborne Neighbourhood Council had just collapsed) and was put in charge of a subcommittee to draw up plans for elections. In April 1974 the Covent Garden Community Forum was elected, with a combination

Figure 3.8
*Part of the GLC's 1971
proposals for Covent
Garden showing commer-
cial redevelopment on a
massive scale around the
Royal Opera House and
the old flower market
halls.*

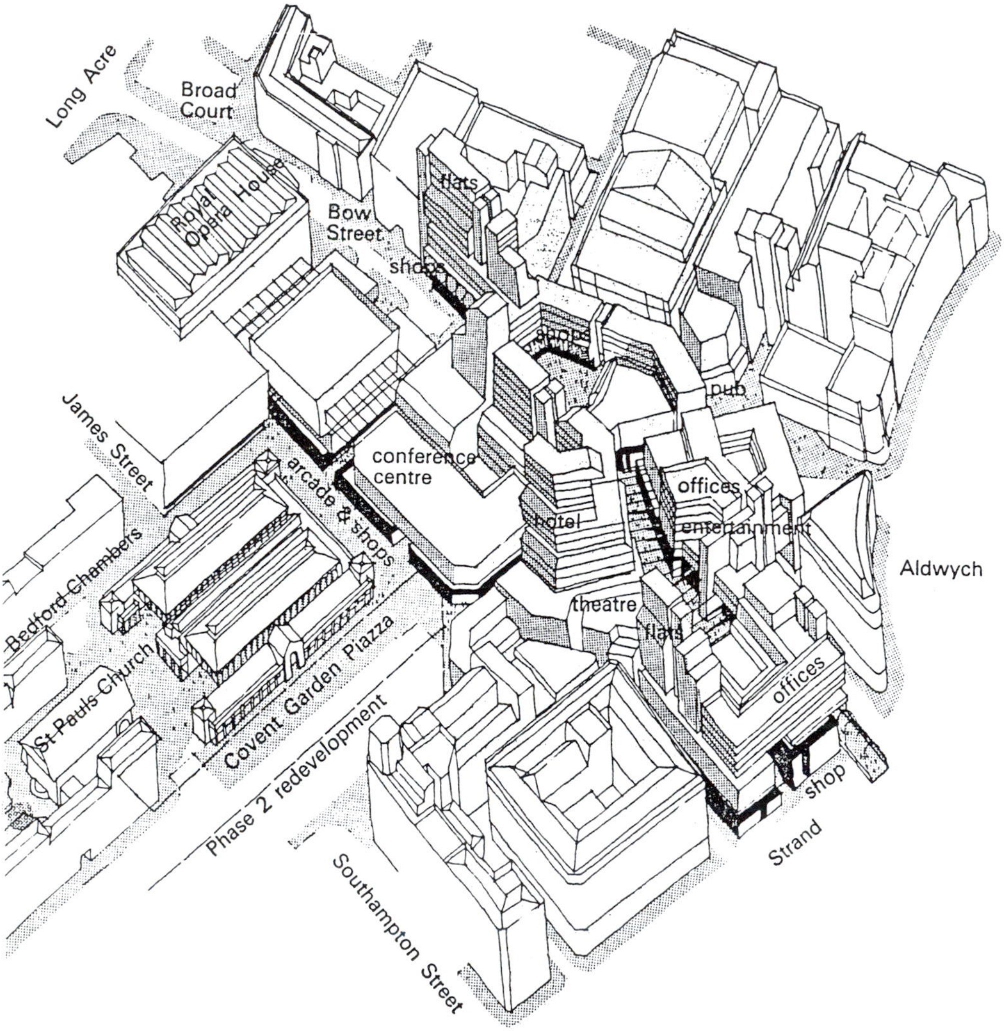

of 21 members representing business and services in the area and only nine representing the residents. The Forum began negotiations with the GLC for a new plan. Within
a year, finding itself outnumbered and increasingly a bystander in the process, the
Covent Garden Community Association withdrew from the Forum and concentrated
on direct action. It set up a food co-op, shops, a social centre, organized community
festivals, and built temporary gardens on redevelopment sites. In 1976 a new plan
emerged that concentrated on retaining the residential community, increasing the
amount of housing in the area, and reducing redevelopment to carefully selected infill
sites.[17]

Closing the motorway box

The new roads the GLC was planning to impose on Covent Garden in the late 1960s were just a pale reflection of its plans for London as a whole. A double ring of new urban motorways was to have been imposed on the capital. The outer ring would have been a surface road, running through low-density suburbs but, nonetheless, it would have caused the demolition of many houses. Even more controversial was the inner ring, known as the London "Motorway Box". This was to have been an elevated motorway eight lanes wide, running through Kilburn, Swiss Cottage, central Islington and Hackney, to join the East Cross Route – the only part of the inner ringway actually built – and pass under the Thames at the Blackwall tunnel. In south London a road on a similar scale would have run from Greenwich to Wandsworth. The construction of these roads would have caused untold destruction and environmental damage to these densely populated inner urban areas. Enormous opposition arose, and three London-wide pressure groups were formed – London Motorway Action Group, London Amenity and Transport Association, and Homes Before Roads – to fight the proposals, backed up by a plethora of local organizations.

The battleground became the western arm of the Box – the West Cross Route – which the GLC wanted to build in advance of the rest of the ringways. At the Public Inquiry in March 1972 the umbrella groups joined forces with a consortium of local organizations to fight the proposals. They detailed the 1,225 homes that would be destroyed and the environmental damage that would be caused to the area surrounding the road. They argued that new roads only generate new traffic and that the real answer was improved public transport accompanied by traffic restraint. And they were partly successful. In 1973 the Environment minister dismissed the case for building the West Cross Route separately, but left open the proposals for the ringways as a whole. This appeared only to delay the evil day but, once again, the political process intervened. Although the Labour Party had controlled the GLC at the time the ringway plan was prepared, they now faced stiff opposition, from both their own activists and the voters in the threatened inner areas, most of which were Labour strongholds. The same Labour GLC that reprieved Covent Garden also tore up the plans for the Motorway Box, and the outer ringway.[18]

Success or failure?

Thousands of hours of committed and unpaid effort was put into community action, much of it without apparent effect. The atmosphere in these campaigns was intense, with seemingly incessant plots, betrayals or suspected betrayals, and feuds developing between individuals and rival groups. There were, perhaps, good reasons why this was so. The activists identified with the working class and could establish a rapport with working-class people. But to be any use to the campaigns, they had to have the ability to lead, the skill to organize, and the will to fight – mainly against bureaucracy and institutional power. But these very qualities made it difficult for them to work with equals and just as likely to fight each other. Faced with obstruction or outright rejection by the authorities, divided by conflicting objectives and choice of tactics, their frustrations often boiled over into serious conflict. Many retired early from the fray, temporarily defeated and demoralized.

So was it all worth it? Brian Anson's verdict is bleak:

The Covent Garden struggle is generally regarded as a phenomenal success: an object lesson in how to take on the system at its own game and beat it. The GLC was forced to abandon its brutal plans for the area and assume a more caring approach to development. The historic area, that in 1971 faced obliteration, survived and on the surface is alive and well . . . [but] There is another story behind the present glamour of Covent Garden. a story of failure of tragic proportions. A failure to see that bulldozers are only weapons in the war; that those who wage it, the variety of the methods they use and the laws under which they are protected remain not only unscathed but . . . through the experience of Covent Garden, infinitely stronger than they were in 1971.[19]

In other words, the campaign neither preserved the social and economic character of the area, nor prevented its rampant commercialization. Covent Garden is now a tourist magnet with street entertainers, a thriving craft market and expensive boutiques.

Most community action can best be judged as a partial success. All too often, success came to late, when much of the damage was already done. The housing campaigns in North Kensington succeeded only after too many had lost their homes and been driven from the area. Stopping the bulldozers, stopping the motorways and the tower blocks, was no mean feat. But it was only the beginning. The motorways were stopped in the early 1970s, but the alternative approach to urban transport has never been taken seriously. In 20 years, London's public transport has hardly improved at all, and the efforts to restrain motor traffic have been feeble and half-hearted. Too often what appeared to be a victory was just the start of a much more prolonged battle.

What happened to the community campaign to develop the land under Westway is a prime example. The North Kensington Amenity Trust is worth examining because it has been cited as a model for community development[20] and has received a major award.[21] Formation of the Trust did seem like a victory for the community, but although the GLC handed over the land, it gave no money to develop the empty shell it had created. For the first few years the Trust encouraged local groups to develop their own projects and a few were set up: an adventure playground, a social centre, a nursery, a community laundry, and two training projects for black youth. But community groups were not equipped to act as developers, and the Trust gave no technical support. Progress was painfully slow and, in the late 1970s, the Trust lost patience and decided to build in the remaining space as a comprehensive development (Fig. 3.9). This turned out to be mainly commercial shops offices and workshops, with only the thinnest veneer of community benefit and participation. Given the promise and the expectations, the end result was a cause of great disillusionment. Perhaps it was the best that could be done in the circumstances, but if the authorities had put up adequate finance, if local groups had been given more help in the techniques of development, organization and fund raising, it could all have been very different

Partial successes are also partial failures, and the shortfall in the high expectations generated by community campaigns helps to explain the cynicism felt by many at the outcome. What community action did was to focus attention on the continuing problems of what were the slums but were now more grandly identified as "areas of multiple deprivation of the inner cities". It also exposed the obstacles facing locally based groups in their attempts to play a direct role in urban development. The groundswell of local action and the publicity surrounding it forced the government to re-examine the problem seriously and the urban design professionals to re-assess their role in the development process.

Figure 3.9
Space under Westway
elevated motorway.
Fought over and won
for community use —
much of it was eventually
developed for commercial
purposes.

The government response

The campaigns around the London motorways and in Covent Garden had a clear impact on the political process, albeit at a local level. Where there is determined social action, politicians cannot afford to stand idly by and grass-roots movements are often the motor of change in government policy and practice. The exposure of Rachmanism was instrumental in the introduction of the 1965 Rent Act, which gave security of tenure and allowed "fair rents" to be fixed. Growing opposition to redevelopment stimulated the introduction of General Improvement Areas in 1969 and the more effective Housing Action Areas in 1974.

In response to the first stirrings of community action, and in the face of growing evidence of urban deprivation from official reports, the government first began to focus on the inner cites with the introduction of Urban Aid in 1968. Under this programme, local authorities could apply for grants for specific projects. The government would fund 75 per cent of successful applications with the local council finding the balance. In 1969 the Home Office introduced Community Development Projects. Twelve CDPs were started in deprived urban areas throughout the country.[a] The CDP were set up in co-operation with the local authorities, each with an action team and research team. No extra money was forthcoming, but by the mid-1970s the CDPs had stimulated a variety of local initiatives.

a. The 12 CDPs were in Batley (Yorkshire), Benwell (west Newcastle), Cleator Moor (Cumbria), Canning Town (east London), Glyncorrwg (South Wales), Hillfields (Coventry), Vauxhall (Liverpool), North Shields (Tyneside), Clarksfield (Oldham), Paisley (Glasgow), Saltley (Birmingham), and Southwark (southeast London). From *Gilding the ghetto* (London: Home Office 1977).

In 1972 the Department of the Environment took a parallel initiative, appointing prominent private architecture/planning consultancies to conduct "inner area studies" in Liverpool, Birmingham and Lambeth. These were finally published in 1977[22] and they confirmed that the inner cities exhibited an abnormal degree of housing stress, social deprivation and physical decay. This much was already evident to those living and working in these areas, but the reports also laid new emphasis on economic degeneration and the decline of employment. In response, the government published its intentions in a White Paper, "Policy for the inner cities". Urban Aid was to be increased from £30 million a year to £125 million and was to be targeted at selected "Partnership Authorities" in the most deprived areas of large cities. At about the same time the central government grant to local authorities was restructured to channel more help to the urban areas. Here finally, then, was official recognition of the scale and nature of the problems or the inner city. And not just recognition; much more money was made available to tackle to urban deprivation. The government saw local authorities as ". . . the mainspring for the revival of the inner areas." But there was a recognition of the role of community action. "Public policy should aim to stimulate voluntary effort and help voluntary bodies play a constructive role. In some places, elected Neighbourhood Councils may have a role in representing the community's view and mobilising voluntary effort".[23]

A new role for the professions

While architects and planners, as individuals. had been involved from the beginning, it took some time for the professions to organize a more co-ordinated response to the demands arising from community campaigns. In this, the planning profession was first in the field. Participation in town planning issues had been stimulated by the proposals of a government-sponsored committee in 1969. The Skeffington Report[24] was concerned to involve conventional bodies such as Civic Societies and Councils of Social Service, rather than seek the radical views of community activists. Nonetheless, it established the principle of participation, and new information and consultation requirements were enshrined in the 1971 Town and Country Planning Act.

Unlike architects, almost all town planners were employed by local government. Their involvement in community action presented potential conflicts of interest and required a certain amount of prudence. It was clear from the events in Covent Garden that the risks to the committed individual could be considerable. One senior local authority planner, prominent in the anti-motorway campaign, felt it necessary to hide his identity behind a *nom de guerre*. If individuals were to be protected, collective action was necessary to legitimize such activities. In 1972 the Town and Country Planning Association – formerly the Garden Cities Association – set up Planning Aid. A register was compiled of town planners, many of whom were working for local councils, who were willing to volunteer their expertise, in their spare time, to support community groups. Three years later the Royal Town Planning Institute set up its own version of technical aid, which was organized through its local branches.[25]

At about the same time Chartered Surveyors began a similar service, providing free technical advice through Citizens' Advice Bureaux. Progress was slower in the architectural profession, and considerably more controversial. It was complicated by the fact that, although all architects were required by law to subscribe to the official registration body, ARCUK, by no means all of them belonged to the professional institute: the Royal Institute of British Architects (RIBA). The non-conformist minority included many of those who had been active in community campaigns. In 1974, just after he left Covent Garden, Brian Anson set up a small ginger group, the Architects Revolutionary Council. As well as becoming involved in several community-based projects, the ARC trained its rhetorical guns on the professional establishment. It saw the RIBA as dominated by the principals of large private practices – the very practices that had gained most from commercial redevelopment in inner urban areas – and by chief officers in local government, pillars of the state machine. Most architects at that time were salaried employees, and their interest were seen as unrepresented by RIBA. The ARC recognized that its radical views would not have widespread appeal, but it sought to capitalize on the general disaffection with the RIBA that had led Louis Helman to dub it "Royal Institute of Boss Architects".

In 1975 the ARC called a conference aimed at setting up a broader movement. From this emerged a new group with the more anodyne title New Architecture Movement, which attracted a membership of over a hundred architects. Much of NAM's energy was absorbed by none too successful attempts to unionize salaried architects. It also mounted a drive to revitalize ARCUK by sponsoring candidates in the annual elections for its council. In this it was more successful and for several years NAM candidates swept the board in seats elected by the 5,000 architects outside the RIBA. NAM also developed, through its regular newsletter *Slate*, increasing awareness of the need to develop closer links with users, with the building trades and of the concerns of women in the building industry. In an atmosphere where there was heightened discussion of the architect's role in the community, the RIBA took its own initiative by setting up the Community Architecture Working Group in 1976.[26]

By 1978 both groups had formulated policies to focus and develop architectural services for the community. The RIBA published its proposals for a community aid fund[27] that would provide grants to self-help organizations and community groups to enable them to pay fees for architectural service. NAM's ideas had developed along two, somewhat different, lines. In *Community architecture: a public design service*[28] – it developed the view that, given substantial reform, local authorities could develop a service that genuinely responded to the needs and wishes of building users. Meanwhile, some NAM members had become involved in setting up co-operatives to work for community groups and tenants' organizations, and they believed that direct technical aid could be provided through new organizations independent of the state structure.

By the late 1970s, new models of participatory design had emerged and key battles had been fought and won around planning and development issues. Young architects and planners, whose social commitment might have led them a generation earlier into the service of the welfare state, now sought a more direct means of using their expertise for the benefit of the poorer members of society. Three broad strands of a community architecture had emerged. The first was to bring design support to the variety of self-help and locally organized groups that had emerged from community action. The second was to develop new forms of professional practice that would channel technical aid directly to community groups. The third was to reform the leviathan of local government and its large technical departments to involve the users of its products and provide a genuine service to the community.

References

1. Robert Owen, *Report to the County of Lanark* and *A new view of society* (London: Penguin, 1970).
2. See, for example, Dennis Meadows, *The limits to growth* (London: Earth Island, 1972).
3. *The Ecologist, A blueprint for survival,* vol. 2(1) 1972 (London: Penguin, 1972 (revised edn)).
4. *The architecture of Darbourne and Darke* (London: RIBA, 1977).
5. *A design guide for residential areas* (Essex County Council, 1973).
6. N. J. Habraken, *Supports – and alternative to mass housing* (The Netherlands: Scheltema & Holkema, 1961; London: Architectural Press, 1972), 60.
7. Richard Hatch (ed.), *The scope of social architecture* (New York: Van Nostrand Reinhold, 1984): contains illustrated examples of SAR projects in Holland, Austria, France and Britain.
8. Lucien Kroll, "Anarchitecture", in Hatch (ibid.), 179.
9. Ralph Erskine, "Designing between client and users"; Vernon Gracie, "Pitfalls in participation: a cautionary tale (of success)", in Hatch (ibid.); and Alison Ravetz, "Housing at Byker, Newcastle-upon Tyne", *The Architects' Journal* (14 April 1976), 735.
10. Michael Hook, "New homes for old", *The Architects' Journal* (1 July 1970), 15.
11. *Another chance for cities – SNAP 69/72* (London: Shelter 1972); "SNAP Toxteth, Liverpool – bridging the estrangement between public and authority", *The Architects' Journal* (10 June 1970), 1452; and "SNAP: a final evaluation", *The Architects' Journal* (31 January 1973), 249
12. Ken Coates & Richard Silburn, *Poverty: the forgotten Englishman* (London: Penguin, 1970), 95 ff.
13. Nicholas Deakin & Clare Ungerson, *Leaving London; planned mobility and the inner city* (London: Heinemann, 1977): based on interviews with migrants from Islington to new towns, the study showed that migrants were predominantly skilled people in the 16–35 age group, the majority with young families.
14. Report of the Committee on Housing in Greater London, Chairman Sir Milner Holland (London: HMSO, 1965).
15. Taken from Jan O'Malley, *The politics of community action* (Nottingham: Bertrand Russell Peace Foundation for Spokesman Books, 1977), and from unpublished studies and papers by myself.
16. Jamie McCullough, *Meanwhile Gardens* (London: Calouste Gulbenkian Foundation, 1978).
17. Brian Anson, *I'll fight you for it! Behind the struggle for Covent Garden* (London: Jonathan Cape, 1981); Terry Christenson, *Neighbourhood survival* (Dorchester: Prism Press, 1979), and *Covent Garden – the next step* (London: GLC, 1971.)
18. Graham Towers, "West Cross Route", *Built Environment* (December 1975).
19. Brian Anson, op. cit., xiv.
20. David Rock, *The grassroots developers – a handbook for town development trusts* (London: RIBA, 1980), 56–9.
21. Winner of Chairman's Award, *The Times*/RIBA Community Enterprise Scheme 1991, reported in *The Times* (9 July 1991), 35.
22. DOE, *Inner area studies: Liverpool, Birmingham and Lambeth* (summaries of consultants' final reports) (London: HMSO 1977).
23. *Policy for the inner cities* (London: HMSO, Cmnd 6845, 1977).
24. *People and planning.* Report of the Committee on Public Participation in Planning, Chairman Mr A. M. Skeffington MP (London: HMSO, 1969).
25. Nick Wates & Charles Knevitt, *Community architecture – how people are creating their own environment* (London: Penguin, 1987), 129.
26. Anne Karpf, "The pressure groups", *The Architects' Journal* (19 October 1977), 728; and "NAM Congress" *The Architects' Journal* (15 November 1977), 925.
27. *The practice of community architecture: the case for a community aid fund* (London: RIBA, 1978).
28. *Community architecture: a public design service* (London: New Architecture Movement, 1978).

CASE STUDY
Swinbrook: housing redevelopment to a community brief

In July 1970, Michael Heseltine, then a junior Transport Minister, arrived to open the GLC's new Westway officially. He was faced with a barrage of abuse from a group of protesters who had evaded the police cordon. Barely 15 metres from the elevated motorway, hung across a terrace of four-storey houses, a huge banner delivered the message "GET US OUT OF THIS HELL – REHOUSE US NOW". Half of Acklam Road had been demolished to build the new road, and residents of the houses that were left had already suffered the noise and disruption of three years of construction. Now they faced the prospect of heavy traffic thundering past their bedroom windows. Their protests were successful. Within a year they were rehoused, and shortly afterwards the Acklam Road houses were demolished. In a sense they were lucky; their neighbours had to wait longer for new homes.[1]

Acklam Road was on the southern edge of Swinbrook. Behind it were four streets of 400 multiple-occupied houses that had some of the worst levels of overcrowding in London. And it had always been so. From the

67

People whose homes were within a few feet of the new elevated motorway mounted a high-profile protest to coincide with its official opening.

occupied these houses in the late 1960s had lived in the area a long time, their families and friends living nearby. They wanted new homes but they didn't want to move away. In 1970 the Golborne Social Rights Committee had commissioned a community plan for rebuilding the area for the benefit of the people already there.

The Acklam Road campaign had forced the GLC to intervene in the area and, in 1971, it undertook to redevelop Swinbrook. The election of the Golborne Neighbourhood Council in 1971 created a forum with a legitimate claim to represent the community. Early in 1972 the GLC was persuaded to set up a Steering Committee for Swinbrook, with equal representation of its own members and the Neighbourhood Council giving community representatives an effective voice in key decisions on the scheme. Through the Steering Committee, participation was broadened in a series of related exercises, the most important of which was the survey: the Swinbrook Community

time they were built, in the late 1860s, the Swinbrook houses were subdivided and let. From the turn of the century it had been a densely populated area of low-income housing, where families lived in one or two rooms, several sharing each house with a single toilet and kitchen between them. Despite the conditions, many of those who

Site plan. Redevelopment along the existing street pattern in a five-phase rolling programme designed to rehouse 70% of the existing community.

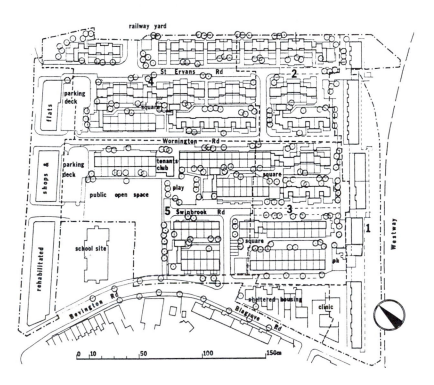

The "barrier" block turns its back on the motorway. Flats are planned so that only utility rooms face the motorway. Living rooms and bedrooms face away. Residents of the block are protected from the noise just as the block itself protects the rest of the site.

Rehousing Census. This was a comprehensive scientific social survey, far more elaborate and expensive than would normally be carried out in such circumstances. But the GLC was anxious to involve as broad a base as possible to test the claims that people wanted to stay in the area. In the event the census revealed a high level of "community consciousness", with just under half those interviewed identifying with the immediate area and almost 70 per cent with North Kensington. The census had confirmed what was little understood by middle-class professionals: that, even in cities, the social focus of poorer people, who did not own cars and could afford little public transport, was predominantly localized.[2]

Meanwhile the GLC opened an office in the area and appointed a Community Rehousing Officer to act as a locally based link. Publicity for the survey and the participation process was organized through the Neighbourhood Council's own weekly newsletter. Once the draft results of the survey were available, the Steering Group was able to brief the GLC Architect's Department. Five key points had emerged from the participation process. First was the demand for community rehousing, and the GLC promised to rehouse everyone who wanted to stay in the area within the new scheme. Secondly, a wish to see community and leisure facilities included in the new development. Thirdly, there was strong opposition to high-rise housing, although there was no rejection of flats as

such. People had become used to living in tenemented houses and the key issue was better standard apartments. Fourthly, was the concern about the impact of the Westway motorway on the Swinbrook area. Finally, people wished to retain their local shopping centre on the northern edge of Swinbrook. These points were incorporated in the architects' outline scheme that was put to the test at a public meeting at the end of 1972, followed by a series of street meetings to develop the details.

Seventy per cent of people wanted to stay in Swinbrook and, to make good the promise to preserve the community, the scheme was planned as a five-phase rolling programme.

Plan of typical flat in barrier block

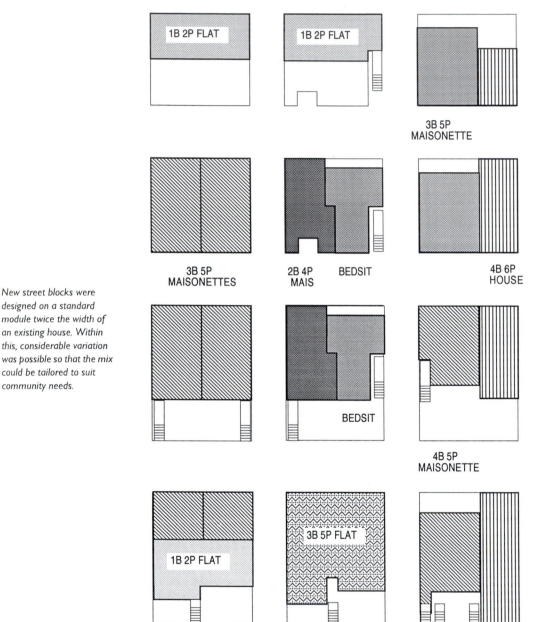

New street blocks were designed on a standard module twice the width of an existing house. Within this, considerable variation was possible so that the mix could be tailored to suit community needs.

VARIATION OF UNIT TYPES WITHIN STREET BLOCKS

70

Left – old Swinbrook, exposed to motorway noise.

Below – phase I of the redevelopment, a protected environment.

As one phase was complete, residents from the next moved in, making their homes available for demolition. Development started by building a five-storey block of flats on the vacant Acklam Road site. This was designed as a single aspect "barrier" block. All the flats have their utility rooms backing onto the motorway, with the main rooms facing away. Flats in the block are protected from motorway noise, and the block itself forms a barrier shielding the rest of the site against motorway noise and visual intrusion. This was the principle developed in the Byker "wall". The difference is that, in Swinbrook, the motorway is actually there. Built into the barrier block were several social facilities: a day nursery, a youth club, a laundry and community rooms

The rest the site was to be developed in four-storey blocks similar in scale to the existing buildings. The design of these offered considerable flexibility. Development was planned along the old street pattern, and new units were based on a module twice the width of existing buildings. In this way the option of keeping some of the old houses could be maintained. Conversely, new modules could be slotted into the existing streets in advance, to replace houses in an advanced state of decay. Within each module, a variety

of combinations of flats and family maisonettes was possible. This offered a certain
amount of choice, but more importantly it
meant that the final design could be tailored
to meet the space requirements of every
family to be rehoused from the next phase.
The final element in the scheme was the
preservation of the Golborne Road shops.
The buildings were comprehensively rehabilitated, with the upper floors brought into
use as housing. Existing shopkeepers were
kept in business by moving them to new
shops as the programme progressed.

The architect's scheme was an ingenious
and flexible solution to a community brief
and it represented a remarkable turnabout
by the GLC. Only a few years earlier, on an
adjoining site, the same authority had dispersed the community throughout London,
razed the houses and erected the massive
Trellick Tower. Nevertheless, Swinbrook
was not without controversy. Only 12 per
cent of the householders were owner-
occupiers and many of these were resident
landlords letting off rooms in houses where
they lived. This practice enabled immigrants
to secure a toe-hold in the property market
and it was common in the West Indian community The compensation available for compulsory purchase would not have enabled
such people to buy elsewhere and a group of
Black house-owners put up determined
resistance to the scheme. Rehabilitation
would have met their objections, but it was
judged to be an extremely expensive option,
given the advanced state of decay of the
houses. In any case there was no significant
demand for it – the great majority wanted
new homes. The difficulty of the owner-
occupiers' position was recognized and, unu-
sually, they were granted the right to be
rehoused as council tenants.[3]

The Swinbrook scheme was a sensitive
response to the demand for community
rehousing, but in the long term it must be
judged only a partial success. The nature of
the scheme meant that implementation
would take a long time, each phase of construction and rehousing taking place over
two to three years. By 1978 only two phases
were complete and phase 3 was still being
built. At this crucial juncture the GLC decided
to divest itself of its housing responsibilities,
and the final phases were handed over to the
Borough Council. The council architects had
little understanding of the innovative nature
of the scheme and scant regard for participation. Without consulting the community,
they abandoned the GLC designs and completed the development in the far more
mundane fashion of a conventional council
estate.

References

1. Andrew Duncan, "Taking on the motorway –
   North Kensington Amenity trust 21 years"
   (London: Kensington and Chelsea Community
   History Group, 1992).
2. R. U. Redpath & D. J. Chilvers, "Swinbrook:
   a community study applied", *Greater London
   Intelligence Quarterly* 26 (March 1974)
3. Graham Towers, "Swinbrook: testbed for
   participation", *The Architects' Journal* (12 March
   1975), 547.

PART 2

The practice of
community architecture

CHAPTER 4

Helping themselves

THE CO-OPERATIVE REVIVAL

The protest movement of the late 1960s began as a reaction against the old order, but the intellectual upheaval that followed caused general questioning of established conventions. Many people became dissatisfied with their lot; with employment in which they were expected to behave as small unquestioning cogs on the machinery of large organizations; with a housing system that offered a choice between being exploited by private landlords, crippled with a mortgage, or having to run an obstacle course for the privilege of living in a barrack-like council estate. There had to be a better way and the seeds of an alternative lay in the nature of community action. In the local groups that formed around the campaigns of the early 1970s, people had to work together in order to succeed. Largely voluntary, and outside the established hierarchies, they had to co-operate – if not always with good grace. Co-operation was often a necessity in creating alternative structures, but in many respects it seemed to offer a better way of doing things – the revival of an ideal that had seemed long-since dead.

Co-operation in various forms became a key element in the community architecture that began to emerge in the early 1970s. The co-operative revival saw the instigation of a multitude of small-scale co-operatives in housing, in building, and in community industry and services. Within the broad range of locally based self-help initiatives, there were three key strands: community self-build – groups coming together to build housing or community facilities for themselves; producer co-operatives, which created a new relationship between designers and builders, and new forms of organizing small-scale production; and housing co-operatives, which forged an alternative to the perils of private landlords and the insensitivity of public housing.

The co-operative ideal

Starting with Robert Owen, co-operation had been a key element in the early responses to urban industrialization. Building on Owen's experiments, in 1828 Dr William King of Brighton began publishing a monthly tract, *The Co-operator,* and he set up several co-operative trading associations. Although these fell foul of organizational and legal difficulties, the co-operative ideal was advanced and soon achieved more lasting success. In 1844 the Equitable Pioneers Society was formed in the northern industrial town of Rochdale. The Pioneers, contemporaries of the Chartists and sharing many of their ideals, aimed to set up co-operative initiatives in distribution, services, housing, manufacturing and agriculture. Their productive pursuits did not prosper, but the distribution and services enterprises of the movement mushroomed. A network of Co-operative Societies was established throughout the north of England, providing profit-sharing shops and a range of insurance and financial services to support their members "from the cradle to the grave".

Agricultural and industrial co-operatives never prospered on any significant scale in Britain, largely because of the pattern of landownership and the capital-intensive nature of industrial mass production. Co-operation in housing and community services was smothered by the all-embracing provision of the Welfare State. By the mid-twentieth century the Co-operative Societies themselves had degenerated in the face of large-scale competition and had become virtually indistinguishable from their commercial rivals. Co-operation had seemed a dead letter, a thing of the past. But in the widespread search for alternatives, the creation of small-scale co-ops seemed to offer new scope for personal fulfilment, satisfaction and participation in decision-making.

Whether the aim is the pursuit of profit or the implementation of public policy, most organizations are structured like military hierarchies, where rank signifies power and personal relations are largely on a "master and servant" basis. Unlike conventional hierarchies, co-operatives are organizations whose members come together freely to work constructively with each other for their mutual benefit. They operate democratically on the basis of one-member one-vote, and all positions of authority are open to regular elections. Each member has an equitable stake in the organization. Members normally hold equal shares, and little or no interest is paid on share capital. Surpluses and benefits from the endeavour are either distributed equally or on democratically agreed criteria of fairness, such as varying needs or measurable contribution to the work. Generally they provide equal opportunity for their members, with education, training or assistance provided for the less skilled or inexperienced.

Forms of co-operative

There are various forms of co-operative (Fig. 4.1). Primary co-ops are the organizations that actually arrange the production of goods or the supply of services to their members. Secondary co-ops are set up to service several primary co-operatives, supplying them with organizational support and advice, and services such as design or accounting, that they could not organize efficiently for themselves. Primary co-ops can be divided into producer and consumer organizations. In producer co-ops the members come together to make or manufacture goods or to organize services that are then sold or distributed to customers. Consumer co-ops are organizations that people join in order to receive goods or services. Usually this distinction is quite clear. A workers co-op set up to make and sell clothing is quite clearly a producer co-op. A grocery co-op set up so that members can receive goods at cost is equally clearly a consumer co-op.

Where the distinction become blurred is that in many co-ops the members are both the producers and the consumers. In a child-minding co-op, for example, the members undertake child-care duties in rotation. They both supply and consume the service. Resolving this confusion helps to unravel the various forms of housing co-operatives. At one end of the scale is the self-build co-op set up by a group to provide housing for themselves. Once complete, the houses are owned by the indi-

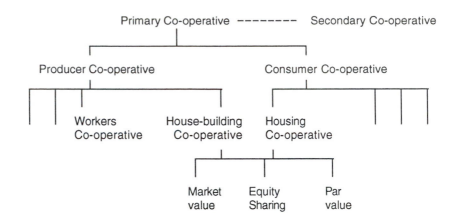

Figure 4.1
Forms of co-operative organization.

vidual members and the co-op ceases to exist. At the other extreme is the tenant co-operative that is set up to manage the housing its members occupy. The one is a producer co-op, the other a consumer co-op. In between these extremes are various combinations of the two. Most housing co-ops are set up to provide housing for their members rather than manage existing housing. Provision may be through self-build or part self-build, or through organizing and managing new construction or conversion. Once complete, the houses are distributed to the members. This can be done in one of three ways:

- *market value*, where the ownership of each house passes to the occupant who can eventually recoup the full sale value; the co-op then ceases to exist;
- *par value*, where ownership remains with the co-op and each member becomes a tenant; the members collectively own the houses and become a consumer co-op;
- *equity sharing*, a mixture of individual and collective ownership which can take various forms; the co-op again becomes a consumer co-op, part owning the housing.[1]

Community self-build

Self-build housing is common throughout the world. In rural communities in China and Africa, villagers come together to build new houses collectively, using traditional materials and time-tested building techniques. In rural India, families build their own houses with adobe walls roofed with hewn saplings and hand-made tiles. In the squatter communities of Third World cities migrants put their rural skills to good use in building their own shelter. In the developed world, self-built housing has, for many years, played a small but significant part in the provision of houses, particularly in Scandinavia and North America, where there are strong local traditions of timber-framed housing.

In urban Britain self-build was another early response to industrialization. In the Midlands and the North in the 1820s and 1930s, many building clubs were formed. Working men would pool their capital and labour to build homes for themselves, balloting for turn in occupying the finished houses. These were "terminating" organizations, closing down once the last house was complete: temporary building societies, precursors of the permanent building societies that grew to become the predominant source of financing private housing. It was an inauspicious start for urban self-build, for the building clubs did not always achieve high standards and were responsible for many of the unlamented back-to-back houses. Faced with increasingly higher construction standards demanded by building regulations, and the competition of the building societies, self-build had virtually disappeared from British cities by the mid-nineteenth century.[2] It was not to be seen again until the 1970s. Its revival then owed much to the pioneering efforts of two architects – Rod Hackney and Walter Segal – who, in their distinctively different ways, breathed new life into an old form.

Rod Hackney

Now the best known exponent of community architecture, Rod Hackney's involvement began in the early 1970s when he was pitched into the world of community action almost by accident. Returning to England in 1971 after three years working abroad, he settled in Macclesfield, an industrial town 15 miles from Manchester, where he bought a run-down early nineteenth-century cottage in Black Road. The houses in Black Road had been condemned as unfit three years earlier and were about to be declared a slum clearance area. Early in 1972 Hackney applied for an Improvement Grant to install a wash basin in his house. The grant was refused on the grounds that the house had a "life" of only 5–10 years before redevelopment. Hackney could not accept the council's reasoning that, because the 160-year-old houses were neglected and lacked basic amenities, they must also be structurally unsound. His training told him that the buildings could be improved at reasonable cost to provide sound and comfortable homes.

A prolonged and subtle campaign commenced to save the Black Road houses. A residents association was formed, the local press was alerted, councillors and the local MP were lobbied, and a detailed structural and condition survey carried out. A cost study was prepared showing that the houses could be improved for only 35 per cent of the cost of redevelopment. Eventually, over a year later, the campaign succeeded when Rod Hackney's house, together with 32 of his immediate neighbours, was declared the first Black Road General Improvement Area (GIA). During the course of the prolonged struggle, many of the residents had managed to buy their homes through various arrangements of loans and mortgages. A group of houses that had been 70 per cent tenanted four years earlier had become 90 per cent owner-occupied by the time the GIA was declared. This was to become a key factor in the development.

During the period since the campaign started, building costs had risen alarmingly. To keep within budget, residents decided to do much of the building work themselves. Rod Hackney's house was improved first and became a model, not just of what could be achieved but how to go about self-build. Over the next year the other houses were improved with the Residents' Association acting as general contractor. Residents worked on their own houses and collectively on the improvement of the common area in the centre of the block. Specialist subcontractors were employed for the more difficult tasks, and friends and relatives helped out the elderly who were unable to do the work themselves. The work to each house was purpose-designed to meet individual requirements and to keep within the various budgets of what each household could afford (Fig. 4.2).

Black Road was a tiny scheme, but it was highly innovative. What started as a battle

Figure 4.2
Black Road, Rod Hackney's
influential experiment in housing
rehabilitation through commu-
nity self-build.

to save to save peoples' homes evolved into a new model for urban renewal. Although not a co-operative in any formal sense, Black Road demonstrated that co-operative action could benefit a community and serve the self-interest of its members. Of necessity, the residents adopted a self-build approach and, with the help of their resident architect, demonstrated that a method could be worked out to make community self-build a viable alternative. Public relations was a key factor in the campaign, and Rod Hackney's abundant flair for publicity made Black Road famous. It has received awards, been featured in national newspapers and magazines and on television, and it has been visited by Ministers of the Crown and by Royalty. More immediately, the publicity helped stimulate others into action.

In 1974 Hackney was approached by a group of residents from the Saltley area of Birmingham, who had seen a television programme on Black Road. George Arthur Road was a multi-ethnic area of Victorian "tunnel-back" terraced housing, threatened with demolition under the City Council's rebuilding programme. Much of Saltley had already been rebuilt as a hotch-potch of tower and slab blocks, and the residents of George Arthur Road did not relish the same fate. They persuaded the Saltley Community Development Project to fund a community campaign. As at Black Road part of the problem was ownership. Many of the houses were leasehold, with the freeholds held by a large London firm. Pressure was mounted to persuade the freeholders to sell. Eventually they did – either to the householders or to a local housing association. After fifteen months of campaigning, a Housing Action Area was declared and Rod Hackney set up a site office to carry out the work. In the main this was "enveloping". All the exteriors were improved in one package contract – roof, chimneys, extensions, external walls and windows, paths, fences and gates, Nothing was done to the interiors under the building contract, although the residents were helped to carry out their own improvements, often on a self-build basis (Fig. 4.3).

Rod Hackney's approach, in co-ordinating a community campaign to stimulate the intervention of outside agencies and the support of private funding, proved extremely helpful to Saltley CDP which, like the other community development projects, did not have access to large-scale funding. It was to be repeated at the Cleator Moor CDP in Cumbria and in similar run-down areas of Leicester, Belfast and Stoke-on-Trent. Although all these schemes relied on community co-operation, the self-build element was limited to individuals' efforts, supported by the technical expertise of Hackney's architectural staff.

Community self-build was to realize its full potential when, in the early 1980s, Hackney was approached by the City Council of Stirling in Scotland. With its capital programme constrained by government cuts and faced with a housing waiting list of thousands, Stirling Council offered Hackney a large site fronted by a derelict terrace that it could not afford to develop. Working with the council and the Scottish Building Society, applicants from the waiting list were interviewed over a period of 18 months, starting in 1984. Thirty-eight families were found with the skills and/or motivation to spend up to 3,500 hours building their own houses. Part of the exercise was to rehabilitate the existing terrace, but along the back of the site new houses were built. These were designed in advance in traditional construction but some conces-

Figure 4.3
George Arthur Road – an area of Victorian tunnel-backs in Birmingham, saved and rehabilitated through Hackney's work with the Saltley CDP.

sions were made to custom design. Extra-thick ground slabs were used so that party walls, stairs and partitions could be configured differently according to individual preferences. External walls, in Scottish tradition, were 200 mm concrete block, rendered both sides, which is considerably easier to build than brickwork. As in all his schemes, Hackney employed an architect, living and working on the site, whose job was to lead the self-build process by example, teach basic building skills, organize the supply of materials, and bring in specialists for the difficult tasks. The houses were constructed for the cost of materials plus the cost of the site, the architect's fees and about 10 per cent for specialist labour. Houses worth £34,000 were completed for £18,000 each (Fig. 4.4).

Meanwhile Hackney had been carrying out a string of developments in Macclesfield, all along Black Road. The last of these was Roan Court, a new development of 60 terraced houses (Fig. 4.5). Rod Hackney acted not only as architect but as developer, builder and estate agent as well. Most of the houses were sold at design or construction stage and, to a degree, have been customized for their purchasers. Once again there was a self-build element, with buyers being offered anything from a serviced slab to a complete house. In practice, few buyers took the self-build option, with most of the building being done by Hackney's construction firm Castward. In what he called phase 2 of community architecture, Hackney aimed to draw most of the labour from those who had learned new skills in the earlier self-build schemes in Black Road. The houses are designed in the vernacular tradition and there was an emphasis on craft skills and quality. Many of the materials were second-hand – oak timbers, bricks, tiles, slates flagstones and cobbles were salvaged from elsewhere – which meant they had stood the test of time and were better than new. They also had the conservationist virtue of recycling.

Figure 4.4
Self-build in Stirling. On the left, the rehabilitated terrace. On the right, the new-build houses.

Figure 4.5
Roan Court, Macclesfield
New housing built by
those who had learned
new skills through com-
munity self-build.

Hackney's economic formula

Starting in his living room in Black Road in 1972, Rod Hackney's practice mush-roomed over the next few years. By 1982 he had nine offices all over northern Britain employing 30 staff. By 1985 there were twelve offices and 70 employees, including 46 architectural staff. From Black Road onwards, most of his schemes have a similar economic rationale. He strongly takes the view that community architecture is not just about housing – it's about re-creating wealth.

Take an area of run-down housing with poor residents, many of whom are unemployed. Property values are low and so is the income of the neighbourhood. There is a culture of dependency on subsistence level welfare benefits. Lack of work and very low incomes create a breeding ground for crime, which further stigmatizes the area. Individually these families can do nothing to change the situation and the building owners are equally powerless. Co-operative action, though, can work wonders. First, the residents need to band together and organize. Next, they need to acquire their homes. In a depressed area they are worth next to nothing, and mortgages can be arranged even for the unemployed. They then have an asset against which they can borrow or apply for grants. With the assistance of the community architect they then learn skills – not just building trades but organizational and communication skills as well. Using their own free labour – which is paid for by state benefits – they repair and improve their houses or build new ones. During the process, the local economy benefits because specialist builders are employed and builders merchants increase their trade. Residents end up owning a house that is worth twice as much as it cost. They have gained confidence in their ability to achieve. They also have skills that they can use to get employment or to set up small businesses. The poverty cycle is broken and the area and its residents increase in value.

There is no doubt that Rod Hackney made this economic formula work in several of his schemes. Finance was one of the keys. In a period of rising property values, mortgage lenders could be persuaded to invest in an appreciating asset. The general availability of improvement grants was another critical financial advantage. With successive government cuts, these have become increasingly difficult to obtain. Significantly, too, he has been highly selective in the choice of projects to take on. The determination of the participants is critical. Relatively few people have the stamina or the skill to take on large-scale self-building. Location is even more important. All Hackney's schemes have been in areas of small-scale terraced housing suitable for single family occupation. It would be much more difficult to make them work in inner areas of large cities, where blocks of flats or multi-occupied tenements are the norm. Even if the daunting organizational problems could be overcome, high land values would break the economic formula.[3]

Walter Segal

Walter Segal did find a way to make self-build work in the dense inner city, if only on a small scale. His approach differed from Rod Hackney's in two key ways. First, he chose to work through the local government system rather than outside it. Secondly, and most significant, he had developed a simplified method of construction that made self-build possible for people with only the most rudimentary skills. What has become known as the "Segal Method" began in the early 1960s when Walter Segal needed to built a temporary home quickly for his own family. Over the next decade he developed and refined his simplified approach in several commissions for individual houses. Eventually it became apparent that the method was so simple that it provided an ideal approach for self-builders.

During the era of large-scale high-density housing, there was little scope for individual houses in the inner cities, much less self-build. But by the early 1970s the atmosphere had changed. One person who helped to change it was architect Nicholas Taylor. In 1973 he published an influential book, *The village in the city*[4], which attacked multi-storey housing, called for a reduction of densities, and for social housing to concentrate on houses with gardens rather than flats: in effect, for inner city to become "Garden City". By 1975 Taylor was a leading councillor in the Labour-controlled inner London Borough of Lewisham. When introduced to Walter Segal, he found a man after his own heart. One of the virtues of the Segal Method was that it could be used on small sites, where difficulties of access or steep slopes made conventional development impractical. In 1976 Lewisham identified four small sites and advertised among its tenants and waiting-list aspirants for potential self-builders. Seventy-eight families expressed keen interest, and a ballot was drawn for the 14 who would form the first self-build group. Finance was to be through the government capital allocation for council housing and, when complete, the houses would be jointly owned by the council and the families who built them.

The choice of equity sharing funded by public finance led to extended delays while the government reviewed the funding rules. Segal's innovative system also had to be proved to satisfy the building bylaws. All this took more than two years. In the meantime each family met Walter Segal so that their house could be custom designed to meet their needs. Once work started on site, the simplicity of the building method proved its worth. Essentially, Segal tried to eliminate all the most difficult of the traditional building skills. The houses are timber framed, which eliminates bricklaying.

82

The legs of the frame sit on simple concrete pads, which minimizes foundations and makes a site slab unnecessary; it also raises the buildings above the ground, so that they can easily be built on sloping sites. Designs are based on a modular grid of that matches the standard sizes of building materials. Whole sheets of plywood and plasterboard can be assembled into the frames and secured by timber battens, eliminating much of the cutting required by traditional methods. Plumbing and electrics run in the voids created by the framing, which cuts out the chasing and drilling that is normally needed. Plasterboard is finished with paint, so plastering skills are not required. Even complicated assemblies such as windows and staircases can be built up from simple standard materials.

Drainage was one thing that could not be simplified, and the Lewisham self-builders found this one of the most difficult and demoralizing tasks. Once the drains and foundation pads were in, the next step was to assemble the frames. The basic frames for each house were assembled flat on the ground. A team effort was required to hoist the frames erect and secure them by temporary bracing, The connecting members, floor and roof joists were then fixed, and the basic structure became stable. From this point on, each family continued the work on their own house as an individual exercise for which Walter Segal provided a set of simple drawings as an instruction manual. The fourteen houses in the Lewisham pilot scheme were based on 8 standard types, one or two storeys high, that were adapted to suit individual needs. The pilot was followed by a second scheme of 13 houses on a single site dubbed, appropriately, "Walter's Way" (Fig. 4.6).[5]

The Segal Method and the houses it has produced has been widely acclaimed. Not only is it popular among its users, it has attracted widespread admiration among architects. Modernists admire the rigorous simplicity of the construction method and see it as a development of the discipline of system building – Segal houses bear a superficial resemblance to the 5M system (see Fig. 2.9). For others it is a new vernacular. Nicholas Taylor's verdict was:

> My own inspiration, William Morris . . . would certainly have understood the creative enthusiasm and fulfilment of the self-builders . . . he would probably have understood the style too, because after all, what Walter has done is simply to update half-timber . . . the essence of what has been achieved here is real vernacular – not a cosmetic vernacular of gables and leaded lights but a vernacular in the true sense of ordinary people building with ordinary people's skills.[6]

Segal's legacy

Walter Segal's work was an object lesson to those who believe only the young are capable of radical initiatives. By the time the first Lewisham scheme was completed, he was well over 70 and had not many years left. At his funeral in 1985, a plan was hatched to create a permanent organization to propagate his ideas. The Walter Segal Self-build Trust was formed in 1988 and it exists to provide information and training in the Segal Method and to give organizational support to self-build groups. Meanwhile, Jon Broome, who became closely associated with Segal while working in Lewisham Architects Department, has perpetuated his legacy. In 1983 he founded the co-operative practice Architype, which has successfully applied the Segal Method in a range of projects, both self-built and builder-built.

Figure 4.6
*"Walter's Way" – the second, and
larger, Lewisham scheme self-built
using the Segal method.*

84

The Segal system has been successfully used by self-build housing groups throughout the country and is now recognized as a simple and cheap method of providing permanent housing that fully complies with the standards achieved by conventional construction. The method has also been successfully adapted to other types of project. In 1981, Peter Suzner and Peter Hubner, Professors at Stuttgart University, developed the Segal system in a design for a 30-room student hostel that was built room by room by small groups of architectural students.[7] More recently the method has been used in several community projects. Most significant of these was the Mill Lane Garden Centre in West Hampstead, completed in 1992 (Fig. 4.7).[a] With the help of a trainer, the centre was built by a group of young people with learning difficulties, vividly demonstrating the simplicity and adaptability of the Segal Method.

Figure 4.7
Mill Lane Gardening Centre, a training and activity centre self-built by young people with learning difficulties (architect: Simon Yauner).

The scope for self-build

Considerable claims have been made for self-build housing both in its achievements and its potential. A lot of publicity has been given to self-build co-ops. Disadvantaged groups from the urban unemployed and ethnic minorities are portrayed building themselves out of poverty and back into employment This laudable image is often juxtaposed against figures showing that up to 5 per cent of annual house construction in supplied by self-build. These figures need to be treated with caution. Of the 13,000 self-built houses completed in 1990, almost 10,000 were built by enterprising individuals and couples. These were, almost exclusively conventional houses on suburban or

---

a. Other community projects built using the Segal method include Calthorpe Project community nursery and meeting room, Camden [architects: Architype]; Ecology Centre, Sunnyside Road, Islington [Constructive Individuals]; Surrey Docks City Farm [Architype]; Maldwyn Nursery and Family Centre, Newtown, Powys [Benedicte Foo].

ex-urban sites, where the self-build element might only comprise managing direct labour and supply of materials. A further 1,000 were completed in a similar way by farmers and businessmen. Only 2,000 were completed by self-build housing associations.[8]

There are successful self-build groups. Some have used the Segal method, some conventional construction and some have converted large houses into flats. Many of them have overcome formidable obstacles. It often takes years to organize skill training, find and secure a site, and – most difficult of all – secure a backer. Groups can receive Housing Action Grants through the Housing Corporation, but to do this they have to register themselves as a housing association and obtain backing from an established housing association or secondary co-op. They still need to borrow the bulk of the money, and conventional funders such as building societies have shown extreme caution. With more help, more people could self-build. In Lewisham, the local council gives initiation grants to self-build groups and helps to find sites. A secondary co-op – Co-operative Housing in South East London (CHISEL) – gives organizational support. Without more help of this sort, many self-builders will be frustrated and their number will continue to be tiny.

Producer co-operatives

The co-operative revival that spawned community self-build coincided with a revival in interest in producer co-operatives. Few old-style industrial co-ops had survived from earlier times but, during the 1970s, several attempts were made to establish new industrial co-operatives on a significant scale. Public attention was focused on the industrial reorganization attempted at the Scottish Daily News, the IPD works in Liverpool and, particularly, the motorcycle works at Meriden near Coventry. In all these cases the original firms had run into financial difficulties and the workers chose to set themselves up as co-operatives rather than accept closure of the plants and loss of their jobs. Given their financial background, these initiatives faced an insuperable uphill task. They also faced legal difficulties, which had so often been the downfall of co-operative initiatives. Despite government support, all these experiments failed and their high profile undermined public confidence in the co-operative approach. Meanwhile, with far less publicity, smaller-scale and innovatory approaches to producer co-operation were more successful.

Design and build

In the radical atmosphere of the early 1970s, while many architects sought a new relationship with the users of their buildings, others sought to establish closer links with the craftsmen who built them. Self-build was one way of bringing together designers, users and builders. But this could only scratch the surface of a major problem. Competitive tendering and inadequate regulation put the building industry amongst the most backward of employers. Men were hired and fired on one hour's notice, and they worked in dirty and dangerous conditions. They were subjected to rigorous pressure on pay rates and often employed on an illegal "cash-in-hand" basis that became known as The Lump. All this placed a premium on maximizing output and minimizing costs. which often had a disastrous effect on standards. To make matters worse, the terms of building contracts placed the architect in an antagonistic relationship with the builder. All communications had to be channelled through the management structure and were often disputed. Any meaningful relationship between designers and the craftsmen actually doing the work became almost impossible.

Long ago in *The ragged trousered philanthropists* (one of the few novels written about the building industry), Robert Tressell graphically described the frustrations of a skilled craftsmen compelled by the system to produce shoddy work for low wages.[9] Repeated attempts have been made to forge a new approach to the organization of building. The building clubs were one early example. In 1833 an attempt was made to establish a Builders Guild on co-operative lines, but it was defeated by a lock-out by the employers. After the First World War a new attempt was made by the Trade Unions to establish a Builders Guild financed by the Co-operative Bank and Insurance Society. This met with more success, and it completed work worth more than £2 million, largely building housing for local authorities: the Homes Fit for Heroes of the Addison Act. This co-operative experiment met its end when the housing programme was slashed by the 1921 economic crisis.

From the early 1970s a considerable number of building co-operatives were set up, often involving architects working directly with craft workers on a design and build basis. The largest and best-known of these was Sunderlandia. The co-operative was set up in 1973 in the northeast city of Sunderland, an area with chronically high unemployment. It was founded by architect Mick Pearce, who had practised for several years in Zambia; Robert Oakshott, a financial journalist, who had spent some time training building workers in Botswana; and Peter Smith, an experienced trade unionist. They set out with high ideals. With everyone drawing equal pay and exercising equal voting rights, they would re-create the crafts skills of traditional building. This was to be achieved largely through training. Initially nine craftsmen were employed and 36 apprentices, including two women bricklayers. Sunderlandia soon found this ratio was far too high to succeed, and the number of apprentices was reduced to 22. Initially, Sunderlandia was successful in getting work. They modernized many cottages for owner-occupiers and successfully negotiated with local housing associations. They also designed and built some new houses.

By 1977, though, they were beginning to suffer from cutbacks in public housing. There were also difficulties on making a non-hierarchical structure works and some people left, disillusioned.[10] By 1980, Sunderlandia was in considerable debt and, despite reorganization was soon to fall victim to the recession of the early 1980s.[11] Sunderlandia was the best known and, perhaps, the largest design and build co-op. But it was not alone. Several smaller building co-operatives were formed at this time, including Collective Building and Design, which has successfully operated in northeast London for 20 years and, in 1994, still had 8 members.[12] While they were inspired by high ideals, most of these co-ops suffered from a lack of marketing and financial management skills. Competition with professional contractors was always difficult and many fell by the wayside in the switchback economy of the building industry. But they did revive the ideal of craft work, and of co-operation between designers and builders. They were good employers and they highlighted the inadequacy of skill training in the building industry.

Figure 4.8
*Ormond Road Craft workshops – a training
and resource centre in Finsbury Park, north
London – designed and built by Collective
Building and Design.*

Working communities

Meanwhile, a novel form of co-operative endeavour was developing, with groups of producers banding together in working communities. Traditionally, small businesses have had to fend for themselves. In dense urban areas particularly, they often occupied cramped and poorly maintained premises. Many were hampered by the lack of specialist services, which were expensive and difficult to organize. In 1971, in the midst of the campaign to preserve Covent Garden, architects Rock Townsend took over an empty warehouse in Dryden Street. They brought together a range of small professional firms – engineers, quantity surveyors, model builders and designers. Collectively the professionals could feed off each others' services. They also pooled common services such as reception, messages, typing, reprographics and conference faculties. By co-operation, all the firms were able to enjoy higher standards of space and services than any of them could afford individually.

The concept was soon applied to non-professional enterprises. In the mid-1970s the GLC leased a disused schoolbook depository to a community initiative called Urban Small Space. The building was converted by architect Mike Franks to form Clerkenwell workshops. The idea here was to provide a range of small cheap spaces as "start-up" accommodation for craft industry and other small enterprises. To keep the costs down, standards were fairly low and the range of common services minimal. But it did provide space that was easy to occupy on a short-term basis and made good use of a redundant building. Similar conversions soon followed, at Barley Mow in Chiswick and in redundant Docklands warehouses.[13] Since then the concept of "managed workspace" has become established and widespread. Although most now originate in initiatives by local authorities or developers, the interaction between occupants and the sharing of common services ensures that co-operation remains a key element.

Housing co-operatives

Although the provision of housing was among the aims of the Rochdale Pioneers, none was ever built by the co-op movement. Housebuilding was capital intensive and the movement did not have access to large-scale capital. The accumulation of housing capital from small savers fell to the building societies which, in their early days, were a form of locally based co-operation. The lead in social housing was taken by the philanthropic societies and the model town initiatives. One of the few early co-operative enterprises was in the Cadbury model town, Bournville. Bournville Tenants Ltd was formed in 1906 and raised capital by offering shares to small savers and through mortgages. The society built 145 houses for rent, with each tenant becoming a shareholder.[14]

From the end of the First World War, the provision of social housing in Britain increasingly concentrated on the state-funded developments of local authorities. In other countries of northern Europe, particularly in Scandinavia, co-operative housing became a significant component of the social housing stock. Even in the countries of eastern Europe, which under the yoke of the Russian communism were generally assumed to be state monopolies, housing co-operatives prospered. In Czechoslovakia and East Germany in 1973, about 25 per cent of housing was managed by co-operatives and in Poland almost 45 per cent.[15] Meanwhile, in Britain, housing co-operatives were virtually unknown, but several initiatives were brewing that would revive this neglected form of housing provision.

The Liverpool Co-ops

The most co-ordinated development of housing co-operatives took place in Liverpool in the 1970s and 1980s. It grew out of the earliest attempts to promote rehabilitation as an alternative to wholesale demolition and redevelopment. One of the initiatives of the Shelter Neighbourhood Action Project, which started its pioneering work in Toxteth in 1969, was the foundation of the Granby Co-operative Housing Association. By the time SNAP closed in 1972 the Granby Co-op had succeeded in buying a few houses for rehabilitation as rented homes using mortgages provided by Liverpool City Council. During 1972 a group of council-owned houses became available nearby and the Granby Co-op encouraged the residents to set up their own self-help organization – the Canning Housing Co-operative. The two nascent co-ops had to learn the hard way and make progress largely through the voluntary work of their own members. It became evident that pooling their efforts would not only help their own organizations but provide a means of propagating the co-op idea. In 1973 the two co-ops set up Neighbourhood Housing Services as a secondary co-op to provide technical and support services. NHS started with only two employees – architect Tom Clay, who had previously worked for SNAP, supported by a part-time typist. By 1977 it had grown to 20 staff serving 8 co-operatives. In addition to technical staff – architects, surveyors, quantity surveyors, clerks of works – it employed housing maintenance, management and administrative staff. By then, NHS was completing 100–129 housing improvements each year. Its mode of operation is typified by its approach to improvement for the Corn and Yates Street Co-op (Fig. 4.9). In 1976 the co-op bought a terrace of 27 houses in Corn Street and another of similar size in Yates Street. NHS took over one of the empty houses as an office for an architect, a clerk of works and a housing worker. A programme of immediate repairs was carried out and plans were developed for phased improvement of the houses. Under pressure from the co-op the council made the area a General Improvement Area eligible for enhanced improvement grants. The houses were typical two-up two-down with back extensions. Within the constraints of the existing structures, improvements were customized to the tenants requirements – some chose to put a bathroom in the small back bedroom, others in an extension behind the kitchen; some chose to keep separate living and dining rooms, others to knock them together into a through room. Many of the residents were elderly and temporary accommodation was ar-ranged for them in one of the empty houses, while their own houses were improved. A few of the elderly were rehoused in a small block of flats built on an infill site.[16]

At this point the development of housing co-ops in Liverpool took a new turn. The new Labour Housing Minister, Reg Freeson was keen to develop housing co-ops and appointed Harold Campbell to chair a working party to investigate legislative changes. This resulted in the 1975 Housing Rents and Subsidies Act under which co-operatives became eligible for Housing Association Grants. To provide practical support Campbell founded Co-operative Housing Services to encourage tenant management and develop the co-operative ideal. In 1975 a group of back-to-back houses in the Weller Street area were taken over, from a bankrupt property company, by CHS. A local office was set up which, in 1977 became independent under the name Co-operative Development Services. The Weller street area was one of 57 scheduled for

Figure 4.9
Corn and Yates –
two streets in Toxteth,
Liverpool, rehabilitated
and improved by a
housing co-operative.

redevelopment by the council. Council housing offered to residents of clearance areas might well be miles away and, in any case, much of the council's stock was poor quality and classified "hard to let". Supported by CDS the residents decided to set up a co-operative to develop their own housing.

The Weller Streets Co-op was formed in August 1977 and faced a task quite different from the earlier co-ops. Rehabilitation presented a relatively limited range of options. Organizing the design and construction of new housing presented a far more open ended problem. Their first task was to appoint an architect. The co-op was quite adamant that its members should control the design process, not letting themselves be hoodwinked by professionals. CDS provided a list of local architects and the co-op prepared a shortlist. At the interviews they made their approach clear: "Our idea is that we design the houses and you hold the pen". Some aspirants were completely fazed by such an attitude but eventually Building Design Group[b] were appointed and Bill Halsall became project architect. With some difficulty a nearby site was secured and Halsall commenced a long series of discussions with the design subcommittee. It was a condition of funding from the Housing Corporation that the new housing should be built to Parker Morris space standards but this still left plenty of scope for alternative designs. Co-op members had clear ideas about what they didn't want. They did not want to live in terraces which they associated with the slums they were leaving. They did not want to live in blocks of flats – flats had become stigmatized by the state of the Liverpool tenement blocks. The elderly members did not want to be isolated in sheltered housing. Interviews were carried out with the co-ops 61 members and a brief was drawn up for a mix of 45 houses – with 2, 3 or 4 bedrooms according to members needs – and 16 flats for the elderly. Visits were organized to view new housing schemes in Merseyside and a preference developed for courtyard housing. The scheme which emerged was based on small L-shaped blocks of houses, each with two flats built into the corner. The blocks form a series of small courtyards from which vehicles are largely excluded (Fig. 4.10). The layout is designed to create a sense of community and discourage the intrusion of outsiders. The co-op placed a strong emphasis on egalitarianism with everyone having the same. The basic design is standardized in a simple traditional style but individuals had a degree of choice in the internal layout of their own houses.[17]

The initiative and determination of the Weller Streets Co-op inspired others. Under the guidance of CDS a rash of co-ops were formed in other redevelopment areas and these were able to benefit from a new funding commitment from the City Council. Later on, tenants in run-down tenement blocks trod the road of new build co-operation. Eventually 30 odd new-build co-ops were formed and their success overshadowed the earlier work of the co-ops committed to rehabilitation. By the mid-1980s, Neighbourhood Housing Services, champion of the rehab co-ops had run into organizational and financial difficulties and closed down, its functions taken over by CDS and others. The Liverpool co-ops started because people rejected the process which broke up and dispersed communities and were unenthusiastic about the quality of new council housing. But their success made them controversial. Instead of seeing the co-ops as a fresh approach to social housing from which valuable lessons could be learned, they were presented as an alternative to council housing itself.[18] As a result the co-ops became something of a political football and, for a time,

---

b. The practice is now known as Wilkinson, Hindle, Halsall and Lloyd Partnership.

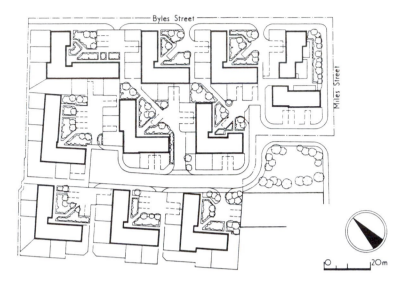

Figure 4.10
(a, above) Weller Street — the courtyard layout that emerged from extensive discussion of options amongst the co-op members.
(b, right) The new housing — a simple but attractive traditional design with generous landscaping.

council funding and recognition was withdrawn. The uphill struggle was made even more difficult by a change in the national funding regime in 1988 and by more stringent rules for registration introduced by the Housing Corporation. The established co-ops still flourish but it is now extremely difficult for community initiatives to found new schemes.

The London Co-ops

In the much larger and more densely developed area of inner London the development of housing co-operatives was more diffuse than in Liverpool. The earliest initiative grew out of the student protests of the late 1960s. Student Co-operative Dwellings was founded in 1968 to provide communal housing for students. It was not able to carry out its first development until 1973 when a site was secured in Lewisham. The Sandford co-op was a new development of 14 houses each of which contained 10 bedrooms for single students who shared bathrooms and large farmhouse kitchen. There was also a block of 6 self-contained bedsit flats for couples. The co-op also founded a community laundry in association with local tenants association. Changing its name to the Society for Co-operative Dwellings, SCD carried out several developments for single people, both new build and rehab, throughout the 1970s and 1980s.[19]

A good deal of co-operative housing activity in Inner London concentrated on rehabilitating large buildings which had fallen into disrepair or degenerated into substandard multiple occupancy. During the early 1970s some small co-operatives sprang up in the form of Co-ownership Housing Associations. The members concentrated on housing themselves by converting large houses into flats, often on a partial self-build basis. Co-ownerships foundered over problems of equity and eventually became owner-occupied dwellings. A larger-scale rehabilitation initiative was the Holloway Tenants Co-operative. This grew out of a campaign begun in 1970 by the NE Islington Community Project. Rather than develop its own housing the Holloway co-op worked with a local housing association which bought up slum houses from private landlords and converted them. The completed housing was handed over to the co-op which became responsible for allocation an management. By mid-1975 the Holloway Co-op had acquired more than 100 houses and had over 200 members.[20]

During the late 1970s there were a variety of co-operative initiatives. Some developed through tenants organizations in rented housing, some through squatters groups. Some were set up to serve the specific user groups – ethnic minorities, the disabled, the young, the homeless. Some groups succeeded in building new, some improved or converted, others simply took over the management of existing housing. From the mid-1980s development by co-ops, like all other housing development, declined through lack of funding. What was established was the principle of co-operative management. There are still many housing blocks managed by co-ops and the principle of tenant self-management has now become recognized as an alternative to the remoteness of municipal landlords and the paternalism of traditional housing associations.

The impact of self-help initiatives

The range of self-help initiatives which took place during the 1970s grew out of the change in the political climate created by community action. But they all drew, wittingly or unwittingly, on historical precedents. They all relied, to a greater or lesser extent, on a revival of co-operative principles. Some may not seem to fit comfortably under the co-operative umbrella. Many see co-operation as an end in itself – a socially desirable alternative to individualism and competition. To purists, self-build groups and working communities may seem motivated more by personal gain than by co-operative spirit. The contradiction between idealists and those with more material motives was a cause of considerable conflict in many of these enterprises. It should not have been. The basic aim of co-operation is that, through working together, the participants gain something for themselves they would not otherwise have had. For many of those involved, personal gain was the only way they could understand the purpose of co-operative enterprise.

Despite mixed motives, despite conflicts, self-help initiatives did achieve a great deal and provided new models for managing and developing the urban environment. They created alternatives to demolishing buildings just because they were old. Through community initiatives new methods were found to preserve and improve areas of old housing. New uses were found for old buildings which had lost their original function – renovating and re-vitalizing them. Where new development was essential, novel and more sensitive forms were developed which reflected the aspirations and preferences of the users. A different approach to design and construction emerged which created new relationships between designers and users and between designers and builders.

All this was not achieved easily. Co-operation does not fit within the framework of either the private or the public sector. It is a third way. In some countries this has been recognized and, where co-operation has been given legal and financial support, it has made a significant economic contribution. Britain's legal and financial structure is primarily geared to supporting the market philosophy of private enterprise or to provision through the organs of the state. History is littered with failed attempts at co-operative enterprise, many of which fell foul of legal, financial or organizational problems. The new co-operators found it no easier. The early initiatives had little assistance, but with perseverance sufficient support was gained to show that they could succeed. They revived and re-established the co-operative ideal which was to become a key thread in the organization of community initiatives and the practice of community architecture.

References

1. John Hands, *Housing co-operatives* (London: Society for Co-operative Dwellings, 1975); diagram adapted from that on p. 22.
2. John Burnett, *A social history of housing 1815–1985*, 2nd edn (London: Routledge, 1978, 1986), 94–5.
3. Michael Hook, "Macclesfield: the self help GIA", *The Architects' Journal* (12 November 1975), 995; "Down your way – current projects by Rod Hackney", *The Architects' Journal*

(5 October 1977), 30; Nick Wates, "CA is here to stay", *The Architects' Journal* (9 June 1982), 43; Nick Wates, "The Hackney phenomenon", *The Architects' Journal* (20 February 1985), 47; and Rod Hackney, *The good, the bad and the ugly – cities in crisis* (London: Frederick Muller, 1990).

4. Nicholas Taylor, *The village in the city* (London: Temple Smith, 1973).

5. Wilhelm Kainrath, "Walter Segal's houses", *The Architects' Journal* (30 September 1970), 769; Charlotte Ellis, "Do–it yourself Vernacular", *The Architects' Journal* (17 December 1980), 1186; Jon Broome, "The Segal method", *The Architects' Journal* (special issue, 5 November 1986). For an extended description of the method, see Jon Broome & Brian Richardson, *The self-build book* (Bideford, Devon: Green Books, 1991).

6. Quoted in *The Architects' Journal* (17 December 1980), 1187.

7. Peter Blundell-Jones, "Student self-build in Stuttgart", *The Architects' Journal* (27 July 1983), 33.

8. Murray Armor, *Building your own home*, 13th edn (Bridport, Dorset: Prism Press, 1991), ix.

9. Robert Tressell, *The ragged trousered philanthropists* (London: Lawrence & Wishart, 1955; Grafton Books, 1965). Tressell probably wrote the book about 1906. When he died in 1911, he bequeathed the manuscript to his daughter. It was published in an abridged version in 1914. Only in 1955 was the full text published by Lawrence & Wishart.

10. Mike Fleetwood, "Sunderlandia's struggle", *The Architect's Journal* (19 October 1977), 747.

11. Robert Oakshott, *The case for workers co-ops* (London: Macmillan, 1978, 1990).

12. Tom Woolley, "Collective building and design", *The Architects' Journal* (18 January 1984), 46.

13. Charles McKean, "Working community entrepreneurs", *The Architects' Journal* (19 October 1977), 749.

14. John Hands, op. cit., 107.

15. Ibid., 55.

16. Michael Hook, "Housing co-operatives", *The Architects' Journal* (29 June 1977), 1215.

17. Alan McDonald, *The Weller way* (London: Faber & Faber, 1986).

18. Nick Wates, "The Liverpool breakthrough: or public sector housing phase 2", *The Architect's Journal* (8 September 1982), 51.

19. John Hands, op. cit., 110, 76 ff.

20. Chris Holmes, "Self-help housing" in Peter Hain (ed.), *Community politics* (London: John Calder, 1976), ch. 10.

CASE STUDY
The Bramley co-op:
new-build co-operative housing

On the edge of North Kensington is a strip of land that nobody wanted to know – no-one in authority, that is. Physically, the Freston Road area was part of Kensington, but, because of a quirk in the borough boundaries, it was actually in the London Borough of Hammersmith. In the 1960s much of the land became owned by the GLC and it met a fate that will, by now, be familiar. On part of it the GLC built an estate of tower blocks. Down the edge they built an urban motorway that was intended to be part of the London motorway box. The new road severed the area from Hammersmith completely and it became a forgotten land. Much of it degenerated into marginal uses – small-scale industry, yards and depots guarded by ferocious dogs, a large and unsightly scrap yard. Part was taken over as a gypsy encampment.

There were also houses: modest, and poorly built, Victorian cottages, part of a development known as Brickfields and quite unlike the grand regency terraces of the adjoining Norland Estate. In 1972 the 77 cottages were declared slums and half of them were demolished. This brought more dereliction to an area that was already depressed and for which none of the local authorities had any positive plans for improvement. Nothing happened for several years until in 1977 the GLC proposed developing the housing land with industrial units. By this time the houses that were still standing were occupied by about a hundred squatters and they had achieved some security under a squatting "amnesty". Some of them set up an action committee and enlisted the support of tenants on the adjoining council estates who did not want to live next to an industrial development. Feeling they were part of a no-man's-land, the squatters declared their houses "The Free and Independent Republic of Frestonia". The new "Republic" attracted national and international attention[1] in the autumn of 1977, with its application to join the United Nations and the appointment of 25 "Ministers of State" and a dozen "ambassadors".

At the Public Inquiry into Hammersmith's structure plan, Frestonia's "Minister of State for the Environment" put in an appearance to argue against industrial use and in favour of housing and small-scale craft workshops.

Eventually, the publicity and lobbying paid off and the housing site was re-zoned for a mix of housing and workshops. At this stage the Notting Hill Housing Trust became interested in the site and appointed architects Pollard Thomas and Edwards to draw up a scheme for both the housing area and the surrounding land. The zoned mix was resolved by a scheme for new housing and a separate proposal for small industrial units on another site on the other side of Freston Road. The squatters set up the Bramley Housing Co-op and – possession being nine points of the law – established their claim to rehousing on the site. Again nothing happened for a long time while the Housing Trust negotiated first with the GLC and then with Hammersmith Council. In 1983 NHHT finally acquired the housing site and recognized Bramley Co-op as a client group.

The architect's first drawings showed 12 shared houses, each for 6 single people, grouped around a communal garden. This was not what the co-op wanted. They may have been squatters but they did not consider themselves a commune. But, after such long delays, the prospect of developing a scheme spurred them into action. They organized a survey of co-op members and formulated a brief for 16 houses that could be for families or shared-singles, and 24 self-contained one person flats. From then on, regular meeting were held between the Co-op Liaison Committee, project architect Steve Fisher, and representatives of NHHT. Several key constraints emerged which helped shape the design. First the co-op housing had to be built on the cleared land, leaving the existing houses standing until the occupants could be re-housed. Secondly, the squatters had turned the derelict land into an extensive communal wild garden. Thirdly, the NHHT wanted to reserve the option of taking over some of the new housing if it was not required by the co-op. There were also funding constraints. The Housing Corporation would not fund shared housing. Nor would it fund bed-sitting room flats, which was what the co-op wanted.

After trying out several alternative layouts, the scheme that emerged shows an ingenious resolution of these constraints. The core of

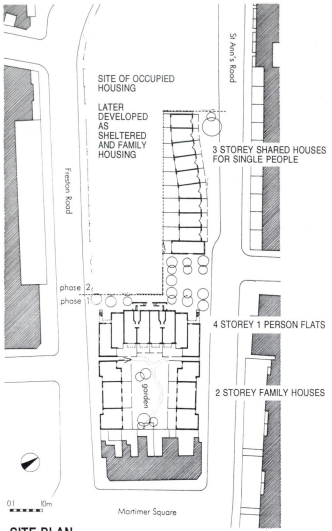

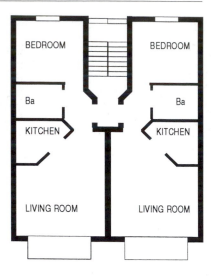

The Housing Corporation would not fund bed-sitting room flats. These small and tightly planned single person flats were developed instead.

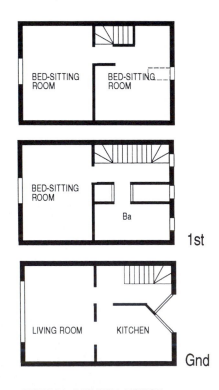

SITE PLAN

The new housing was built on the vacant land while the co-op members continued to occupy the run down cottages on the adjoining site.

the co-op housing is grouped around a communal garden. Each side is formed with four- and six-person two-storey houses. A four-storey block provides flats for single people – planned as small one bedroom flats to overcome funding objections. This block completes the enclosure and has balconies facing south over the communal garden. The development was completed by a separate terrace of ten three-storey houses. These are designed for occupation by three single people, each having a large bed-sitting room and sharing bathroom, kitchen and dining room. To satisfy the Housing Corporation these were officially four-person family houses and

TYPICAL SHARED HOUSE

"Officially" four-person family houses, these were, in fact, each designed to house 3 single people sharing.

The closed public face of the family houses, with the four-storey block behind and the shared houses to the right.

Entrance to the single person flats at the side of the four-storey block.

were designed in such a way that they could equally well be occupied by families. The separation of the terrace from the core housing meant it could be used by the Trust as ordinary rented housing if not required by the co-op.

Throughout the development of the scheme there was a continuing dialogue between the architects and the client group. Detailed discussion took place with a liaison group of five people who reported major issues back to a full meeting of the co-op. Communication was helped by the fact that the co-op members were living next door to the site during the whole development process. New and revised drawings were put on public display for instant discussion and comment. Nevertheless, it seems clear that the users were less involved in the design process than in smaller-scale co-op developments such as Weller Street. Designing multi-storey housing on a tight urban site is a much more complex exercise than producing layouts of individual houses. Given the tough constraints, the project would probably not have benefited from group discussion of alternative layouts. Co-op members felt they did not have much influence on the look of the scheme. Nonetheless, it is clear that the overall form derives from a detailed community brief and has emerged as a distinctive and unusual solution quite different from social housing developed from a standard brief.[2] The basic contrast between open and airy facades on to the communal garden and

The snaking crescent of houses for shared singles

The communal garden – a key feature of the scheme that developed from the garden made by the squatters on the derelict land.

defensive brick walls, with small openings on the outside, also reflects the users' concerns to be protected against traffic and against crime and vandalism. At the same time the architects have introduced distinctive window designs and brickwork patterns that undoubtedly reflect their own ideas rather than those of the users. There was also limited user input into the interiors. Internal layouts were standardized through discussion with the user committee. Houses were allocated only two months before completion and, at that stage, choice was limited to kitchen layouts and finishes. Steve Fisher feels that all design issues were discussed with the user group but there were conflicting ideas among the members. Besides, many co-op members were interested less in design details and more in the basic problem of securing decent housing. By the time building work started, they had been living for years in tumbledown houses, served by temporary water and electricity, with outside toilets and inadequate washing facilities.

The co-op housing was completed at the end of 1985. Once the co-op members were re-housed, the old houses were demolished

and a second phase was completed by the same architects to a brief by the Notting Hill Housing Trust. A terrace of family housing has been built and a group scheme of sheltered housing for the elderly. The whole development sprang from the ingenuity of a group determined to improve their lot and with the patience to pursue their goal over several years. The co-op housing came directly from the detailed brief they provided, but in its very precision lies the only drawback. The scheme has limited flexibility and the co-op has no claim on alternative social housing. With so many single members, as they form couples and have children, the precise brief will no longer fit, creating considerable strains both on the housing and those who live in it.

References

1. Reported in the *Daily Mirror* (4 November 1977), the *Daily Mail* (5 November 1977) and in press reports in Germany and Scandinavia
2. Ruth Owens, "Dreams and realities – Bramley Housing Co-op", *The Architects' Journal* (29 April 1987), 37.

CHAPTER 5

The direct approach

COMMUNITY TECHNICAL AID

In the variety of projects developed under self-help initiatives, design services were normally provided by architects in some form of private practice. At one extreme was the relatively large organization created by Rod Hackney, physically dispersed but centrally directed; at the other was Walter Segal, who always worked entirely alone, never employing an assistant or even a part-time secretary. In between were more conventional small or medium-size practices where most of the work was done by salaried staff under the direction of the partners in the firm. For some architects there seemed an inherent contradiction between the co-operation they were fostering in their client groups and the hierarchical structure of their own working lives. If co-operation was a successful model for the development of community based projects, perhaps it could also form the basis of new, more democratic approach to professional practice.

At the same time there was increasing concern that the very term "community architecture" had a ring of exclusivity. It seemed to imply that architectural design was the only service community groups needed and that only architects could provide it. In truth, those professionals who had begun working with community groups in the early 1970s had provided them with a variety of technical and design support – planning, architecture, building surveying, landscape and even graphic design. There were also other services groups needed to get building projects off the ground – advice on funding, on the acquisition of land and buildings, and on how to organize themselves as effective clients and developers. The range of these services, and the new forms of organization that sprang up to provide them, became known as community technical aid.

New forms of professional practice

The challenge to established conformity of the 1960s brought with it the upsurge of community action and new approaches to the development of the inner cities. It also brought new forms of practice in which professions could organize themselves to serve the interests of poor urban communities better. Not just building designers, but lawyers and other professionals were creating new models of professional practice. Some of these models were developed in deprived urban areas in Britain. Others came from abroad.

102

Trans-Atlantic models

During the 1960s the pressure for inner urban redevelopment was as strong in the United States as in Britain, probably stronger. Whereas much of the British urban development was ostensibly in the public interest, and carried out by local authorities, the American system was much more commercially orientated. Social housing programmes were minimal and the planning activity of city authorities was largely for the benefit of commercial redevelopment. Most often it was slum housing that was demolished to make way for new office blocks and industrial buildings. In New York, in 1964, a group of volunteers set up the Architects' Renewal Committee of Harlem (ARCH) to help poor tenants in this largely Black and Puerto Rican area. A major campaign was mounted around the East Harlem Triangle which the City had designated as an industrial "park". With the assistance of ARCH, residents resisted plans for the demolition of their homes and successfully demanded rehabilitation and the provision of social facilities.

The late 1960s were a period of urban riots and political revolt in the USA. Attention was focused on the problems of inner urban areas, and others followed the lead given by ARCH. Similar community design centers (CDCs) sprang up in other cities – in Philadelphia, Los Angeles, Cambridge (Massachusetts). In San Francisco a CDC was set up in 1967 on the initiative of the University of California. Architecture and planning students from the university worked on community projects under the supervision of staff. The center provided both a learning resource and a service to the community. One of their key projects was in the Yerba Buena district, where a large commercial redevelopment was planned displacing about 4,000 people. The CDC prepared an alternative housing plan, which would have allowed the residents to be rehoused nearby, and this formed the basis of legal action against the City authorities. Although the alternative plan was rejected, 1,500 people did win the right to new homes provided by the City.

In 1969 the American Institute of Architects became involved, stimulated by pressure for change in the inner cities. It also wanted to appeal to younger architects who had been failing to join the AIA for some years. Local chapters of the AIA took the initiative in setting up community design centers, often in conjunction with universities, and by the early 1970s there were almost 70 CDCs across the USA.[1] But the development of these centres was not without controversy. According to Richard Hatch, founding Director of ARCH,[2]

> . . . the movement was known from the outset as advocacy planning. The original efforts focused on tenant-landlord issues, on preparing communities to halt the urban renewal bulldozer and on the spreading of citizen participation. The work of the groups was largely political – sharpening the issues and raising consciousness. The AIA re-dubbed advocacy organizations Community Design Centers. Under the aegis of the AIA the movement became service orientated and non-political . . . established [architects'] offices run by members of sponsoring AIA chapters surely found it all quite cost-effective when, by rule, they received the commissions and the fees generated by the local CDCs.

What had begun as a radical movement became primarily a means of providing more work for private architectural practices. On the way it broke new ground. Architects and planners had organized a service to bring design support direct to low income groups and had set up locally based centers to deliver these services. Through the involvement of universities, students had helped to provide a free service and, at the same time, had learnt something of the needs of people who would not normally be able to afford architects fees. The CDCs were something of a flash in the pan. By 1975 the inner cities had passed out of the political spotlight and there were severe cuts in the Federal housing budget, which had provided much of their income. Some closed down, others were reduced to a skeleton service. Only a few CDCs remained fully operational. Nevertheless, the American initiatives were to provide useful models for building designers seeking to respond to the demands created by community action in Britain in the 1970s.

The Glasgow initiative

One of the earliest technical aid initiatives in Britain took place in Glasgow, a city notorious for its housing problems. Nineteenth-century developments in Glasgow had taken a form quite different from other British cities. Whereas mass housing elsewhere had been provided by back-to-backs or subdivision of large houses, Glasgow had purpose-built flats. Almost all the city's housing – even for the middle classes – had been in the form of four-storey tenements. Typically, these were built in continuous terraces enclosing a street block, with the courtyard in the centre providing outdoor washing and drying space. Each block of flats was reached by a central stair with a single shared toilet on each landing. The tenements were well built, usually of stone, with generous ceiling heights and solid floors. Except for the wealthy, though, space standards were appalling. Whole families, often with many children, were crammed into one- and two-room flats. By the time of the First World War, densities were very high – over 1,000 per acre – and more than 100,000 people lived in one-room dwellings.

Abercrombie's post-war plan for the city had been rooted in the need to reduce overcrowding. In the years that followed, densities were reduced, but by means that were questionable to say the least. Much of the population was decentralized to large, ill serviced peripheral estates such as Easterhouse and Castlemilk, which have become notorious for their continuing social problems. Many of the tenements were demolished – including much of the Gorbals, one of Britain's most infamous slums – and replaced by multi-storey blocks. By the end of 1970s there were 200 tower blocks in Glasgow, housing almost 20,000 people.[3] By then, densities had been much reduced, but the city's public health department continued to issue closing orders on the tenements. Indeed, housing was being condemned at a rate far faster than it was possible to redevelop. Coincidentally, the 1969 Scottish Housing Act introduced substantial finance for house improvement. The sheer scale of the problem, coupled with the availability of new finance, was enough to tip the balance in favour of improvement rather than demolition.

In 1970 Raymond Young, an architectural student at the University of Strathclyde, submitted a thesis on *Public participation in planning* – a subject made topical by the newly published Skeffington Report. He concluded that, if tenements were to be improved, a catalyst organization was needed to provide technical support for the residents' collective efforts. After graduation, working alone from his own tenement home in Govan, Young set up a Tenement Improvement Project and succeeded in persuading the City Council to declare the Taransey Street Housing Treatment Area.

After some delay, a show house was completed in early 1972. Working through his old tutor, Jim Johnson, Young persuaded the university's Department of Architecture to set up a Research and Development Unit that would become the catalyst organization. Assist, as the unit was called. was initially set up with a two-year life and established a local office, in a converted bicycle shop, to service the Taransey Street area.

Assist's aim was to provide a free technical service to enable the tenement housing to be improved on a voluntary basis. The idea of voluntary improvement was similar to the SNAP initiative in Toxteth, but the improvement of tenement housing was complicated by two key problems. First, in order to reach adequate space standards it was necessary to combine flats – replanning three tiny flats to make two of reasonable size. The second problem was divided ownership. Within each block there was a mixture of owner-occupied and tenanted flats. Those that were rented were owned by a multiplicity of trusts and landlords. All owners shared responsibility for the common areas through a complex system of tenement law. The solution was to help the residents form a housing association. Given the difficult management problems, most owners were happy to sell. The community-based housing association was able to buy up enough flats to allow improvement to proceed. A rolling programme was developed for renovation, one complete "close" of 8–12 "houses" being improved at a time. Some people were rehoused to facilitate the process, but much of the improvement work was carried out with tenants in residence (Fig. 5.1).

The success of the Taransey Street scheme engaged the active support of the City Council who co-operated in declaring further improvement areas. The Housing Corporation also became involved and set up a local office in Glasgow. Raymond Young went on to lead the Housing Corporation office and Jim Johnson became full time director of Assist. Under Young, the Housing Corporation played a pro-active role, training a development officer to work locally in each chosen action area stimulating the residents to form their own housing association. By 1977, there were 10 community housing associations, covering about 12,000 tenement flats, jointly funded by the City Council and the Housing Corporation. All were based on the improvement principles and participation techniques developed by Assist Meanwhile, Assist had broadened its activities from its community housing role, preparing schemes for the landscaping and improvement of tenement back courts; an infill development of sheltered housing. and conversion schemes for Glasgow Free School and Dixon Halls Old Peoples Day Centre.[4]

The urban renewal initiative in Glasgow had echoes of the centres set up by American universities. But it went further. Strathclyde University's technical aid unit generated a creative partnership between academic, local and national institutions. This partnership stimulated local groups to organize and participate in the improvement of their housing conditions. In one respect this was another early initiative based on enlightened intervention by the authorities. Elsewhere self-help initiatives had come from community groups and the institutions had been reactive rather than proactive. The architects and designers involved worked either as pioneering individuals or as part of conventional practices. What Assist demonstrated was that if design professionals were brought together in an organization specifically geared to community needs they could develop new and special skills to sponsor and support locally based self-help groups.

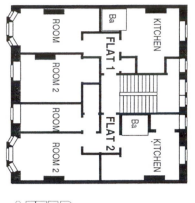

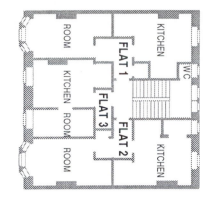

AFTER

BEFORE

Figure 5.1
(top) Assist's improvements
to the Taransey Street tenements. New bathrooms
built in and three small
flats combined to make
two of reasonable size.
(foot) 20 years after
improvement, a lasting
and successful alternative
for many Glasgow tene-
ments otherwise scheduled
for demolition.

Neighbourhood law centres

Outside the process of urban renewal, other professions were recognizing the unmet demand for their services in the inner cities. The Notting Hill Summer Project had revealed a considerable need for legal advice. This was not just the need for representation against criminal charges but advice on claims for social security and other benefits. There was also massive demand for help with housing problems – enforcing tenancy agreements. rent registration, getting repairs done, rehousing rights. The North Kensington Neighbourhood Law Centre was set up to meet this demand. Charitable funding was raised to employ solicitors to provide a free legal service for the local community. The Law Centre was not just an agency for advice on individual cases. Through research and analysis of their casework it was able to mount pressure

106

and campaign around general issues of local concern. For example, a conference called by the North Kensington Law Centre in 1977 resulted in a new pressure group to highlight local employment problems.

The North Kensington initiative was soon imitated and during the 1970s Neighbourhood Law Centres were established in many inner city areas, often funded by local authorities. These organizations introduced three new and important principles into professional practice. They were organized on a localized basis to relate to a defined area. They were independent of the institutions and the state structure and could take up issues on behalf of individuals and the local community without fear of compromise. Most important they provided a free service to those who would, otherwise, not have access to professional advice. These principles created a new way in which committed professionals could organize to assist deprived communities. They were to serve as a model for new departures in providing design services for community benefit

The new voluntary sector

Most of the community action which developed from the early 1970s focused on preventing destructive new development. Much of this activity was around the housing issue – preventing the destruction of communities and familiar environments and, at the same time. generating initiatives to produce improved housing conditions, designed with more sensitively to the views of those who would live in it. Housing was the key issue and is the main land use in most inner urban areas. But good housing alone is clearly not enough. Employment is almost equally important and many self-help initiatives had revolved around job creation and employment issues. While bread and shelter are enough to sustain life they do not, alone, ensure personal fulfilment or the enjoyment of leisure. Social and recreational facilities had long been recognized as essential components in humanizing the urban environment.

Until the 1960s, community facilities in the inner cities had been provided by philanthropic bodies or by the state – a process which was much the same as the provision of social housing. From the early days of industrialization social facilities were provided in centres run by philanthropic institutions. Chief among these were the established churches which provided schools and general purpose halls for youth clubs, dances, sports and other recreational use. Among secular providers were the social action centres in the settlements, and these were supplemented by the work of large national charities and "improving" organizations such as the Boy Scouts. Various clubs and societies provided recreation centres including political parties, groups like the British Legion and the Masons and, in the north of England a widespread network of working men's clubs. From the late nineteenth century, education and training, child care, facilities for the elderly and a range of recreation and sports faculties were increasingly provided by the local authorities. By the 1970s provision was widespread, but often still inadequate. In many areas of the dense inner cities state provision was lacking or insufficient. Access to the facilities run by an institution usually required commitment to its creed or cause and often had an atmosphere of paternalistic "character formation". Many people felt excluded by such institutions particularly the ethnic minority communities which were a growing proportion of the population of the inner cities. In the upsurge of community action new groups sprang up to make good this shortfall – people began to organize to provide new facilities for themselves. Some of the earliest of this direct action developed around the lack of open space. In the search for outdoor play and recreation, demands were mounted to open private spaces for public use and to take over derelict land for adventure playgrounds, community gardens and other outdoor facilities.

Major demands grew around the needs of ethnic minorities. New cultural and religious centres were founded to serve minorities from Asia, Africa and the West Indies. Groups were formed to develop ethnic arts and culture. Discrimination in employment was tackled by new organizations for skill training and employment generation. Facilities were developed for other groups seen to be disadvantaged by existing provision – women, the elderly, the physically and mentally handicapped. Throughout the 1970s and early 1980s new groups mushroomed throughout inner urban areas. It became a substantial new sector of the inner city and soon spawned its own umbrella groups like Play Associations, and its own support services such as community transport. In origin and culture it was quite different in from the world of the traditional charities and institutions run by well meaning men of the cloth, Colonel Blimps and ladies bountiful from the shires. The army of long-haired blue-jeaned radicals who ran the new foundations created, in effect, a new voluntary sector

The growth of technical aid

All these new groups needed space – indoor premises in which to operate, outdoor space suitable for their needs. To get their space they needed the services of designers. From the mid-1970s several initiatives were developed by independent groups to provide design services to community organizations. The free service provided by law centres was one model although it never proved possible to provide technical aid on so localized a basis. The stimulation to new development demonstrated by Assist was another but the new groups sought independence of institutions answerable only to their client groups. Behind it all lay the trail blazed by the Community Design Centers in the USA.

Appropriately, the first technical aid service developed from the work of an American in London. Ed Berman founded Inter-Action in 1968 when the search for radical alternatives was at its height. Inter-Action was a co-operative of community workers teachers and artists and developed several initiatives to improve environmental awareness and help inner London voluntary groups organize their own projects in the arts, media and education. The operation was a considerable success, raising large grants both from government and private industry. By the mid-1970s Inter-Action had 60 staff and had its own purpose-built centre in Camden. In 1975 they founded NUBS – Neighbourhood Use of Buildings and Space – to provide a free architectural service to community groups. Initially NUBS employed only one architect, and never more than 2 or 3, but it demonstrated the need for the new service it provided and its potential in generating new facilities for community use.

In its first two years NUBS was involved in three key projects. In 1975 the completion of a new public baths in North Kensington made the Victorian Silchester Baths redundant. The council wanted to demolish the old building but a consortium of community groups decided it could be put to good use. NUBS prepared a scheme for converting the old building for use as a sports and horse riding facility and a centre for

Figure 5.2
Two of NUBS early projects. Above, the Riverpoint Project, a disused church hall converted to A hostel for the single homeless. Below, the first city farm established by Inter-Action in Kentish town.

craft workshops The old baths was a listed building and the community campaign attracted the support of the Ancient Monuments Society. In the end Silchester Baths was demolished but NUBS involvement was an early demonstration of a commitment to preserve the urban heritage and find new uses for old buildings. This principle was demonstrated with more success in the Riverpoint project in Hammersmith. NUBS helped a local group to convert a vacant church hall into a hostel for single homeless. The project was completed very cheaply with the help of volunteer labour, support from building contractors and the help of the local building college (Fig. 5.2).

The third project was in Kentish Town. There Inter-Action set up the first city farm – a real working farm in the inner city which would provide a source of education and pleasure for children and young people unused to close encounters with farm animals. NUBS designed and organized simple buildings for the farm which were built by volunteers and local residents. In its early work NUBS succeeded in establishing principles which were to become the hallmark of the work of technical aid groups – conserving and re-using redundant buildings; finding ways to complete building projects cheaply for client groups with limited resources; support and sponsorship of innovatory organizations who aimed to create unusual projects to meet hitherto unrecognized demands.[5]

Although NUBS succeeded in demonstrating the value of its service to community groups it could not offer a model for alternative forms of architectural practice. At that time architects Code of Professional Conduct bound them to a fixed fee and they were prohibited from providing a free or speculative service. Furthermore, no form of practice could qualify for charitable status. In 1976 a small group of staff and students from the Architectural Association School of Architecture set up Support Community Building Design. Support aimed to provide a service similar to NUBS but to practice in a form acceptable to the established rules. Tom Woolley, founder member of Support, wrote "NUBS . . . creates a false impression of the realistic cost of a community architecture service to society. It is doubtful whether NUBS, precisely because it is a charity, provides a model which would be widely applicable. We [in Support] are beginning to function as a conventional practice because that's the service which a number of groups have asked us to provide. We have to exist as a conventional practice to be acceptable to local authorities – and, of course, we have to charge according to the minimum fee scale".[6]

Support recognized the potential demand created by the plethora of new community groups but also realized that if new organizations were to be established to meet these demands they would need a realistic financial base. If voluntary groups could secure funds for building projects they could also raise money for professional fees. Support may have accepted the professional constraints of the Code of Conduct but in its internal organization and objects it was far from a conventional practice. It was a established as an egalitarian co-operative with the aim of providing its services only to user groups in control of their own building projects. In its early years Support carried out projects mainly for community groups, but also schemes for trade unions and assistance and advice to groups campaigning to improve their housing conditions. Pay was poor and co-operative organization was struggle but they succeeded in demonstrating that a novel form of practice could become financially self-sufficient in providing an independent design service to the new demands created by community action. At this stage the various pressure groups in the professions began to take up the cause.

The New Architecture Movement took Support, and similar co-operatives such as ARCHAID in Leeds, as its models for a new approach to architectural practice. In 1977 the RIBA Community Architecture Group set up an "urban workshop" in Newcastle-upon-Tyne. This was primarily an environmental education initiative and drew on students from the city's School of Architecture to run a city centre advice shop. But money was found from the RIBA and the government's job creation scheme to employ three architects full-time. Eventually the centre became incorporated as Newcastle Architecture Workshop. It now functions as a technical aid centre but continues to provide a educational resource for schools.[7] In 1979 the Town And Country Planning Association founded the Community Technical Aid Centre in Manchester as the northern focus of its "Planning Aid" service. Initially, Manchester CTAC concentrated on planning issues and worked in conjunction with Design Co-op, an architects' collective but after a few years the two services were merged.[8]

The demand for community technical aid had now been clearly demonstrated and the viability of the new centres of professional service had become evident. In 1979 another new initiative took the process a stage further. In Liverpool, architect/planner Leslie Forsyth brought together a consortium of community groups. If voluntary groups were the main beneficiaries of technical aid then they should control the service. The Liverpool group founded Community Technical Services Agency (COMTECHSA) the first centre to be controlled by its client groups. Because of the strong community links, COMTECHSA succeeded in obtaining funding to provide a free feasibility service through the government/local authority Partnership Programme.[9] This initiative helped to set a new pattern. In 1981, the Labour Party regained control of the Greater London Council. Under its young and radical leadership, the new GLC actively supported community action. It established a new funding regime for community groups in general and technical aid in particular.

The availability of new funding stimulated the formation of new London-based organizations. Community Land and Workspace (CLAWS) was founded in 1982, modelled on the concept of user group control initiated by COMTECHSA. Another important initiative gave new focus to the role of women in building design. A re-invigorated women's movement was one of the products of radical intellectual climate of the late 1960s. The practice of architecture had been very male dominated and the construction industry notoriously so. The New Architecture Movement had spawned a feminist discussion group and this led to the formation, in 1980 of a new feminist umbrella group. Matrix was, in part, a propaganda organization and arranged an exhibition and the publication of a book[10] giving a feminist perspective on building design. As a practice – Matrix Feminist Architectural Co-operative – it was funded by the GLC from 1981 to provide a design service to community groups particularly those run by or for the benefit of women.

Statutory funding gave a new impetus to community technical aid. The cause was helped by reforms in the regulatory regime. The mandatory fee scale was abandoned which meant that architects were no longer breaking their Professional Code by providing a free service. At the same time the Charity Commissioners relaxed their stance and accepted technical aid as a charitable object. Community technical aid mushroomed during the 1980s and new centres were established in most major cities. Most of them had a strong local focus, mainly serving groups in their own inner urban areas. Some, particularly in smaller cities extended their reach to assist self-help groups in the urban hinterland. Over the years some groups became quasi-institutional. In Wales and in Northern Ireland technical aid groups were funded directly by the government and acted as consultants on government projects.

The new services

From uncertain beginnings community technical aid had become an established form of alternative professional practice. These alternative practices provided a range of ostensibly conventional technical services – planning, architecture, landscape architecture, graphic design – but to meet the needs of community organizations they had to adopt radically different approaches from their conventional colleagues.

Neighbourhood planning

Town Planners had been trained to carry out surveys, produce development plans for local authorities, and to operate the machinery of the post war planning legislation. Before the influence of Skeffington and the movement for Planning Aid, most of this activity took place behind closed doors. Planners were – supposedly – objective, analyzing scientifically collected data and producing rational solutions to perceived needs. In reality they were often biased by preconceptions and were prey to the pressures for commercial development. In the new atmosphere of community action they were forced to abandon their cloak of objectivity. In serving community groups they became advocates for the particular cause their client groups espoused. The scope of community planning might be small scale – helping a group to get planning permission or framing an objection to a new development – or it might expand to the development of a full-scale neighbourhood plan.

The Belfast group, Community Technical Aid (Northern Ireland), has carried out a range of planning aid. It has recently helped groups in the Springvale area of West Belfast to campaign for the removal of scrapyard and for an environmentally conscious approach to traffic access to a new development. It has also helped disability groups in the province to press for better access facilitates.[11] Manchester Community Technical Aid Centre has helped Residents Associations with advice on traffic and environmental improvements and on conservation area status. It helped a local group campaign for the improvement of a shopping precinct.[12] With the general demise of comprehensive redevelopment, small-scale environmental improvements form the bulk of the work of Planning Aid.

But the large-scale controversies did not go away entirely. One of the largest was created by British Rail's proposals, in the late 1980s, to develop 135 acres of derelict land behind Kings Cross Station in London in conjunction with the new international terminal for the channel tunnel. Working with a consortium of property developers, British Rail wanted a lavish, high density commercial development, 70 per cent of which would have been offices with token amounts of social housing and community facilities. A consortium of local groups prepared two alternative plans with widespread public participation (Fig. 5.3). The community plans proposed a much cheaper solutions with the scale of development reduced by more than half, and the bulk of the site devoted to housing, light industry and secure open space. In their ideal plan, the Kings Cross Railway Lands Group envisaged the whole of the land devoted to local

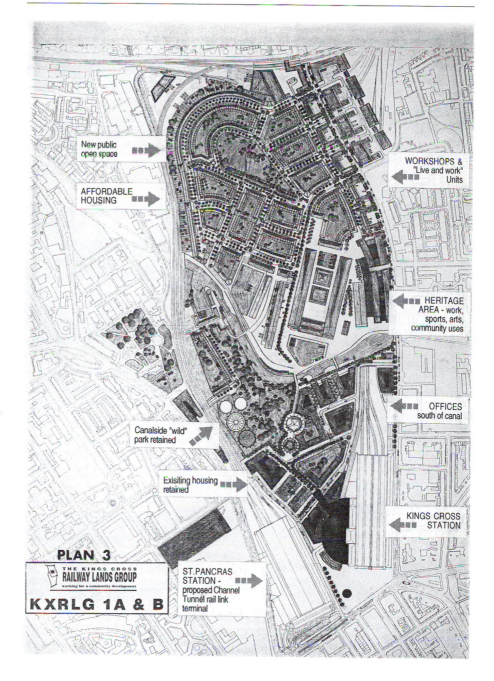

Figure 5.3
Kings Cross Railway Land – the alternative plan developed through community participation as a counterweight to the high density and largely commercial scheme proposed by British Rail.

New public open space

AFFORDABLE HOUSING

WORKSHOPS & "Live and work" Units

HERITAGE AREA - work, sports, arts, community uses

OFFICES south of canal

Canalside "wild" park retained

Exisiting housing retained

KINGS CROSS STATION

PLAN 3

THE KINGS CROSS
RAILWAY LANDS GROUP
working for a community development

KXRLG 1A & B

ST.PANCRAS STATION - proposed Channel Tunnel rail link terminal

113

uses. Their compromise proposal did accept some commercial development and a small-scale terminal for the channel tunnel.[3] The arguments raged for some time with the community plans providing a well worked out focus for socially acceptable development. Meanwhile the recession killed off the commercial plan and several of the property companies with it. The government eventually decided on a scaled-down terminal for the channel tunnel much more like that in the community plan than in British Rail's original scheme. The land itself remains derelict and the Railway Lands Group has prepared an interim use initiative for temporary use of the land and buildings.

New urban space

The design professions also had to find new roles in Community technical aid Until the 1970s the role of architects has been, almost exclusively, to design and supervise the construction of new buildings. The maintenance of existing buildings was the professional function of building surveyors. Community action had, to a large degree, led to the retention of areas of old housing. But it could not simply be preserved. It had to be improved, converted and adapted to modern standards. This required the design skills of the architects and the preservation skills of the surveyor. Most community groups ran on a shoestring. They could not afford new buildings. Retaining old buildings was in tune with the times but for most groups it was an economic necessity. The re-use of redundant buildings became a key component of community architecture and it required new design skills to cheaply adapt and extend − or at the cheapest, make do and mend. Even where groups could afford new buildings severe cost constraints placed new demands on the resourcefulness of designers to come up with cheap methods of construction and new approaches to the construction process which often used the free labour of unskilled volunteers. Almost as strong as the demand for new architectural and surveying services was the need for landscape design. Many of the new community buildings had associated outdoor space and there were new and unusual demands for outdoor space Landscape architects similarly had to learn new skills and cut their coat according to the cloth. Much of the work was small scale − a new fence here, some new paving there, a few plants − and the designers involved had to learn the merits of economy reserving their skills for space creation for the limited number of large projects.

The range of uses of the new urban space are many and various, the interest and objects of the organizations involved so diverse as the almost defy classification. As a rough and very imperfect guide to the new voluntary sector they can be grouped into five categories:

- *Community or cultural centres*   Community centres range from multi-purpose halls or buildings, with a variety of user groups, to centres developed for specific cultural groups. They include centres for minority faiths − Muslim, Hindu, smaller sects of the Christian and Jewish religions, for national minorities − Indian, Turkish, West Indian, Bangadeshi and more. They include resource centres for disadvantaged groups − the homeless, refugees, AIDs sufferers; and for those with special needs − the elderly, the handicapped and disabled. They include minorities of minorities − Turkish elderly, Bangladeshi women (Figs 5.4, 5.5).

Figure 5.4
Proposals for the Liverpool Islamic Cultural Centre designed by COMTECHSA. The new building will be attached to an existing mosque and will provide a centre for children and the elderly, together with a source of advice and support on business, finance and social matters.

Figure 5.5
The Huddleston Centre in east London – part of a large church divided into several levels as a multi-purpose community centre. A project designed and built by Collective Building and Design.

- *Child care*   There had been a phenomenal growth in new groups based around child care. It is indicative of the scale of this provision that in the London Borough of Hackney in 1992, in addition to facilities provided by the public and private sectors, voluntary and community groups ran 10 community nurseries, 6 voluntary nurseries, 20 parent and toddler groups 40 playgroups, 5 adventure playgrounds, and 10 toy libraries,[14] This is probably not atypical of similar inner urban areas throughout the country. It made buildings and spaces for child care activates one of the largest single sources of work for technical aid centres (Fig. 5.6).

Figure 5.6
The Jamoke project in south London. An industrial workshop converted and extended by the Matrix Co-operative to provide a day nursery and training centre for child care workers.[15]

Figure 5.7
An industrial unit converted by SUPPORT in 1984 for Tower Hamlets Advanced Technology Training – a community organization established to offer free computer training to people who would otherwise not have access to such skills. The project was particularly aimed at the disabled, women and the local Asian community.

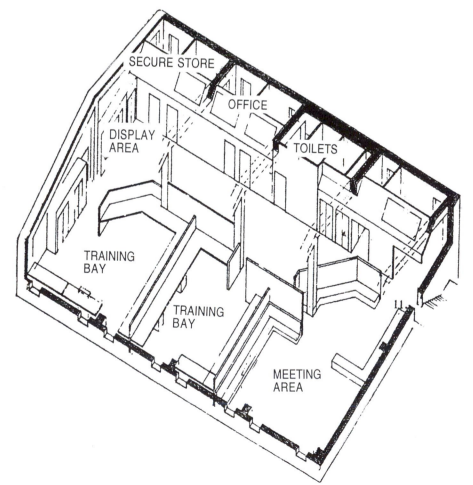

116

- *Training and employment*   The established voluntary sector has long since provided centres for skill training and productive employment of the handicapped and disabled. The new voluntary sector has contributed a fresh emphasis on provision for ethnic minorities. Not handicapped by mental or physical disability, but disadvantaged by cultural or language difficulties and by discrimination, minority communities have commonly underachieved in education and employment. Various initiatives in training and employment have been started by ethnic minority voluntary groups. These include training in business skills, information technology, design, dressmaking and car mechanics (Fig. 5.7).

- *Recreation and the arts*   There are many groups organizing community theatre and a variety of community based arts. A major growth area has been around outdoor recreation. Building on the pioneering community gardens in North Kensington and Covent Garden, a large number of local groups have campaigned to develop new open space by taking over derelict or unused land. Similarly, the first urban farm has spawned many imitations. By 1987 there were more than 60 city farms and community gardens[16] and many more community open spaces (Fig. 5.8).

Figure 5.8
The Calthorpe Project near Kings Cross. A local group fought to prevent a derelict site being sold for commercial development. Over several years they have built a community garden and recreation space. A social centre has been built using the Segal method designed by the co-op Architype.

- *Housing*   Housing was a major focus of community action. The co-ops and community housing associations generally looked to specialist technical organizations or to private practices for design services. As a result, housing has not been a major component of the work of technical aid centres. Some of them have done projects for community housing association, often specializing in minority or disadvantaged groups; refurbishment work for co-ops; and advisory or environmental improvement work for management co-ops and tenants associations.

- *Development services* While some technical aid groups concentrated on architectural services, many em-ployed a wide range of design disciplines and were able to offer a variety of services to the community which could not be matched in the structure of private practice. A few centres offered graphic design to meet the need among community groups to improve their publicity. Community Design for Gwent provide a service in the design of letterheads, logos, reports and also runs training courses in printing, poster design and arranging displays.

Much of the work of technical aid centres is advisory. This includes feasibility studies and general advice on building maintenance and adaptability. Quite often this advice does not lead to projects but it helps voluntary groups assess options and test the workability of their ideas But it doesn't stop at design advice. Many groups also find their clients need other advice – help with establishing local needs and the viability of their projects; advice on structure and organization; help with fund-raising for building work; and with seeking and acquiring new premises. Most technical aid groups offer this sort of support and a number employ specialist staff to provide organizational advice. At its best, community technical aid does not just provide technical services but offers a positive stimulus to the development of new community projects.

From co-op to collective . . . and back

Co-operation was central to the new voluntary sector. People came together voluntarily to work jointly to provide services for themselves or others. In these new independent ventures joint action was the key and the co-operative an obvious model. By the mid-1970s new legal forms had been identified and many groups became incorporated as non-profit making Companies Limited by Guarantee, a form set down by the 1965 Industrial and Provident Societies Act. Groups with a benevolent or charitable purpose could also join the statutory register set up under the Friendly Societies Act 1974. But for many groups the co-operative was a flawed model. True, everyone had equal shares and equal voting rights but this really amounted to a more democratic system of management. Co-operatives still had hierarchies based on different levels of skill or responsibility and this often meant they paid differential rewards.

The co-operative was a suitable model for many self-help initiatives where the main purpose was to produce benefits for the members. Receipt of the benefits were enough to satisfy most members. Besides some of these co-ops were quite large and representative and hierarchical structures were necessary to make them work. The new voluntary sector was composed largely of small groups committed to working together on a permanent basis. Their reward lay as much in their commitment to the project as in any benefits they might get from it. In a joint project nobody wanted to be subordinate to a boss or manager which would make their working lives little different from any other form of employment Hierarchies did not seem appropriate to such enterprises – partnership was a more appropriate model.

Many groups adopted a pure and egalitarian form of co-operative – the collective. In a collective everyone is equal. There are no managers and no subordinates. Everyone shares responsibility equally and is rewarded with equal pay. There is no "division of labour" between skilled and unskilled workers – everyone takes a share of mundane

118

tasks. And there are no votes. Voting leads to division and the "tyranny of the majority" over those on the losing side in any decision. Instead, decisions are made through "exhaustive discussion", arguing through the pros and cons until a consensus is reached. Some law centres, for example abandoned the traditional structure of the lawyers practice – solicitor, clerk, typist/receptionist, trainee, cleaner/factotum – all in a clear hierarchy of descending job skills, responsibility and pay. Instead all the staff were classed as caseworkers, regardless of qualifications or experience. All managed the centre collectively through regular meetings. All took their share of subsidiary tasks such as staffing the switchboard or reception desk. On the face of it ranking a qualified and experienced solicitor the same as a first year trainee was a denial of natural justice. But, it was argued, if all are taking the same responsibility, and are equally committed to their work, then they are expending the same effort and deserve the same reward.

Many voluntary sector groups, providing all sorts of different services, adopted the collective form. Most were small groups with, perhaps, 5–10 staff but some were quite large. Inter-Action, for instance, had more than 20 staff working collectively. So it was with technical aid where many of the groups formed to bring design services to the voluntary sector were in the form of collectives. For building designers the collective was not dissimilar to a partnership in private practice, except that everyone working in the organization was a partner. There were no employees and no ancillary workers. This meant that, as well as learning the new professional skills required for building re-use and economy design, they had to learn new technical skills. Typing their own letters and reports; keeping financial records and preparing accounts – what became known as "self-servicing".

People went into collectives with high ideals and high expectations but many were soon disillusioned. Discussion at the regular co-op meetings often centred on the principles of the organization rather than on the quality and nature of the service they were providing. Hours were spent debating the development of the collective ideal – such as whether to pay more to those with children because they had greater needs; whether to pay maternity leave. Routine work was neglected so more hours were spent on whether to break the pure form of collective spirit by employing a bookkeeper of a cleaner – and if so, whether a cleaner should paid the same as an architect. There may have been no formal hierarchy and no votes but this did not stop strong or difficult personalities dominating or disrupting discussion. When disputes arose, often over money problems and priorities, there was no way of resolving them. "Exhaustive" discussion became exhausting discussion and rather than endure endless and recurring controversy a lot of people left collectives, their ideals tarnished and their expectations dashed.

All this was a considerable distraction from the real work. The projects which came in were generally allocated democratically, at the regular meetings. From then on, though, the individual designers were often left to progress them on their own. There were often no mechanism for monitoring fee costs, progress or public relations. Organizational priorities squeezed out discussion of design standards and quality. It couldn't last. From the mid-1980s the collective form was progressively abandoned, Most technical aid centres appointed managers or co-ordinators and introduced clear structures and differentials. Similar changes were taking place in other groups in the voluntary sector which had functioned as collectives. But all was not lost. The new structures resolved the diversions and disputes and introduced efficient methods of monitoring performance, But the collective spirit remained and many of these organizations are among the most democratic working environments, The collectives had re-formed themselves into a refined form of co-operative.

Meanwhile, the co-operative ideal had had a more general influence on professional practice. In the spirit of the 1970s several architectural practices set themselves up as co-operatives. The best known of these is Ted Cullinan's practice which has run as a highly successful co-operative for more than 20 years. By the early 1980s there were a dozen architectural co-ops[17] and more have been formed since. Most of these are not collectives and the co-operative principle is preserved through equal share ownership and voting rights. Decisions are made democratically but specialization, hierarchies and differentials often develop by agreement. Most do not have any significant involvement in providing technical aid to community groups. Generally, though, they concentrate in socially orientated projects. Mostly they try to extend the democratic practices of their own organizations into the involvement users and clients in the development of their designs. Co-operatives set up by architects and other professions are not an integral part of the voluntary sector and must be seen as a bridge, bringing democratic working practices into the sphere of private practice.

The struggle for recognition

The growth of the new voluntary sector has been fostered by the work of two community architecture umbrella groups. The RIBA's Community Architecture Group, which first proposed a community aid fund in 1978, finally achieved its goal in 1982 when the government agreed to provide £12,000 from its Urban Initiatives Fund. The RIBA approach was to help new groups to get their projects started by donating half the cost of suitable feasibility studies. With these grants they could employ architects and in the first year over 40 community groups took up the offer. It was a modest start but over the next two years the fund was tripled and the RIBA compiled a register of practices interested in working with voluntary groups.[18]

Among the nascent technical aid groups this approach led to concern that the RIBA, like the American Institute before it, was using its auspices primarily to benefit its own members. Most architects working in the technical aid groups were not RIBA members and, in any case, were interested in developing an alternative to private practice. From Liverpool, Leslie Forsyth of COMTECHSA initiated a discussion among technical aid groups about forming a new organization. In the autumn of 1983 an exhibition of the work of 40 new centres launched the formation of ACTAC – the Association of Community Technical Aid Centres.[19] Forsyth became Secretary and John Knights of NUBS took the chair. ACTAC aimed to stimulate public funding for technical aid and to act a resource centre for the exchange of information and ideas, and to organize training in working with community groups. It has continuously maintained a directory of groups and individuals offering technical aid to voluntary groups.[20]

The initial tension between to two groups did not last. They soon recognized their complementary roles. Technical aid groups were among those benefiting from the community aid fund and representatives of the movement were co-opted into the Community Architecture Group. Their joint sponsorship helped community technical aid to establish itself and grow. The minimal funding available acted as seed finance. Both the aid groups, and the community organizations they served, could use it to attract funds from elsewhere. Partly this came from the philanthropic Trusts. To a degree it was provided by commercial sponsorship. Mostly, though, it came from the state. Much of the new voluntary sector was funded by local government, either directly or through government Urban Partnership and other central funds.

The new groups established an uneasy partnership with the public sector. The one resenting the obstructive procedures with which their applications were met and the excessive and detailed conditions attached to their grants. The other, suspicious of the radicalism and unorthodoxy of the new groups and the potential threat they were perceived to present to local government power and the services it provided. Nonetheless, the partnership prospered to a considerable degree. But from the late 1980s it came under increasing threat as a result of government restrictions on local authorities spending power. Many community groups faced increasing cuts and this had a knock on effect on technical aid. By 1992 many groups had reduced their staff and services to a minimum. Some closed altogether including the early pioneers NUBS and Support. Those that prospered did so by reorganizing and placing a new emphasis on presentation and marketing. A few successful centres managed to extend their client base to include the larger established voluntary organizations and the traditional preserves of the public sector such as schools or housing estates. Yet, despite the cuts, the demands were still there, Even in 1992/93, in the depths of the recession, the RIBA community aid fund was oversubscribed with applications from groups wanting to build new space. The potential for technical aid remained as great as ever.

The contribution of community technical aid has been underestimated partly because, with some exceptions, if has failed to produce a coherent body of work of "architectural quality" which would have helped to define the impact of community architecture as a design discipline Here and there the visual expression of cultural diversity shines through but most of the built space produced by technical aid groups is, at best, of modest design standards and, at worst, indifferent. This partly because of organizational problems. Partly because most of those involved see themselves as "enablers" – helping voluntary groups to secure premises and facilities for themselves which they otherwise wouldn't have – rather than as designers. The main problem, however, has been consistent under-funding. Outside the state, outside the private sector, the new community groups are usually seen as part of the third estate – the voluntary sector. Compared with their older cousins – the established charities, churches and voluntary institutions – groups in the new voluntary sector are the poor relations. Ragged infants with the begging bowl struggling to establish their new roles and their new values.

For every £1 they needed to provide decent built space for themselves they might get 10p. Many have had to function in wretchedly inadequate premises and with facilities far poorer than those they really need. If the architecture of community technical aid is largely minimalist it is because they have had to struggle with tiny budgets. This has created considerable resourcefulness, finding cheap ways to salvage and re-use old buildings. Seeking out the most economical ways of building new. Some have described it as "appropriate architecture". Appropriate to the budgets, perhaps, but not an appropriate response to the dedication which many have put into these new ventures. The new voluntary sector has proved a rich source of experiment and innovation. It has produced new forms of organization and established the need for new services. Many of the ideas developed through voluntary action were to provide the impetus for new policy and practice in the work of local government.

121

References

1. Bill Mikesell, "Architectural advice centres", *Architectural Design* (April 1976); Susan Lobbenberg, "Community design centres" *Voluntary Action* (Autumn 1980). See also Robert Goodman, *After the planners* (London: Penguin, 1972).
2. C. Richard Hatch, letter to *Architectural Design* (September 1976), 516
3. Roger Smith, "Multi-dwelling building in Scotland 1750–1970", in Anthony Sutcliffe (ed.) *Multi-storey living – the British working class experience* (London: Croom Helm, 1974).
4. Michael Hook, "Project Assist", *The Architects' Journal* (10 January 1973), 61; John Maule McKean, "Housing: from redevelopment to rehab", *Architectural Design* (March 1976); and Michael Thornley, "*Housing rehabilitation handbook* case studies: Assist [3 parts]", *The Architects' Journal* (10 November 1976, 8 December 1976 and 9 February 1977), 901–8, 1089–100, 269–77.
5. Bill Mikesell op. cit.: and Tom Woolley, "Inter-Action's NUBS", *The Architect's Journal* (19 October 1977), 739.
6. *The Architect's Journal* (19 October 1977), 731–2, 740.
7. Rod Hackney, *The good, the bad, and the ugly* (London: Frederick Muller, 1990), 102; and *Annual Report 1989/90* (Newcastle Architecture Workshop).
8. Nick Wates, "Shaping a service in Manchester", *The Architects' Journal* (4 August 1982), 26–8; and *Annual Report 1990/91* (Manchester Community Technical Aid Centre).
9. *Annual Report 1991/92* (Liverpool: COMTECHSA).
10. Matrix, *Making space – women and the man-made environment* (London: Pluto Press, 1984).
11. *Annual Report 1990/91* (Belfast: Community Technical Aid [Northern Ireland]).
12. *Annual Report 1990/91* (Manchester: Community Technical Aid Centre).
13. *Towards a People's Plan* (London: Kings Cross Railway Lands Group, 1991)
14. *Guide to childrens services in Hackney 1992/93* (London: Hackney Under Fives Association, 1992).
15. Ruth Owens, "Child care challenge", *The Architects' Journal* (18 October 1989), 38.
16. *City Farmer* (Bristol: National Federation of City Farms Ltd, Spring 1987).
17. Cazenove Architects Co-operative, "Co-operative architects", *The Architects' Journal* (16 February 1983), 42.
18. A Turbulent Decade Building Design (21 July 1986)
19. Nick Wates, "ACTAC in action", *The Architects' Journal* (12 October 1983), 56.
20. *National directory of community technical aid*, published twice yearly (Liverpool: Association of Community Technical Aid Centres).

CASE STUDY
Jagonari: a centre for Asian women

Central to the growth of the new voluntary sector was the recognition that certain groups of people were disadvantaged. The handicaps of sickness, disability, old age and infirmity had long been supported by the traditional charities and public institutions. They had been much slower to respond to less obvious disadvantages caused by discrimination and alienation. During the 1970s, feminism had heightened awareness of discrimination against women in employment, education and cultural opportunities. Increasing evidence had emerged of discrimination on grounds of race. Added to this was the isolation felt by many immigrants, raised in very different cultural backgrounds, unused to the mores – perhaps even the language – of the new society they had joined. This isolation had often led those who came to Britain in past waves of immigration to establish their own clubs and institutions.

So, too, the new immigrants, among whom Asian women were disadvantaged in more ways than most. In the Indian subcontinent, women play a full part in economic life as well as taking the leading role in domestic and social organization. The process of migration cast them into the confinement of wholly supportive roles. Usually the men were the first to travel to seek work and new homes. When settled they would send for their wives and children. Marooned in an alien culture, whose ideas they did not understand and whose language they probably did not speak, Asian women in Britain were often restricted to the care of the home and family and the company of each other. Jagonari was one organization set up to end such isolation by mutually developing their education and skills and pooling their resources.

The Jagonari group of Asian women was originally formed as part of the Davenant community centre in Whitechapel. The centre attracted support and funding under the new community policy adopted by the GLC after the 1981 local elections. Next door to the Davenant Centre was a vacant site on which Jagonari wanted to develop their new services, which included language teaching, computer training, seminar rooms and a creche to support the women attending. The original intention was to buy some "portakabins" for the vacant land but it soon became clear that such a large range of activities could not be carried out in temporary buildings. In 1983, Jagonari was put in touch with the feminist design co-operative, Matrix, which already received funding for feasibility work under the GLC grants scheme. Together the two groups developed a brief and approached the GLC's new Women's Unit for support. There was considerable discussion as to whether they should develop a modest proposal or "go for broke" with a relatively large-scale scheme. In the end they chose the more ambitious course and a costed scheme was developed for a new building to fill the vacant site.

Jagonari was a dynamic group and it carried out a lot of lobbying on behalf of its proposals. The group's aims chimed well with the GLC's policy of support for women and ethnic minorities and its ambition and energy eventually paid off. The GLC agreed to fund the scheme from its own resources, avoiding the complication of government sanction. Matrix were committed to co-operation with their user client and it set up a series of group discussions. Initially the Asian women were asked to bring along pictures of buildings they liked. Some attempt was made to get them to draw images of buildings, but this was not too successful. Among themselves, the Matrix members held a "design day" to discuss the suggestions emerging from the client groups and to develop their own ideas The main ideas developed from Jagonari women's images of buildings, and the scheme that emerged reflects the group's functional requirements and concerns. It also visually express Jagonari's cultural purpose with an amalgam of English vernacular and Asian design influences.

A key constraint was context of the site. The adjoining Davenant Centre was a listed building, and the local Planning Department and the Historic Buildings Council wanted a building that was sympathetic in scale and design with its Whitechapel Road neighbours. The Jagonari women wanted a courtyard – a common feature of Asian public and religious buildings – although they also wanted a secular feel that would embrace all

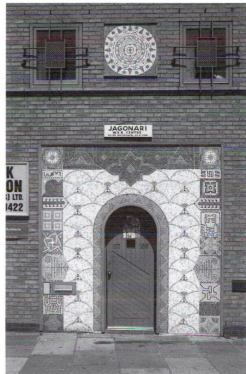

The scale of the Jagonari building ensures that it marries into the context of Whitechapel Road, yet the design makes a distinctive contribution to the street.

The main entrance reflects the need for security but, at the same time, decoratively advertises Jagonari's cultural origins.

religious and cultural groups. Security was an overriding issue, particularly in a part of London where racist assaults have been common, both historically and in the recent past. The solution that emerged is a four-storey building that completes the street facade and presents a secure public face. Behind is an enclosed courtyard that provides light and air to the main building and outdoor space for the nursery – a separate two-storey building at the rear of the site.

The requirement for security played a key part, not only in the overall concept but in the planning and appearance of the building. The main hall and seminar rooms are at first- and second-floor level, giving them privacy and security from the public domain. At ground level, only the small windows of the kitchen face the street and the entrance is kept to minimum size and is well secured. The window grilles also reflect the demand for security, although their distinctive design, with an unmistakeable Asian influence,

makes them both decorative and expressive of the cultural origins of the user group. The use of traditional "English" brickwork gives a solidity and strength to the building. Its distinctive pink colour, though, was a painstaking choice. During the detailed design process, 20 women walked a zig-zag path from Whitechapel to Hampstead Heath on a "brick picnic" to find the right shade. The bicultural approach is finished off by the rooftop "bell tower" (actually a vent for the lift). Such features are to be found on Asian buildings. They are also common on Victorian schools – an early architectural link between east and west.

The building was completed in 1987 and, in the following years, the activities of the centre were developed and refined. The large hall that runs the full depth of building on the first floor is used for a variety of conferences, seminars and workshops as well as for social and recreational activities. Most of the rest of the centre is devoted to child

125

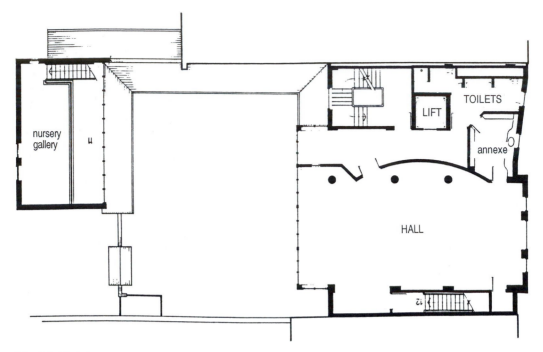

FIRST FLOOR PLAN

Most public uses are concentrated on the ground and first floors. The second floor provides a range of training and craft rooms whereas the top floor contains staff offices and a library.

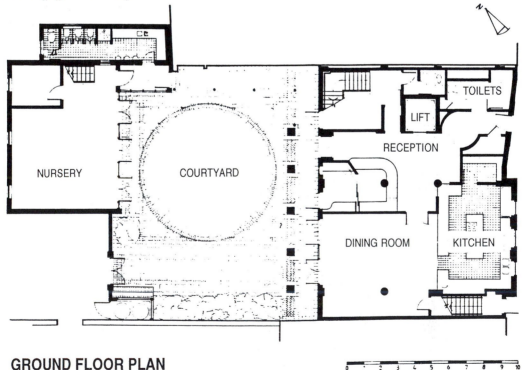

GROUND FLOOR PLAN

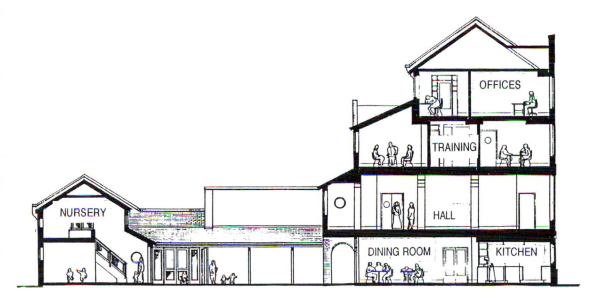

SECTION

care and personal development. The nursery has become a key element. Originally designed for 18 children, in 1993 it was extended to provide full day care for 35 under-fives. The suite of training rooms on the second floor were originally designed as a flexible and multi-purpose facility. There are now only two main day-time activities.

The courtyard – a key feature of Asian buildings – provides a secluded outdoor space for the nursery and allows light and air to the back of the main building.

Jagonari run a full time three-year training course in child care leading to City & Guilds qualification. The successful nursery in the same building provides hands-on training experience. The other main use is training in language skills, which provides a community resource to help women develop their employment prospects. In the evenings the training centre is occupied by supervised homework sessions – an activity that, no doubt, contributes to the high standards achieved by Asian school students.

The Jagonari centre was well designed and well built. Construction standards are high with solid masonry and durable materials such as hardwood windows. A high standard of craft work is expressed in the distinctive metal grilles and the decorative paving to the courtyard. As a new building it meets current safety standards. It is also fully accessible, with level access at ground level, lift access to upper floors and disabled toilets at each level. The scheme is an outstanding illustration of the influence of a committed user group participating in the design of a new building. This is not just evident in the way the functional requirements are resolved. The building is also a strong visual expression of the cultural origins of the user clients. At the same time it respects the context of the surrounding built environment and makes a harmonious contribution to the urban architecture of Whitechapel.

Most user groups would be more than happy to have such a building. Yet it is not typical. Indeed, it is probably almost unique. Very few voluntary groups have received sufficient funding to enable them to construct new buildings. Most of those that have could afford only single-storey buildings, often of cheap, lightweight construction and a more temporary nature. The others have had to make the most of existing buildings – sometimes well adapted but, too often, well short of their needs. Jagonari was the last community project funded by the GLC before it was abolished. The building is a monument to an enlightened policy. It is compelling evidence of the standards that could be achieved by the community architecture of the new vol-

untary sector if only it received the recognition and funding it deserves.

References

1. John Cunningham, "The house that Jill built", *The Guardian* (6 January 1988).

The main hall on the first floor – a venue for large meetings, conferences and social events.

CHAPTER 6

Behind the lines

COMMUNITY ARCHITECTURE
IN LOCAL GOVERNMENT

For many of those involved in community action, and in the self-help and voluntary initiatives that flowed from it, local government was the enemy. Councils were seen as insensitive and monolithic bureaucracies that, in defiance of the popular will, destroyed the physical and social fabric of urban communities, either through their own developments or by aiding and abetting property developers and speculators. By the late 1960s the local State had come to wield enormous power. For community activists it was a power that had to be challenged. One way was to work outside the system, creating socially sensitive alternatives through direct action. The innovations of co-operative organization, from community self-build to social action centre, created important and influential new models. But it was a movement of a relatively minuscule scale. Most of the projects were tiny, and even taken together they hardly amounted to a major force. In ten years the RIBA Community Projects Fund had generated capital projects worth £70 million.[1] No mean achievement, but during the same period a single London Borough might spend as much capital in a single year. The achievement of direct action was dwarfed by public sector spending power hundreds of times larger. Far from challenging State power, it was but a gadfly on a bullock.

The other way was to seek to influence and to infiltrate the corridors of power in the town halls. In fact, the effect of public pressure brought a fairly rapid policy response: a shift from giant redevelopments towards rehabilitation and small-scale rebuilding; but it was hardly more democratic than what had gone before. Developments were still carried out in a standardized manner, with little effort to involve those affected. By the late 1970s the influence of community action began to bite deeper into some local authorities. New approaches were taken that were to bring the influence of participatory democracy into the exercise of local government power. There was greater involvement of, and support for, community groups; some experiments were made in decentralization of power structures to relate to local communities; and, in dealing with the legacy of the past – the housing estates – there was greater participation of tenants in shaping their own environment.

The juggernaut changes course

The widespread community action of the early 1970s was the tip of an iceberg. Beneath it lay a profound public rejection of the post-war approach to urban regeneration, which had reached its peak in the large-scale clearances and high-rise redevelopments of the 1960s. But public opprobrium was not the only factor. It was becoming evident that multi-storey housing was not working. There were the many technical problems: the leaking roofs, the plague of condensation and vermin infestation, the poor construction standards (particularly in system built housing). Worse still, there were growing social problems: the frustration of mothers trapped on upper floors with children who could not play outside; the isolation of the elderly who never set eyes on another soul from one day to the next. Meanwhile, the common stairs and lifts, the open galleries that were supposed to be "streets in the sky", the remote underground car parks – all became prey to crime, vandalism and a variety of abuse.

A change of course became inevitable and local government was not slow to respond. From the early 1970s, local authorities largely abandoned high-rise housing. Birmingham, for example, commissioned its last tall block in 1971. Most other authorities soon followed suit. High-rise, high-density schemes continued to be built, but mostly these were hangovers from the excesses of the 1960s: massive schemes that took ten years and more to design and build. Comprehensive redevelopment of the worst areas of urban housing continued during the 1970s, but the schemes that were produced were, very largely, smaller-scale lower-density developments of houses, flats and maisonettes, usually in low-rise, walk-up blocks of four storeys or fewer. There was a new emphasis on traditional materials and construction: more brick, more timber and tile cladding. Not untypical of the new approach was the Popham Street estate in Islington, completed in 1974 (Fig. 6.1). Here, architects Andrews Sherlock achieved a density as high as many tower block estates, with buildings only three storeys high.[2]

Figure 6.1
Popham Street estate, Islington, as dense as many high-rise developments. It is typical of the more sensitive, but still regimented, approach to council housing in the 1970s.

Popham Street showed the waning influence of the Modern movement. Families were housed on the ground, each with their own private garden, albeit small. Brick is the predominant material. At the same time modernist concepts are retained: the flat roofs, the strip windows, even an underground car park. Above all, there is a repetitive monotony that suppresses individuality and retains the hallmark of "council housing". This was the response of local government to the barrage of criticism of high-rise housing. In one sense it was a radical new course, but at the same time not going far enough to provide any sense that the people who lived there had any control over their environment or any influence in shaping it. While Popham Street was being built in London, similar new public housing was taking shape in Manchester, Liverpool, Glasgow and other inner urban areas throughout the country.

At the same time there was a new emphasis on rehabilitation. As in the 1960s, councils continued to buy up slum houses on a large scale, but no longer on the comprehensive basis that characterized clearance areas. A more sensitive approach developed. Closure Orders and Compulsory Purchase Orders were applied more selectively on the worst houses individually and in small groups. Once acquired, though, the bureaucratic machine began to roll. The tenants were rehoused elsewhere and a standardized approach was developed to rehabilitate, convert and modernize the houses, normally using multiple contracts. The physical environment was preserved, but communities were still disrupted and dispersed. Behind the familiar street architecture, standard plans prevailed: strangers were thrown together in subdivided houses. The uniformity was such that council houses could still be identified by the standardized street doors, with identical ironmongery and all painted the same colour.

Some steps towards participation

While local government moved rapidly, during the 1970s, in the face of the rejection of high-rise housing and large-scale redevelopment, it generally retained a comprehensive and standardized approach to housing development and urban renewal. Meanwhile, here and there, a few experiments were taking place to involve the users of public housing in shaping their own environments. One example, based on the Byker model, was the GLC's approach to the Swinbrook redevelopment, and the experience of this led it to apply a similar method to one or two other schemes. Another example was the support given in 1975 by Lewisham Borough Council to Walter Segal's self-build experiment. Of considerable potential significance was an attempt to apply Habraken's ideas to public housing in Britain.

During the late 1960s, two students at the Architectural Association, Nabeel Hamdl and Nic Wilkinson, developed a application of Habraken's "supports" ideas, using the currently fashionable industrialized building techniques. Their idea for flexible housing went by the cumbersome title "Primary System Support Housing Assembly Kit" (PSSHAK). Unlike Habraken's original concept, PSSHAK did not use a large-scale support structure but concentrated on housing that could be adapted to individual needs within a small-scale standardized shell. In 1971 they were offered the opportunity to develop these ideas in the GLC Architects' Department. A small pilot scheme of 12 dwellings was completed in north London in the early 1970s and a larger scheme was developed for a site in Adelaide Road, Camden (Fig. 6.2).

For the Adelaide Road scheme, Hamdl designed eight three-storey blocks. Each block comprised a "primary support" shell consisting of floors, roof, external walls, windows and doors, and ducts to serve bathrooms and kitchens. The blocks could be subdivided in several ways to provide different mixes of dwellings. Within each home a variety of layouts was possible using prefabricated modular partitions. Prospective tenants were selected and they were given choice of location within the blocks. In this way an overall mix for each block was agreed. Once allocated housing space, each tenant was invited to design its layout, using a specially designed instruction manual. The layout could be designed to suit each tenant's choice of the relationship and size of rooms and also accommodate the furniture and fittings they already had. Once tenants moved in, they had the chance to have the layout rearranged after a trial period, and the system allowed for further changes in the future.[3]

PSSHAK attracted considerable interest at the time and seemed to offer an opportunity for users to have more say in the design of their own housing and greater satisfaction with their homes. In fact the system, as developed at Adelaide Road, offered strictly limited flexibility. Although tenants had some choice in location and in the planning of their homes, they had no control over the form of housing or over its external appearance. Habraken's idea was that individual preferences would be expressed externally in variations in window types and sizes, and in different cladding materials. Personal expression would individualize mass housing, giving it variety and interest. As Sutherland Lyall commented in 1977, "Habraken was against the monotonies of mass housing but, looking at the drawings of the little standard GLC brick boxes designed for Adelaide Road that seems to be precisely what the GLC intends to perpetuate there".[4] This seems a harsh judgement on a scheme of considerable charm

Figure 6.2
psshak housing at Adelaide Road, Camden.
The first serious attempt in Britain to apply
Habraken's ideas on design participation proved
only moderately successful

and variety. Nevertheless, it was perhaps the failure of PSSHAK to produce greater diversity – a physical expression of user participation – that made its results disappointing. Adelaide Road was the first, and the last, large-scale PSSHAK scheme, but it did establish the principle that new housing could be made flexible and adaptable to the needs of those who were to live in it.

Overall, the response of local government to its critics was to produce, during the 1970s, more user-friendly environments: smaller-scale new schemes, a great increase in conservation and rehabilitation. Despite one or two brave experiments in democratic participation, though, this was all imposed by the same remote machine that had produced the tower blocks. The response to criticism of the product was to create a new product, one that was a great deal better but which amounted to a new uniformity. What was at fault was not just the product; it was the very structure and organization of local government and the policy framework that lay behind it. By the late 1970s the new voluntary sector was growing in strength and community architecture was spreading the concept of user participation. All this generated new ideas about how the public sector should be organized and an influx of new people into the town halls as both members and officers. In places this produced comprehensive changes that were to make local authorities more responsive to the wishes of the communities they served.

A policy for the community

Once started, community action had spread rapidly. Some of it arose spontaneously – as a response to threats of redevelopment or to provide for needs unmet by existing provision. Some, in the worst areas, was stimulated by the government-funded Community Development Projects and the Inner Area Studies. Community groups had demonstrated the shortcomings of housing policies and the need for new initiatives in employment and in social and recreational facilities. At first this was seen not just as a challenge to the power of local government but, by generating locally controlled facilities, as a threat to local government services. By the end of the decade, the local State had developed a more sanguine attitude to community initiatives, for both good and bad reasons. On the negative side, community action had become a force to be reckoned with. Better to support it, to channel its energy in non-antagonistic directions, than to let it remain a perpetual thorn in the side of local administration. Besides, voluntary sector projects came cheap, and the services and facilities they provided could help to pacify a rebellious population and divert them from criminal activity.

On the positive side, many community groups had shown a wish to be in control of their own services and faculties, particularly those generated by ethnic minority groups. They had shown the ability to take initiatives and to develop innovative new services. If there was a demand for such services, they should be provided. Who better to run them than those who had set them up. With mixed motives, local authorities began to develop new policies to provide funding and organizational support to community groups. The positive perspective was boosted by a new approach on the part of the activists. A growing army of radicals had, by now, worked in and for the new voluntary sector, and had become committed to its aims and objectives. Originally they saw the local State as an enemy to be fought tooth and nail. They now recognized

133

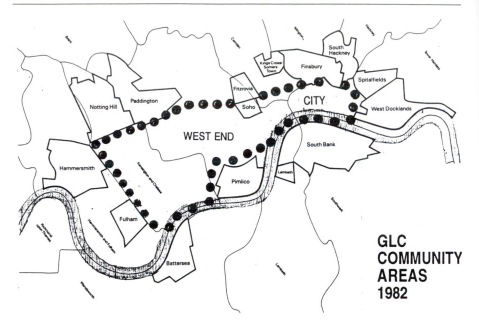

Figure 6.3
The GLC's community areas – designed to focus community development around London's central business district as a bulwark against commercial exploitation.

GLC COMMUNITY AREAS 1982

that the considerable power and wealth of local government could be harnessed to community purposes. Many began to engage in the political process in order to bring about this change.

Nowhere was such a process more comprehensive than in the action of the group of new councillors who took over the Greater London Council in 1981. The new GLC, like many other councils nationwide, developed a new policy of funding and support for community groups. But it also developed a positive framework: the Community Areas Policy.[5] The policy recognized that, while billions of pounds had been invested in new building projects in the City of London and the West End, there were many areas, just outside the centre, that were amongst the most deprived in Britain. A fraction of the fortune lavished on commercial buildings would work wonders in these areas. At the same time the only interest shown by developers in the deprived areas was as cheap sites for profitable commercial development. The new policy identified 16 community areas, all but one around the fringes of the central area. It was intended, reported Jules Lubbock ". . . to throw a *cordon sanitaire*, modelled on the greenbelt, around the whole of the central business area . . . within which no large offices or hotels, which are not of immediate benefit to the local community would be allowed . . . It is a defensive policy for stabilising and rebuilding working-class communities. and for providing jobs appropriate to their skills and housing at an appropriate price."[6]

The impact of the policy was to focus the priorities of the GLC's housing and industry and employment programmes. More directly, priority was given to grant aid to community organizations in the community areas. Between 1982 and 1985 £18 million was given in grants for community centres and facilities, and for environmental improvements. More than 65 community centres were funded. It was the application of the policy in the Spittalfields Community Area that funded the development of the Davenant Centre and the building of Jagonari. At the same time, planning applications for commercial development were restricted as far as possible, although an attempt to

134

change the statutory plan was not supported by central government. The struggle against the encroachment of commercial development is best illustrated by the way in which the long-standing controversy over Coin Street on the South Bank was resolved.

The Coin Street saga

The Coin Street sites were a strip of land, 13 acres in all, behind the arts complex of concert halls, galleries and the National Theatre on London's South Bank. A prominent site so close to Central London would long since have fallen prey to commercial development but for the fact that most of it was owned by public authorities. There were considerable pressures for development, and several schemes were prepared for multi-storey offices and hotels. Coin Street became an early battleground of community action, with the formation, in 1972, of the North Southwark Community Development Group: an umbrella of tenants associations and other community groups. NSCDG was pledged to see the Coin Street sites developed for community benefits and, by 1977, had persuaded the local planning authority that the sites should be developed for housing use. Despite the statutory designation for housing, the pressures for commercial development continued and resulted in public inquiries in 1979 and 1981.

The second inquiry was presented with a stark choice. On the one hand was a proposal by Greycoats Commercial Estates. Although distinguished with a design by Richard Rogers, the Greycoats scheme would have produced a massive string of office buildings, 10 to 16 storeys high, dwarfing the National Theatre and the other riverside buildings (Fig. 6.4). On the other hand was a counter-proposal for a much smaller-scale mixed development – of housing, light industry, shops, restaurants and public open space – prepared by the Association of Waterloo Groups (Fig. 6.5). At the centre of this conflict lay a serious debate about urban planning. It had long been argued that the status of the South Bank, at the heart of London, had been devalued by piecemeal development of small-scale or undistinguished buildings. The wide River Thames needed a well designed large development to create the appropriate urban scale and prestige. At the same time there was concern that the arts complex was, in effect, a cultural ghetto, deserted during the daytime and lacking variety and vitality. One way to enliven the area would be to bring people to live there and allow small enterprises to develop. These would feed off and provide for the theatrical, musical and television complex already there

Faced with a choice in which the arguments of both sides seemed to offer some merit, in traditional planning terms. the Secretary of State for the Environment took an unusual course. He decided not to decide, and granted permission to both schemes. This was where the matter stood when the GLC Community Areas Policy came into force. The long standing "Battle of Waterloo" had been a key generator of the policy, with its aim of restricting commercial development. One of its authors, George Nicholson, had worked for NSCDG and identified with the community cause. In 1982 he became Chair of the GLC Planning Committee, and the resolution of the Coin Street controversy became a key test of the new policy. A special team was formed in the GLC Architects Department to design a scheme for the sites, based on the AWG proposals. A non-profit company – Coin Street Community Builders – was set up, in association with the local community groups, to develop the sites. In 1984 the GLC sold the sites to the new company and organized funding for their development.[7]

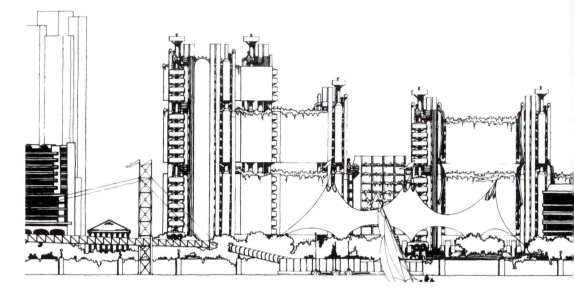

Figure 6.4
*Greycoats scheme –
designed by the Richard
Rogers Partnership – for
large-scale office development at Coin Street,
dwarfing the National
Theatre and the other riverside buildings.*

Figure 6.5
*The Association of Water-
loo Groups alternative
scheme for a mixed devel-
opment of housing, open
space and craft industry,
which preserved existing
buildings on the site.*

By late 1994, only one area of housing – the Mulberry Co-op – had been completed, together with a public open space and riverside walk. Work was progressing
on the development of more housing and industry, and on the conversion of the
eight-storey Stamford Wharf building into flats and managed workspace. The Mulberry housing scheme has aroused considerable controversy. Supporters argue that it
is in keeping with the traditional terraces in the area. Detractors consider it too modest
in scale and design, including the Royal Fine Arts Commission, which described the
scheme as "inappropriately suburban" (Fig. 6.6).[8]

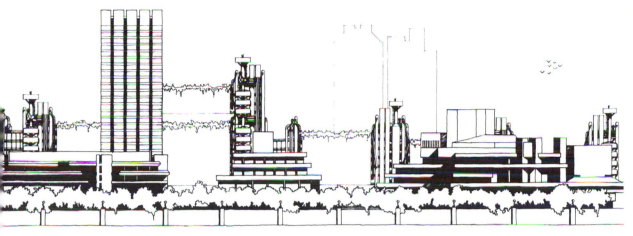

Because of its prominence, Coin Street in general, and the Mulberry Co-op in particular, has been seen as a test case for community architecture. It was certainly a key battle in the struggle to instil community values into the planning process. It can be argued strongly that the mix of uses proposed by the scheme will more successfully stimulate vitality and a sense of community than would a massive office block. But it is questionable whether the Mulberry Co-op is a representative expression of community architecture. For a start, there was no user participation. Instead the brief and an oversight on the design was developed by a "housing and social facilities group" that included some local residents but not the future tenants. Although the scheme is a co-op, the tenants were selected from local authority waiting lists only six months before completion and had no input into the designs. For later developments, Coin

Figure 6.6
Mulberry co-op, the first community development at Coin Street, attracted considerable criticism because of its low density and the limited participation of users in its design.

Street Community Builders have taken the decidedly non-participatory route of asking architects to prepare schemes in competition.[9] It is at least arguable that greater user participation in the designs would have produced more stimulating results.

The key question, though, is the scale. In market terms, the Coin Street sites were worth a very great deal. Even restricted to housing use, the market value would demand a much larger-scale development. It is understandable that community planning would not want to be enslaved by market values. Nonetheless, Coin Street is a very desirable area to live. It would surely have been appropriate to give more people the opportunity to do so than the 56 families who have ended up in the Mulberry Co-op by sheer chance. If Coin Street is not entirely successful, it is because it was a symbolic stand against commercial development. But to produce a scheme that patently under-uses the potential of the sites is not an adequate response to the excessive over-development demanded by commerce. Especially since, by opting for such low-scale development, the Coin Street scheme jeopardizes its key objective – the generation of a lively working and residential community.

The Community Areas Policy was very beneficial to many community groups throughout Inner London, but in its intervention in the large, and very public, stage of Coin Street, it faced a highly polarized situation. Years of adversarial conflict had created only two options – Greycoats office development or the Association of Waterloo Groups plan. The GLC bravely opted for the community plan and created an artificial organizational and financial structure to develop an area where there was no resident community. It has resulted in a development that, although certainly better than large blocks of offices, seems unlikely to realize the full potential of the sites. It might all have been different had there been a more representative local forum and the opportunity for a more open debate about the aims of planning a new community and the means of realizing them.

Decentralization

Although by the early 1980s many councils had started to give active support to community groups, a few local authorities had begun to experiment with new structures designed to direct their services better to local communities and to involve them in the decision-making process. A key to these experiments was the neighbourhood concept. Whereas many local action groups centred on a community of interest, the idea of neighbourhood rested on a geographical definition of the urban community. Neighbourhood theory first emerged in the 1960s when sociologist Michael Young, author of *Family and kinship in East London*, was engaged by the Redcliffe-Maud Commission on Local Government to prepare a community attitudes survey.[10] The survey found that most people in cities identified with a "home area" and could define it more or less accurately on a map. The research impressed one member of the Commission. In a lengthy dissenting report, Derek Senior called for the creation of "common councils" as a counterweight to large local authorities ". . . in every community which recognizes itself as such".[11] The Royal Commission, as a whole was unconvinced and its work resulted in larger local authorities, more remote from the communities they served.

Michael Young was determined to develop his research and he founded the Association for Neighbourhood Councils, which carried out a pilot study in north

London[12] and subsequently a national survey. At about the same time, similar proposals emerged from work in Sheffield.[13] Common to all these proposals was a view that, in large cities, people identified with a geographical area of 10,000 or fewer people, and that these areas formed the ideal unit for the lowest level of representative democracy. It was an idea that gelled with the emergence of community action. Experimental neighbourhood councils were set up in Golborne, Covent Garden and elsewhere. These grass roots initiatives were influential in generating a more community-orientated approach to urban development, but they failed ultimately because of their anomalous position. Set up in a situation where the communities were in conflict with local authorities, the experimental neighbourhood councils had no powers. They could only seek to influence. In doing so, they came to be seen as creatures of the authorities and they lost the support of the communities they purported to serve.

The early neighbourhoods councils became casualties of the conflict between community action and local government. But the idea of neighbourhood remained alive as a basis for the reform of local government. In 1977 the Lambeth Inner Area Study recommended: "Workers from different services should be brought together locally in a multi-service team . . . in a community service centre";[14] and the government White Paper on the inner cities suggested: "There is scope for the development of new methods such as area management or neighbourhood planning – in which both members and officers establish closer links with the people they serve . . .".[15] The idea was simple enough. People identified with geographical neighbourhoods, so it would make sense for local authorities to decentralize services to a local level, making them more easily accessible and more responsive to the needs and views of the separate communities that made up the large urban authorities.

Over the next few years some local authorities did experiment with decentralization. In a pioneering reorganization, Walsall in the West Midlands decentralized its housing services to a network of Neighbourhood Offices,[16] Birmingham introduced area improvement teams and, later, also developed the neighbourhood concept. Other major cities – Manchester, Bradford, Glasgow, Edinburgh – decentralized key services.[17] In London, Haringey and Camden decentralized some services; Islington set up a network of 24 Neighbourhood Offices to provide housing, social and environmental services; and Tower Hamlets divided almost all its services into seven quasi-autonomous neighbourhoods. But although the idea was simple, relatively few authorities adopted decentralization in a comprehensive manner. For those that did, there were considerable difficulties. The problem was that decentralization posed an enormous challenge to the traditional structure and organization of local government.

The pyramid of power

The structure of local authorities is rooted in their history. The early local councils were quite small organizations. They would appoint specialists to advise them and organize services – the Borough Architect, the City Engineer – each with a few staff to assist them. The chief officers would be responsible for carrying out their specialist services and for reporting regularly to council committees where they could be held to account for all decisions. While authorities remained small, the system worked quite well. As local authorities accumulated larger and larger programmes of slum clearance, school building and other social facilities, so the departments grew larger and more numerous. Some authorities grew large during the 1950s or earlier. But the exponential growth took place during the 1960s. For instance, when the London Borough of Islington was created in 1965, one man acted as Borough Architect, Planning Officer and Building Works Manager. He was supported by 18 technical staff and half a dozen administrators. Within a few years there were three separate departments and, by the end of the 1970s, the Architects Department alone had 175 technical staff and 55 administrative and support staff.

It was a process that pointedly illustrates Parkinson's Law of the Rising Pyramid, in which every official required two or more assistants, so that neither could pose a threat. As the tiers of managers multiply, so they create more and more work for each other and spend less and less time solving the real problems.[18] The pyramid perfectly represented the structure of most local government departments. But as the pyramids grew larger, they made nonsense of the concept of accountability. In a department of 20, one person could reasonably be expected to account for all key decisions. In a department of 200 it became impossible for the chief officer even to know about, much less be involved in, all the decisions taken. How much more so in the super-departments, such as the GLC Architects, which, in its heyday, numbered its staff in thousands. Yet the hierarchical pyramid and the notion of accountability of the top dog is endemic in the British system of government, and ministers still claim their "accountability" to Parliament as evidence of democratic health.

The growth of large hierarchies, centrally directed, was accompanied by increasing specialization: social services with specialists in the elderly, child care, the handi-capped; housing departments divided into estate managers, lettings officers, benefits advisers, development managers; and so on. As Dave Church, Walsall's Chair of Housing, commented: "A lot of [staff] were doing jobs that were driving them round the twist – can you imagine, someone doing nothing for 20 years but letting garages".[19] Such "division of labour" was supposed to create efficiency and to take advantage of the "economies of scale" offered by ever-larger units of local govern-ment. In practice it created severe disadvantages for the users of these services. Any enquiry had to be directed to the correct specialist. It might be repeatedly referred as it passed from one official to the next. At the end the line the correct officer might be "in a meeting", "on leave" or unavailable for some other reason. Buck-passing, slow-ness to respond and inaccessibility became the hallmarks of the burgeoning bureauc-racies, together with an inability to deal with issues that did not fit neatly into one of the specialized areas.

In dealing with the built environment, authorities would analyze the problems of their areas as a whole and then develop programmes to deal with them. Each depart-ment would prepare its own programme, and large departments such as housing would break their work down into separate programmes of development, repair and improvement. To meet these demands, technical departments were organized into specialized teams, each dealing with a separate programme area. The system produced widespread anomalies through being centrally derived and implemented through dif-ferent specialisms. Poor definition of sites might leave one side of a street standing while identical housing on the other side was demolished. A potential development site, or an estate in need of repair, might be overlooked. Within a small area, several developments might be taking place simultaneously, each carried out by a separate team and totally unco-ordinated. In some cases several technical teams might be work-ing on the same estate simultaneously, each dealing with a separate aspects of repair or improvement. In such situations there was inevitable duplication of effort and costs.

140

Above all, specialization led to refining the approach to a particular problem within narrower and narrower limits. Design approaches were standardized, leading to a repetition of errors and a failure to consider alternative options.

In 1977 Sam Webb, an architect with experience in several local authorities, analyzed the influence of pyramidal hierarchies in creating the excesses of system building and standardization in the 1960s. He also observed that it created a power elite: ". . . some gave up their drawing board for power . . . Frequently their only role is that of chart maker, or schoolteacher checking on spelling in outgoing letters, or on behaviour at work . . . the introduction of systems, procedures carried often to the "n'th" degree became their prime aim". These "omnipotent adminmen" remained architects but were no longer designers. Design, the real work of architects, took place in the project groups. No design work, Webb notes, took place above group leader.[20] The role of the hierarchy, which often comprised three or four tiers of management, was to develop the programmes and the standardized solutions with minimal accountability to elected members and the complete absence of contact with the community who were the users of their service.

Area Teams

Webb's withering analysis no doubt helped to create a climate for reform. So, too, did proposals for decentralization emerging from the Community Development Projects. These were influential in the discussions taking place in the New Architecture Movement on the development of the community architecture approach in the public sector. In their proposals, published in 1978,[21] they called for the end of specialized teams and the abolition of all posts above group leader. All design services would be provided by a practice group dedicated to a small geographical area. The Area Team would carry out all the project work in the area. To do this it would be "generic" rather than specialist and would include as many design disciplines as possible. The generic team would get to know the land and buildings in its area and could produce more appropriate and better co-ordinated development. It could also get to know the people and come to understand the concerns and views of the various social groups within the local community. It would be better placed to identify the needs and opportunities for new development. Being multi-disciplinary would ensure cross-fertilization of ideas between different disciplines and building types, and feedback of experience from maintenance problems into better new designs.

Decentralization, in general, and Area Teams in particular, provided a real possibility that local authorities could reform themselves to relate directly to the many communities that made up the inner cities. Services would be provided close to peoples' homes, and policies and practice could be developed that were sensitive to local opinion and in tune with local needs. But it was highly controversial because it threatened the specialist structures that had developed almost everywhere. More seriously it threatened the powers and the very livelihood of the legions of highly paid chief officers and senior managers. Almost everywhere it has been tried there has been a bitter struggle with vested interests. It was helpful if the hierarchy itself could be convinced.

Such was the case in Birmingham, one of the first authorities to experiment with area teams. Following Rod Hackney's pioneering project at George Arthur Road in 1974, redevelopment rapidly gave way to rehabilitation of Birmingham's large areas of tunnel-back Victorian housing. By 1977, 105 GIAs and 35 HAAs had been declared[22] and, over the following 10 years, 40,000 houses were improved through "enveloping" schemes. At an early stage the authorities decided on a participatory approach and began to set up locally based project teams. The first of these was in Small Heath and it covered a zone of 8–10 GIAs. In all, eight area teams were set up, covering the worst concentrations of unfit housing. In each area a series of public meetings were held to prepare a "residents' plan". This focused on the housing renovation but also included landscape and environmental work, small infill developments and improvements to shops and schools. Each team comprised three or four architects, together with housing and engineering staff. The multi-disciplinary teams were led by the Environmental Health Department, but the City Architect, Bill Read, was sympathetic to the new approach. He abandoned the specialized structure and reorganized his staff into generic practice groups, some of which were linked with the area teams.

Birmingham provided a partial approach to decentralized area working, concentrating on the worst areas of deprivation. The most comprehensive reorganization took place in Haringey in north London. Haringey developed an early commitment to user participation. In 1976, the council initiated five co-operative housing projects, including a substantial new build scheme, in which the future tenants were invited to take part in the design process.[23] The staff in Haringey Architects Department were familiar with the participatory approach and this commitment was helped by the presence of John Murray, a prominent member of NAM and co-author of their proposals for area teams. In 1978/9 the chief executive prepared proposals for reorganizing the department, which reinforced the traditional hierarchical and specialist structure. Local authority procedures require trade unions to be consulted about structural changes. Through their union, the staff pressed for a non-hierarchical generic structure of area teams and, by extensive lobbying, gained the support of councillors. This alliance produced a partial victory. In 1979, the architectural staff were organized into eight area teams, although other staff retained their specialist structure.

Far from settling the argument, the compromise solution only added fuel to the fire. The next few years were punctuated with intense debate as all the forces generated by community action confronted traditional local government attitudes. In the midst of the controversy the Borough Architect resigned. Some say he was a victim of the conflict, some that it was coincidence. Whatever the reasons, it gave the staff an opportunity for a radical assault on the pyramid of power. They now demanded comprehensive decentralization, with co-operative management and team leaders subject to annual elections. Most of this was achieved. In 1985 the eight area teams became fully multi-disciplinary, comprising architects, surveyors, quantity surveyors and clerks of works. Each team of 25, in effect, became a locally based practice with a high degree of autonomy. Special teams were set up to deal separately with very large projects. Full internal democracy was not conceded, but the council did accept that the team leaders, once appointed, should form a collective management board, electing one of their number as service co-ordinator and, in effect, chief officer.

The success of the new system can be gauged by the work of the Wood Green Team. The team's main work was the Noel Park Estate, about 2,000 houses built at the turn of century (Fig. 6.7). The estate was built by the philanthropic Labourers and Artisans Dwelling Company and was one of the early working-class cottage estates designed to relieve the overcrowded slums. The council bought the estate in 1966 and it became a conservation area. The houses were very small, with no bathrooms and outside toilets. The Wood Green Team improved the estate in phases over several

Figure 6.7
Noel Park estate in Haringey, improved in phases by the Wood Green Area Team with the full participation of tenants.

years, completing 100–200 houses each year. Kitchens were refitted and bathrooms squeezed in while tenants were temporarily rehoused. Tenants were involved in developing the design and there was a show house for each phase. At the end of each phase the team did a tenants' feedback questionnaire and amended their designs as a result

Many of the Noel Park tenants were elderly and the architects suggested that there should be a sheltered scheme on the estate in one rehabilitated block. Housing officers were interested, but it didn't come off. They did, however, find a small site for a new build scheme. The Palace Gates scheme[24] (Fig. 6.8) provided 33 sheltered flats and three family houses. The team didn't know the future users, but there was a local organization for the elderly (Wood Green Pensioners). The architects went to them with the briefing and with the sketch schemes. Project architect David Hayhow had been architect for the first phase of Noel Park. His knowledge of the area and understanding of the local building type no doubt helped produce a scheme that is carefully designed and detailed and fits well in the context of the surrounding built environment. User participation, development of local knowledge, cross-fertilization of experience – ideas inherent in the work of the Wood Green team – aptly demonstrate the benefits of the new approach to public architecture.

The events in Haringey sent ripples through technical departments in the neighbouring Boroughs. Many staff, disillusioned by being typecast into specialist roles, were attracted to the new way of working. Many senior managers, witnessing the fate of their Haringey counterparts, had serious qualms. In Camden Planning Department an alliance of staff and councillors succeeded in introducing area working. A similar alliance developed in Islington Architects Department and, despite the implacable opposition of the Borough Architect, eventually bore fruit. Subsequently, the new approach was adopted in technical departments in some other authorities. Area team working brought a new structure to public service, giving a more accessible and accountable approach to public capital projects.

143

Figure 6.8
Palace Gates shelter housing, Haringey. The brief and the design approach grew out of the Area Team's work in the local community.

At the same time as decentralization began to develop, local authorities had started to adopt a more democratic approach when it came to dealing with their legacy from the past: the substantial stock of run-down estates.

Transforming the social estate

By the 1970s the stock of social housing was enormous. More than six million homes were owned and managed by local authorities (31 per cent of all housing)[25] and a good many more by housing associations. In outer urban areas and smaller towns, most of this was in estates of houses and gardens: the "council houses" that flowed from the Tudor Walters report. In the inner cities, and particularly in inner London, there were concentrations of multi-storey housing. This was not just the legacy from the housing boom of the 1960s, but substantial numbers of earlier blocks, many of them dating from the inter-war period. These were mostly scaled-down versions of the tenements pioneered by the philanthropic societies – estates of four- and five-storey blocks set in grounds of bleak tarmac. Space standards were low, in contemporary terms, and many estates had become overcrowded. Most had been neglected and fallen into disrepair. These were, by now, the worst of council housing. Hard to let, some of these blocks had degenerated into "sink estates" with high concentrations of the poorest tenants and the worst social problems.

Modernizing the old estates

Some councils sought to dispose of the problem by simply demolishing their tenement blocks. But this failed to recognize that many estates had an established community structure. Others repaired and made the best they could of housing of poor standards and quality. In the London Borough of Islington, a co-ordinated effort was made to tackle the problem of its old estates by comprehensive modernization. In 1977 the council set in train a survey all its older estates. Six of the worst estates were earmarked

144

for demolition. The remaining 31 – almost 4,000 flats in all – were put into a rolling programme of modernization. Block by block, tenants were to be rehoused. Flats would be gutted, replanned to modern standards, and refurbished with new fittings, decorations and services. Five storey blocks would be served with lifts. Controlled access systems would be introduced and estate grounds softened with planting and new paving. At the time, government funding rules allowed large-scale spending only on housing more than 30 years old. Nevertheless, Islington also set in motion a more limited programme for improving more recent housing.

These two programmes – the ambitious Estate Action Programme for the older estates and the more limited Post 48 Programme for estates built during the 1950s – started their work in 1978. The identification of this work and its method of organization were a characteristic, if enlightened, operation of the pyramid of power. The programmes were developed by the management hierarchy and, in keeping with tradition, specialist technical teams were set up to carry out the work. But there was a key difference. Because most of the housing would remain occupied during the work, the council recognized that it would be wise, as well as just, to involve those living there in the improvement process. "Tenant consultation" became a key part of the programmes. A housing manager would be based on each estate to develop a dialogue with tenants. The architects and surveyors, used to working in remote offices reporting up the pyramid, would now be brought face to face with the users of their services.

At first, consultation was to play a limited part and there were good reasons for this. Community projects and campaigns had arisen from people organizing themselves and pressing their demands on the authorities. Here, the tenants were being *invited* to participate in shaping their own environment. Many were sceptical – they did not believe the slum estates could be improved or that the council would find money to do it. At the same time many of the architects involved, whether public or private, had little understanding of participation and were finding their way in a new field of design work that was then uncharted. The early schemes stuck firmly to the programme and achieved significant improvement in standards without realizing the full potential for modernization. By the early 1980s both users and designers had gained more confidence in the process, and schemes were emerging that more radically affected both the appearance and the organization of the estates. Family accommodation was being concentrated in ground-level maisonettes. Circulation and access was being reorganized to provide a direct relationship to the public street and to secure the estate grounds. Replacement doors and windows, brick cleaning and redecoration were rejuvenating the appearance of the run-down blocks (Fig. 6.9).

Meanwhile, in the neighbouring borough of Hackney, a march was being stolen. The Borough of Hackney also had a large number of old estates but had no policy to deal with them. It was facing pressure from tenants for improvements. In 1980 it appointed Hunt Thompson – then a conventional practice with no experience of estate work – to carry out a pilot scheme on a run-down estate of 300 flats. Drawing on early experience of estate improvement elsewhere, the architects, working with the tenants, produced a comprehensive scheme for the improvement of Lea View. When the first phase was completed, in 1983, the appearance of the drab 1930s block had undergone the most radical transformation (Fig. 6.10). Widespread publicity was generated for the scheme and large claims made for its achievements.[26] Without doubt, Lea View was a great success, but it was achieved at a high cost and could not be sus-

Figure 6.9
Tufnell Park Estate in Islington. Consultation began in 1980 and the estate was modernized in phases over several years.

tained. For example, the lift towers – a key improvement that had a dramatic visual impact – were not provided to all the blocks. Nor did the scheme generate a knock-on effect in other Hackney estates, which have received minimal improvements, if any.

Islington's estate work continued to develop, without fanfares. A change in the funding regime allowed budgets to increase steadily for the inter-war estates. It also allowed larger-scale improvements on the estates built in the 1950s. Eventually, almost all the Borough's older estates were to benefit from major improvements. Islington's estate work in general, and the Lea View scheme in particular, demonstrated that smaller estates could be transformed into high-quality urban housing. In part this was a technical exercise: replanning and reorganizing the blocks; specifying repairs; improving heating, insulation and ventilation to increase comfort and reduce condensation problems. But tenant participation was a key to the improvements. Partly, this was to build on and strengthen established communities on the estates and to use tenants' intimate knowledge to identify key problems. The main achievement of the most successful participation, though, was to create, through discussion, an environment that tenants could control to a far greater degree. On a basic level, this meant individual choice over detailed planning and finishing of their homes; collective choices of new windows and doors and finishes to common areas. On a broader level, it meant breaking down the estates into controllable units: individual family homes with their own private gardens; estate grounds where the public were excluded and intruders easily spotted; small groups of upper floor flats, preferably with no children, with elec-

146

Figure 6.10
*Hunt Thompson's much
publicized improvement
scheme at Lea View
estate in Hackney.*

tronic security at the common entrance. Participation not only gave tenants greater satisfaction with their own homes but, by giving them more control over common areas, significantly reduced vandalism, abuse and crime.

Tackling the 1960s legacy

If the older, smaller council blocks could be successfully modernized, what of the large estates put up during the housing boom? Could the same principles be applied? This was a problem of a different order. The flats themselves provided good housing, built to the generous space standards introduced by the Parker Morris report of 1963. But many of the estates have technical problems – poor construction, poor insulation, or both – particularly those built using industrialized systems. The overriding problem, though, is the sheer scale. Tall blocks, 20 storeys and over, might contain 80 or 100 flats or more, all reached through a single main entrance and a common lift and stairs. In the lower-scale high-density estates, deck access – "streets in the sky" – means hundreds of flats might be linked together in a common access system completely open to abuse. As with the tenements before them, people had lost confidence in these estates. Those who could had moved elsewhere, leaving behind the poorest, the most vulnerable, and a fair sprinkling of antisocial "problem" families.

The technical problems were difficult enough and usually costly to put right. Sometimes, solutions could be found: structural strengthening or repair, overcladding blocks with a new "skin" to keep the rain out and the heat in, and so on. If the technical problems could not be solved, the buildings would have to be demolished. Even if they could, the most intractable problem lay in the open common areas and access systems. At the periphery, something could be done. Estate grounds could be closed to public access, underground car parks could be closed or converted to other uses such as workshops or warehousing. But early attempts to secure the access systems almost always failed. Electronic intercoms, which worked well enough in securing entrances to 20 flats or fewer, did not work when used by hundreds of people. Most were vandalized and they broke down within days or hours of commissioning.

In 1988 the government recognized the intractable problem of the 1960s legacy of large estates and introduced its own programme to channel large-scale funding for their improvement. The new initiative bore the same name as the early Islington programme – Estate Action – and was based on the same principles. Tenant participation, local management and accountable design teams were key to the process. Breaking down the large estates into smaller units or providing systems for the control of public areas were the keys to the solution.

Under new funding, fresh approaches emerged to security. Some were based on the concept of "defensible space", developed by Oscar Newman from work on housing estates in New York.[27] A similarly quasi-scientific approach was later developed in Britain by Alice Coleman.[28] The essence of this solution lay in closing through-routes, demolishing high-level walkways and reducing the common parts to small areas that could be secured, controlled and surveilled by residents, reducing the opportunities for vandalism and abuse.

Another new approach borrowed from the traditional French "concierge" (the formidable lady who supervises the entrance to every Parisian apartment block). From the late 1980s, "concierge" systems were developed for large council estates. In a tower block this might mean a receptionist monitoring the comings and goings in the entrance hall. In a more dispersed estate the "concierge" might monitor the entrances, lifts and halls through hidden cameras on a bank of television screens. In theory, vandals would be deterred and wrongdoers caught in the act. In practice these systems are heavily dependent on technology and a high price is paid in loss of privacy: in concept, perhaps, not so much "concierge 1994" as "Big Brother 1984".

At its worst, the government Estate Action Programme has minimized tenant participation and placed a heavy reliance on new technology aimed less at social well-being and more at social control. At its best, it enabled tenant organizations to take initiatives to improve and control their environment, to play a larger part in the management of their estates, and to develop community projects as a counterweight to the temptations of crime. It is still too soon to say whether it will work, whether the giant estates of the 1960s can be made into good housing, whether they should be given over to more appropriate uses, such as student hostels or sheltered housing, or whether it might be better, as some authorities have concluded, to tear them down and start again.

A new model for local government

By the mid-1980s the challenge to local government power mounted by community action had born considerable fruit. Gains were not made without struggle and conflict, but, at root, local authorities are democratic institutions. They can be influenced by the tide of social movements. In many authorities the tide flowed in through two democratic routes. New members, convinced of the benefits of community democracy, began to press for policy changes. New staff, schooled in community action and the new voluntary sector, used the influential weight of trade unions to challenge the power of the management hierarchy. These forces created a new model of local government: supportive of the work of community groups; committed to the participation of tenants in controlling their own environment; above all decentralized into small offices at community level, staffed by people with multiple skills responsive to local needs, and accountable to the communities they served.

The forces that regenerated local democracy brought a new wave of social architecture – more democratic, more responsive to the needs of its users. What the best of local authority practice has demonstrated is that community service requires detailed knowledge of an area and its buildings, and a dialogue and a development of trust with local groups and tenant organizations. This can best be achieved through the continuity and developing expertise of locally based teams. In recent years, public practice has faced a hostile climate. Capital cuts and competitive tendering have demolished local authority technical teams, sweeping away the best with the worst. But the record of decentralization and commitment to community participation remains a model for the reform and democratization of local government.

References

1. Letter from Ian Finlay, Chair of RIBA CAG, to the author.
2. Featured in *The Architects' Journal* (27 March 1974), 661.
3. Douglas Frank, "Habraken in Hackney", *The Architects' Journal* (15 September 1971), 573; and "PSSHAK makes it at last", *The Architects' Journal* (12 October 1977), 692. See also Richard Hatch (ed.), *The scope of social architecture* (New York: Van Nostrand Reinhold 1984), 48 ff.
4. Sutherland Lyall, "PSSHAKed up at County Hall", *Building Design* (17 June 1977), 18.
5. *Community areas policy – a record of achievement* (London: Greater London Council 1985).
6. Jules Lubbock, "Citizen takeover", *The Architects' Journal* (2 April 1986), 24.
7. *Coin Street Briefing Paper* for Lambeth and Southwark Councillors 1986, and *Coin Street Design Team Report* 1989; both unpublished.
8. Reported by Jules Lubbock op. cit.
9. Robert Cowan, "Community choice", *The Architects' Journal* (4 September 1991), 24.
10. *Report of the Royal Commission on Local Government in England and Wales*, Chairman Lord Redcliffe-Maud (London: HMSO, 1969).
11. Ibid., volume II: *Memorandum of dissent* by Mr D. Senior.
12. *The Hornsey Plan* (London: Association for Neighbourhood Councils 1971).
13. William Hampton & Jeffrey Chapman, "Towards neighbourhood councils", *The Political Quarterly* (July–September 1971 and October–December 1971), 247–54, 414–22.
14. *Inner London: policies for dispersal and balance* (London: HMSO, 1977).
15. *Policy for the inner cities* (London: HMSO 1977), Cmnd 6845, para. 37.
16. For a vivid account of decentralization in Walsall, see Jeremy Seabrook, *The idea of neighbourhood – what local politics should be about* (London: Pluto Press, 1984).
17. Paul Hogget & Robin Hambleton (eds), *Decentralisation and democracy – localising public services* (Occasional paper 28, School for Advanced Urban Studies, University of Bristol, 1987).
18. C. Northcote Parkinson, *Parkinson's Law or the pursuit of progress* (London: John Murray, 1958).
19. Jeremy Seabrook op. cit. p123
20. Sam Webb, "Architecture, alienation and the omnipotent adminman", *The Architects' Journal* (19 October 1977), 751.

21. *Community architecture: a public design service* (London: New Architecture Movement, 1978)

22. Nick Wates, "Public alternatives", *The Architects' Journal* (19 October 1977), 759.

23. Tom Woolley, "Designing with tenants", *The Architects' Journal* (19 October 1977), 759.

24. Bill Ungless, "Shelter at the Palace Gates", *The Architects' Journal* (27 May 1987), 23.

25. *Facts in focus* (London: Penguin, 1975), tables 43 and 44.

26. John Thompson, *Community architecture: the story of Lea View House* (London: Hunt Thompson Associates, 1984). Made into a film with the same title 1985; Jon Rowlands, "Estate improvement by community participation", *The Architects' Journal* (29 July 1983), 52.

27. Oscar Newman, *Defensible space* (New York: Macmillan, 1972; London: Architectural Press, 1973)

28. Alice Coleman, *Utopia on trial – vision and reality in planned housing* (London: Hilary Shipman, 1985).

CASE STUDY
Wakelin House: modernization of a pre-war housing estate

During the Victorian housing boom of the 1850s and 1860s, Islington, like North Kensington and other parts of inner London, was developed with speculative estates of large terraced houses designed for middle-class families with servants. As the better off deserted the cities for the new suburbs, these houses, unwanted by their intended occupants, degenerated into multiple occupancy and became overcrowded slums. With the development of the peripheral cottage estates for the working classes during the 1920s and 1930s, it became possible for the local authorities to begin clearing the worst slum housing. These were generally small areas (two or three blocks of houses), but large enough for about a hundred new flats.

Between the wars, Islington was a small authority and had few technical staff. For its new housing it turned to a local architect, E. C. P. Monson. Although Monson was in private practice, almost all his work was in Islington and, between the late 1920s and the early 1950s, he designed more than 50 small estates in Islington. He also designed the Town Hall and virtually monopolized council development during the period. He was, in effect, the borough architect. Wakelin House, built in 1933, was one of the earliest Monson estates. Its layout drew on the established tradition of philanthropic housing for the working classes. Indeed, in form, it bears a remarkable resemblance to Henry Roberts' pioneering Bloomsbury scheme of 1849 – five storeys of family flats reached by open stairs and access balconies. In appearance it was an eclectic mixture of Georgian features and vernacular influences that stemmed from the Arts and Crafts movement.

The new flats of the 1930s were, in their day, a great step forwards. In the surrounding slums the urban poor lived in cramped, damp and insanitary accommodation infested with vermin. Whole families would share a single room, and several families shared a kitchen on the landing and a toilet in the yard. Estates such as Wakelin offered their new tenants clean and dry accommodation. They provided self-contained flats, admittedly small, but each with its own kitchen and bathroom that offered each family the dignity of privacy. Over the years the slums around disappeared. Many were demolished and replaced with new housing. Those that remained were rehabilitated and converted to high-quality flats. Successive improvements in housing standards left Wakelin far behind. By the late 1970s the estate had become overcrowded and fallen into disrepair.

The flats were well below the space standards established by the Parker Morris report and were poorly planned. Tiny kitchens, with equally tiny bathrooms leading off them were not only cramped, they were a health hazard. Some of the bedrooms led directly from living rooms and did not meet modern standards of fire safety. Outside, the communal courtyards were a sea of tarmac, where children played among the washing lines, parked cars and the rubbish piled around the bin stores. On the street frontage a strip of inaccessible grass with a few trees was the only relief to the grim environment. In its turn Wakelin had become an urban slum, and, in 1978, it was one of the run-down estates scheduled for comprehensive improvement under Islington Council's Estate Action Programme.

Design work on the modernization of Wakelin House began in 1981 and a series of public meetings were held. A group of tenants assembled in a local community centre, many obviously poor, quite a few elderly. At first they treated the council architects with diffidence, unsure what to expect or what was being asked of them. Many, convinced that Wakelin was beyond redemption, would have preferred to be rehoused. Starting with a feasibility study carried out some years earlier, the basics of the improvement programme were explained. Gradually, as the tenants realized what was possible, they began to talk about the problems on the estate. Two major concerns emerged from the meetings; first was the damage and nuisance caused by large numbers of children; second was a general unease about security. Everyone was concerned that the estate was completely open to public access, with the risk of assault and burglary and the nuisance of outsiders parking cars, dumping rubbish and generally treating the estate as an exten-

"Before" and "After". Once a bleak sea of tarmac, the courtyards have now been secured, landscaped, and provided with play areas.

sion of the public street.

These two concerns were interrelated. Large groups of children can be very destructive and government-sponsored research had established that high child density was associated with high levels of vandalism.[1] The solution was to convert the lower floors to maisonettes by combining flats vertically. Families with children could live at ground level with direct access to outdoor space. With the family accommodation concentrated on the ground the upper floors could be converted largely to one-bedroom flats housing the elderly, single people and childless couples. New lifts were built into the fabric to serve the upper floors, and access balconies were extended to make all the flats suitable for elderly or disabled ten-

ants. With this clear division, families would be better housed and children would be kept out of the upper floors.

The general concern about security triggered a more radical response. It was decided to turn the estate inside out. Originally, all access was through the courtyards — to the doors of the ground-floor flats and up the stairs to the access balconies. If the access system could be turned around so that all the entrances were off the street, only the tenants would have access to the courtyards. And that is what was done. New entrances were cut for the maisonettes, with each entered through its own private garden. For the upper floors, new common entrances were created. Each is entered directly from the street via an "entryphone"

153

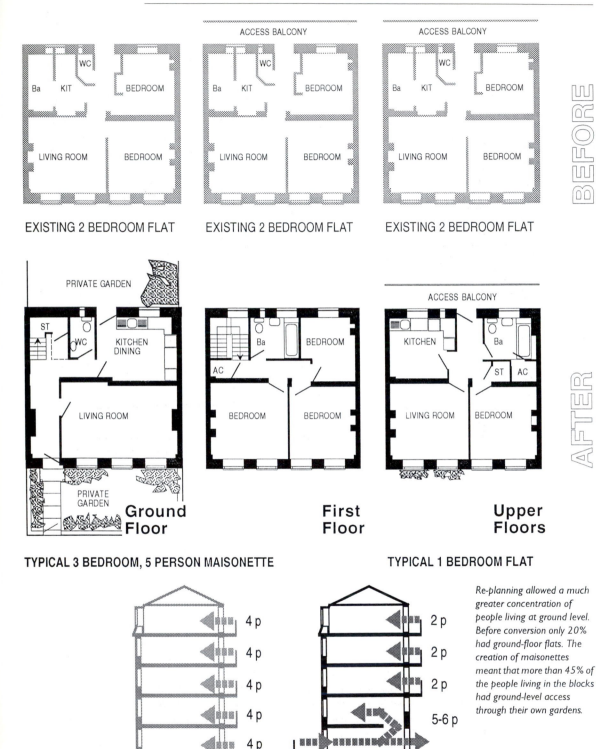

BEFORE

ACCESS BALCONY

WC
Ba KIT BEDROOM
LIVING ROOM BEDROOM

EXISTING 2 BEDROOM FLAT

ACCESS BALCONY

WC
Ba KIT BEDROOM
LIVING ROOM BEDROOM

EXISTING 2 BEDROOM FLAT

ACCESS BALCONY

WC
Ba KIT BEDROOM
LIVING ROOM BEDROOM

EXISTING 2 BEDROOM FLAT

AFTER

PRIVATE GARDEN

ST
WC KITCHEN DINING
LIVING ROOM
PRIVATE GARDEN

Ground Floor

Ba BEDROOM
AC
BEDROOM BEDROOM

First Floor

ACCESS BALCONY

KITCHEN Ba
ST AC
LIVING ROOM BEDROOM

Upper Floors

TYPICAL 3 BEDROOM, 5 PERSON MAISONETTE

TYPICAL 1 BEDROOM FLAT

4 p
4 p
4 p
4 p
4 p

BEFORE

2 p
2 p
2 p
5-6 p

AFTER

Re-planning allowed a much greater concentration of people living at ground level. Before conversion only 20% had ground-floor flats. The creation of maisonettes meant that more than 45% of the people living in the blocks had ground-level access through their own gardens.

154

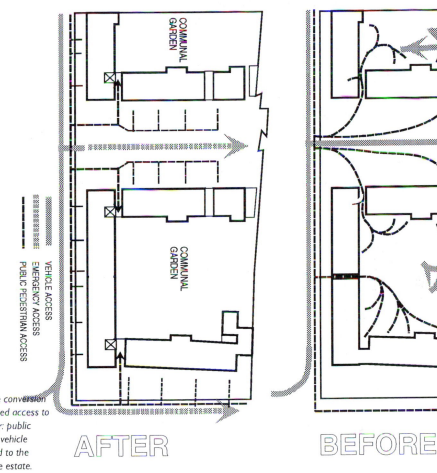

COMMUNAL GARDEN

COMMUNAL GARDEN

VEHICLE ACCESS
EMERGENCY ACCESS
PUBLIC PEDESTRIAN ACCESS

AFTER

BEFORE

Site plan before conversion showing unlimited access to the estate. After: public pedestrian and vehicle access is limited to the perimeter of the estate.

controlled door. Turning round the access gave the estate a more traditional relationship with the public street. It also meant that the old courtyards could be made private to each block. The tarmac was dug up and replaced with planting, sitting space and play areas. In these new communal gardens, children can be left unsupervised while their parents have peace of mind, knowing they cannot stray, be run over, or be approached by strangers with malicious intent. For the tenants on the upper floors, the communal gardens greatly improve the appearance of the estate and allow residents to sit out in sunny weather.

Some of those who had wanted to move got their way. To carry out the large-scale

work, one third of the estate had to be emptied. During construction of the first phase, each flat was pre-allocated to a particular tenant. Each future occupier was given a choice of colours and finishes — wallpaper, paintwork, wall tiling, and kitchen fittings. Front door colours were also subject to tenant choice, giving a degree of personalization to the outside of the estate. When the first modernized flats were completed in 1983, most tenants were surprised by what had been achieved and were delighted with their new homes. Many had lived on the estate for a long time; one or two had moved in when it was built. Over the years they had made friends in the area and some had extended families on Wakelin and neighbouring

Each maisonette is now entered direct from the street through its own front garden.

The new communal garden to the large block – secure for children to play and planted for the enjoyment of all the residents.

Wakelin was not the first estate to be improved. Earlier schemes had achieved significant improvements in housing standards and had followed the same pattern of phased renewal to preserve established communities. Completion of the first schemes established a benchmark, but it was evident that more could be achieved. Through extensive discussions of the tenants' concerns, over a series of consultation meetings, solutions emerged that made fundamental changes to the organization of the Wakelin estate. Two key changes – the concentration of family accommodation at ground level, and the creation of a secure environment in almost all the common areas – led to longer-term success. By reducing opportunities for crime and abuse, the high standards achieved by modernization have been maintained. Apart from some limited vandalism outside the common entrances, and damage to the communal gardens by boisterous children, the estate was still in remarkably good condition seven years after the improvements were completed.

estates. They were now able to move, with their neighbours, to new homes nearby and maintain their links in the community. Modernization rolled through the estate in three phases. When the final phase was completed in 1985, many of the flats were taken by tenants from an adjoining estate that was about to undergo similar treatment.

References

1. Sheena Wilson, "Vandalism and 'defensible space' on London housing estates", in *Tackling vandalism* [Home Office Research Study 47], R. V. G. Clarke (ed.) (London: HMSO, 1978).

CHAPTER 7

Involving people

THE TECHNIQUES OF PARTICIPATION

The common theme that emerged from the various approaches to community architecture was participation: the involvement of the people affected by development in taking decisions about their own environment. Participation was never an easy process. From the start it was bedevilled with controversy about whether user involvement genuinely affected decisions or whether participation was an elaborate facade to protect the powers of professionals and development agencies and siphon off protest. Some saw the only guarantee of democratic design in users taking control of the design and development process. But user control proved an illusion. Regardless of ownership and control, effective participation requires a sincere commitment on the part of designers and funders to enter a creative partnership with those who use their products. Even where there was a genuine will to involve users, there was considerable uncertainty about how to do it and how to make it effective. Over the years, through trial and error, a range of techniques has emerged that allow the consumers of the built environment an effective input in shaping its form.

Effective participation starts with a recognition that people with no experience of building design need to understand something of the process, and that design needs to be demystified through better communication, so that users have some appreciation of the choices that are available. Once the options are opened, decisions need to be made. In most participatory projects this is done by creating a dialogue so that users, working in partnership with professionals, can make choices collectively or individually. While decision-making through discussion has become the central process of participation, techniques have also been developed that use pre-prepared kits. Using tools or components, people are invited to play "design games" manipulating or putting together a kit of parts to produce the basis of a solution. A wide range of participation techniques have been used in many community architecture projects. Undoubtedly, these have produced results radically different from what would otherwise have happened. Yet controversy remains, about both the process and its products.

The ladder of participation

It is now well established that there are several levels at which people can be involved: a hierarchy. The earliest and most influential expression of this is the "ladder of citizen participation" by the American sociologist Sherry Arnstein (Fig. 7.1). Drawing on experience of urban social programmes during the 1960s, Arnstein sought to demon-

157

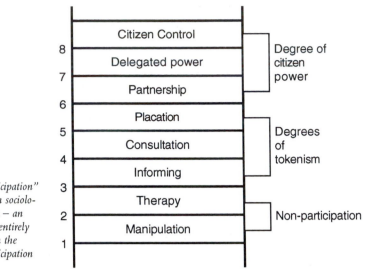

8	Citizen Control		Degree of
	Delegated power		citizen
7			power
6	Partnership		
	Placation		
5			Degrees
	Consultation		of
4			tokenism
3	Informing		
	Therapy		
2			Non-participation
1	Manipulation		

Figure 7.1
The "ladder of participation" devised by American sociologist Sherry Arnstein – an early, although not entirely helpful, influence on the development of participation in Britain.

strate that, for the most part, participation was simply a means of manipulating public opinion. ". . . participation without redistribution of power is an empty and frustrating process for the powerless. It allows the power-holders to claim that all sides were considered, but makes it possible for only some of the sides to benefit. It maintains the status quo".[1] Most of the rungs on the ladder are, therefore, a sham. Only near the top, where some power is transferred, does participation become meaningful.

The ladder of participation was formulated in the late 1960s and first appeared in Britain in 1971 when community action was in its infancy and community architecture had yet to be invented. What may have appropriately detailed the shortcomings of a social programme in a completely different system of local government was not necessarily applicable to participatory projects in Britain. Nonetheless, Arnstein's analysis helped to create a climate in which all forms of participation became questionable and efforts would better be directed at achieving the ultimate goal of citizen control. Colin Ward, for instance, advocating tenant control of housing estates in 1974 observed, "In many fields the word participation has already become suspect because it has been associated with token gestures for winning public approval for decisions which have already been taken and which there is no intention of altering".[2]

By the demanding yardstick of "citizen control" almost all participatory projects can be criticized and most have been condemned in one way or another. From one point of view, participants were "manipulated" by activists for their own personal or political ends. From another they were subjected to the "therapy" of professionals paternalistically imposing preconceived solutions to powerlessness and poverty. Or they were "placated" by solutions developed by architects more interested in promoting their own careers than the concerns of the community. Condemning many architects involved in participation as ". . . glory seeking self-publicists". Nigel Cross, of the Open University, laid into the early models of participation. Of the medical faculty at Louvain he demanded, "If I asked you whose work it was, you would identify the architect, Lucien Kroll. But wasn't it supposed to be designed by the students and staff?". Particular venom was directed at the Byker scheme. "Perhaps the most cynical example of the architect's own ideas masquerading as the outcome of a participatory process is the Byker Wall. This is clearly an 'Erskine' building, and not something designed collectively by the Byker residents. Yet an elaborate charade was gone through of setting up an architect's branch office 'in the community' ".[3]

No such claims were, in fact, made of the Byker wall and Cross's attack is wide of the mark. But the mud stuck. Along with better founded criticisms of the scope for manipulation, the idea grew that participation was inadequate because users did not control the design process. The pitfalls of participation – real and potential – led many to define community architecture purely in terms of "citizen control". The concept of the "user/client" developed in the practice of community technical aid. Some groups would only work with users who were in control of their own developments, and deliberately suppressed the expression of their own design ideas. The straight and narrow path to the top rungs of the ladder came to be seen in self-build housing associations and co-operatives and in community facilities managed by their users. It was a hard road with limited achievements. Alison Ravetz recorded in 1980:

> The top two rungs have never yet been seen in British town planning except, perhaps, with the partial and very localized instances of Black Road and a few other GIAs, or a handful of housing co-operatives where citizens groups have been able to use official machinery. grants and professionals to build what they wanted to build.[4]

Yet, for many, the user/client remained the ideal form, and citizen control the true goal. Naturally, this excluded any project carried out by or for a local authority, a large housing association or, indeed, any large organization. In such projects, the policies and objectives of the hierarchy would, inevitably, lead to compromises if not to disaster. In an estate improvement in Westminster, which the council dubbed the "Martlett Court Community Architecture Project" 85 per cent of a limited budget was spent on major repairs on which the council was not willing to negotiate. Only a tiny sum was allocated for improvements chosen by the residents. The tenants' association withdrew from the consultation process, complaining that their ideas and their views had been ignored. Journalist Robert Cowan, reporting on the controversy, concluded "Community architecture is what happens when a community is the client".[5] It is more than likely that the cause of the breakdown in communications lay in the parsimony of the budget which, even after improvement, left the flats without lifts, seriously undersize and with no central heating. Nevertheless, such failures reinforced the notion that user control was the ultimate objective. In reality, reaching the top of the ladder was neither a guarantee of satisfaction nor of genuine control of the design process, and the achievements of such projects have been strictly limited.

Limits to citizen control

The scope of user-controlled projects has been constrained primarily by the availability of resources: lack of land or space, lack of available skills in building, or the management of development; above all, by lack of money. Wealth is power and the one thing community groups never controlled was the funding for their projects. If funding could be obtained, it was rarely sufficient and often had strings attached. The many community groups seeking to develop their own facilities certainly reached the goal of "citizen control". Without doubt. they were "user/clients". But almost all of them had the greatest difficulty getting land or buildings for their projects. All but a very few had to manage with the most minimal funding for building or improvement. As a result, the facilities they created were usually barely adequate.

Lack of financial power was the generator behind community self-build. The inhabitants of the Black Road GIA did not embark on the do-it-yourself approach out of love of the process. It was a financial necessity. The same is true of the majority of self-build groups, most of whom would probably have preferred to have someone else do the dirty and physically demanding work of building their homes. Making a virtue of necessity, many have found the process rewarding, and have produced impressive results. But, even at its best, self-build is a limited process; groups must be kept small and the building skills of their members are relatively minimal. Small groups of low-scale simple buildings are the best that can be achieved.

Because of these limitations, the housing co-operative is often seen as the ideal form for community control of development. Funding has been available and the establishment of secondary co-ops has provided technical and organizational support. Free from the constraint of self-building, schemes of a substantial scale have been possible. But co-ops too had their limitations. Those that took over existing housing or flats usually had limited room for manoeuvre. Because the housing was already occupied, there was often little scope for the comprehensive replanning and conversion that would have been necessary to produce housing of a really high standard. New build co-ops avoided these problems but often had extreme difficulty acquiring suitable sites. When they did, the rules attached to funding frequently provided considerable constraints on standards and on the nature of the schemes produced.

Although many self-help and community groups achieved a degree of control over the development process, it was hedged around by some fairly severe constraints. In the search for the ultimate in participatory design, the key question was whether these "user/clients" had control over the process of design. Simply being the client was, in itself, not enough. In the traditional relationship between architect and client. the client provides the brief and the architect prepares the design. There is a very clear division between the dialogue, which sets out the functional requirements and the arcane technical process through which the design is developed. Many user groups had just such a traditional relationship with the architects they employed. Putting users in control of the brief was a big step forwards but it was a long way from control of design. Indeed, this conventional relationship between designer and client did not even ensure participation of the users. In the better schemes, groups were able to work with their architects to develop the schemes together. But in all cases the users were dependent on the technical expertise of the designers. The building collectively designed by its users proved to be a chimera.

The scope of partnership

The best that could be achieved through "citizen control" was a situation in which users could take part – "participate" – in the design process. A form of partnership developed between users, with little understanding of the design process, and sympathetic design professionals committed to their involvement and empowerment. If "participation" in an effective partnership was the most that could be attained, it could equally well be accomplished in many projects where large organizations were involved, but with a crucial difference: the engagement of a local authority or a large housing association in a community project brought with it greatly increased resources.

160

The availability of existing land or buildings was often the key to opening up development options, and access to substantial funding meant that high standards of design and construction could be reached.

The involvement of large housing associations was critical to the SNAP project in Liverpool, to Rod Hackney's schemes in Birmingham, Leicester and elsewhere, and to projects such as the Bramley housing co-op. The commitment of local authority funding and resources was the key to housing projects such as Byker and Swinbrook. The most successful community facilities were developed when local authorities could be persuaded to commit substantial funding. The most far-reaching rehabilitation of existing housing was accomplished where local councils were able to use their stock to offer rehousing – emptying sufficient dwellings to make possible comprehensive replanning and modernization. The availability of large-scale resources made a great difference to what could be achieved. But it added a new and powerful player to the partnership between designer and user: in the term coined by Ralph Erskine, "the sponsor client".

Almost all the funding for these projects came, ultimately, from central government. But, because they controlled the purse strings, the development officers in local government and in housing associations held a powerful influence. Their power was constrained by the policies of their organizations and they were ultimately accountable for their decisions. Within this framework, the development managers had considerable scope to frustrate or promote participatory projects. The powers of fund managers on the one hand and designers on the other were the key to successful participation. While designers were able to control through the power of knowledge, funders could control through the power of patronage. Where these professionals were protective of their powers, consultation became a public relations exercise or a relatively meaningless facade. Where they were committed to participation, successful user involvement became possible, possible but not guaranteed. For genuine participation to take place, the commitment to the process of the development managers and the designers, a willingness the share their powers, is a prerequisite. For the process to succeed, an understanding is needed of both how it can be achieved and what it can accomplish. Without understanding, the best will in the world can lead to frustrated expectations and destructive conflict. The first step to success is in empowering the users by opening up the design and decision-making processes to public scrutiny.

Demystifying design

It is extremely difficult for anyone to understand building designs. Architects themselves only have an approximate idea of how their schemes will look when they are built, and are frequently surprised and even alarmed when they see their concepts emerge in built form. How much more difficult, then, for those with no design training – and, perhaps, with limited formal education of any sort – to understand proposals put before them. There is a wide gulf to be bridged and this requires building designers to develop new skills in communication: to learn to explain their ideas, the options available, and the possible solutions to particular problems in a clear and simple manner.

The power of words

Most professions create a mystique. For the sceptical lay-person, this mystification is a deliberate tactic to give an exaggerated impression of expertise and protect the power of the profession against anyone wishing to question its decisions. Architects talk and write in florid terms about the poetry of space and light, even when extolling the merits of participation. For example, ". . . the recurring motifs of Hertzberger's architecture that can be formulated in various ways: e.g. polyvalent form and individual interpretation, structure and infill, warp and weft, order and chaos, competence and performance, labyrinthine clarity, casbah organisäe, langue et parole . . . Here one sees and example of user orientated architecture conducive to participation".[5] Perhaps. Certainly not an example of user-orientated language conducive to communication.

Even if they do not always wax lyrical, architects commonly lapse into terms such as "scale", "massing", "solid/void relationship" as a form of shorthand. Local government officers often speak in abbreviations – DoE, HIP, EAP, PC2, LBA, CCT, etc. – and some seem to take pleasure in inventing new ones to mystify each other. Such jargon means nothing to the average person and its use is a serious obstacle to real communication. Professionals involved in user participation must make a conscious and sustained effort to speak simply and plainly, using words that most ordinary people understand. It might help communication, and would certainly be good practice, if they started talking to each other like this.

Speaking plain English is difficult enough, but in some circumstances even that is not enough. In many urban areas in Britain there are significant communities from many parts of the world. Many ethnic minorities do not use English as their first language and quite a lot of people, particularly among first-generation immigrants, have a limited understanding of it. Participatory projects are commonly of a multi-cultural nature, and ethnic minorities are frequently client groups for community projects. Special efforts are needed to appreciate and surmount language barriers. At meetings this is often not a problem, as there is usually someone present who can translate. It is often useful, though, to publish leaflets in more than one language, and for one-to-one meetings it may be necessary to find an interpreter among the minority community.

Making simple images

Drawings are the building designer's stock in trade – the standard method of communicating schemes. What may be appropriate in communicating a scheme to a builder or to another designer is not necessarily suitable for communicating to non-professionals. There is an increasing tendency among architects for the drawing to become an artefact in itself, inventing new concepts of representation that are often not even understood by other architects. This is another aspect of mystification. For effective user participation, greater simplification is needed. Simple plans can usually be understood, particularly if these are presented as coloured diagrams rather than strict projections. Simple drawings also have the benefit of easy adaptation; it is no good embarking on user participation with a beautiful set of drawings that look as though they are the final solution. Sketch perspectives are a useful tool in communicating the appearance of a proposal (Fig. 7.2). It is also helpful if a proposal can be presented against a similar representation of something that already exists – the plan of an existing flat or the elevation of an existing building – to which people can more readily relate.

Figure 7.2
Sketch of new maisonette entrances and private gardens in an estate project. The three-dimensional drawing stimulated discussion among users on the correct height of fencing — high enough to provide some privacy, low enough that the surveillance of passers-by could guard against intruders.

Theoretically, models can be very helpful. They present a complete three-dimensional representation of a proposal as it will look when complete. In practice there are severe limitations. Detailed models are very expensive to build and they cannot easily be altered. The sheer investment in a model may make the designers reluctant to consider alternative solutions. Simple models are not easily understood, but they can be a useful communication tool. The Matrix Co-operative made extensive use of rough models to develop schemes with user groups (Fig. 7.3). Given adequate explanation, basic models made of card or balsa wood can be an aid to exploring design options, particularly if they can be taken apart and adapted during discussions. The development

163

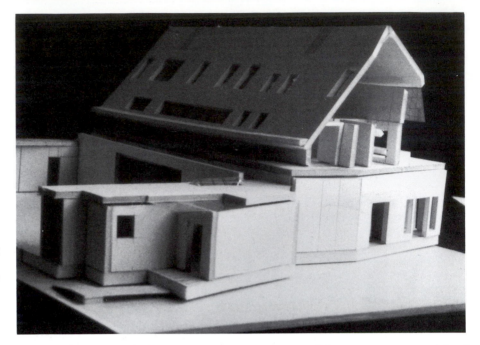

Figure 7.3
Rough model built by Matrix of a new centre, attached to the Weslyan Holiness Church in Waltham Forest, east London, combining a day centre for the elderly and a 25-place nursery. During consultation the model could be taken apart and quickly adapted to incorporate changes. Once the design as complete, a more highly finished model was prepared to help in fund-raising.

of simple computer aided design opens considerable possibilities. Computer models of proposals can be built from which a series of perspectives can be generated representing a walk-through or walk-around a project. This can be as time-consuming as building a real model, but part-models can be built relatively quickly (Fig. 7.4). The great advantage of computer models is that they can be changed very easily, making it possible to generate a wide range of options at very little cost. Computer drawings could also be extremely useful in developing kitchen designs or furniture layouts. On a one-to-one basis, elements can easily be moved around on the screen, generating solutions tailor made by designer and user working together.

Sampling

Sampling is a technique designers themselves use when considering options, and it can be equally valuable in user participation. It can be done in several ways. Visits can be made to similar schemes, particularly if they are nearby. Once they had appointed their architect, the first venture of the Weller Street Co-operators was to organize coach trips to housing schemes in Merseyside and the northwest to see what was possible. It was the ideas generated by the schemes they had visited that eventually led them to settle on a courtyard layout for their own development. If visits are not possible, then pictures are the next best thing. Photographs or slides can be taken to meetings to illustrate a general approach or the appearance of details or components.

The technical aid group CLAWS has developed a refined version of this approach that they call "ideas boards". Large cards are prepared with photographs or sketches of different methods of solving the same problem: types of fencing, different seat designs, and so on. Topics will vary according to the project. In a participation exercise in Brick Lane in East London, boards were prepared on different ways of arranging outdoor restaurant tables, using examples from Covent Garden, Amsterdam and elsewhere. When

164

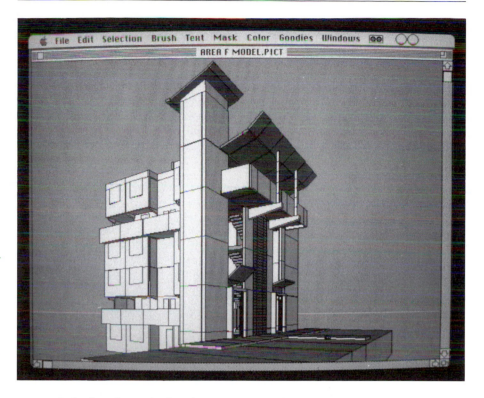

Figure 7.4
Full blown computer models can be time-consuming and costly. Part-models such as this one can be built relatively quickly, although designed to be viewed only from one direction, they can create a vivid realization of a proposed development.

prepared, the boards are displayed at a meeting, exhibition or open day. CLAWS use a caravan where the ideas boards are displayed. People are given self-adhesive red spots to stick on the board next to their preferences. To make ideas boards effective, a large photographic library needs to be built up.

The third way of sampling is to collect real bits of buildings. Sample components can be obtained from manufacturers and presented to users for discussion and choice. Samples of finishing materials – wallpaper, tiles, finishes for kitchen units – are indispensable. But larger components can also be sampled. In estate modernization schemes in Islington, samples of windows of different types and in various materials were taken to meetings to help tenants decide their preferences. The danger of sampling is that "off-the-peg" solutions can easily be misapplied. A detail or component might be very appealing in the context of another scheme, but may be quite inappropriate if copied into the project in hand. The skill of the designer is required in both selecting suitable samples and conveying an understanding of the overall design implications of using them.

Creating a dialogue

The key to breaking down the mystique surrounding the design process is better communication so that users have some understanding of the possibilities and the options available. The essence of better communication is simplicity, clarity and adaptability. User participation is meaningless if people cannot understand what is being proposed.

165

It is worse than meaningless if, having understood, they are then unable to change it. Having opened up options, decisions have to be made. In most projects this is done through discussion: an informed dialogue between users, designers and sponsors.

The number of people with an interest in a development varies enormously. In a small self-help project it may be as few as six or eight people. Usually it will be more. A community centre might have a management committee of a dozen or so, but there may be as many more user groups, all of whom will want their say. In a housing project there could be 50 or 500 families involved, and a large development can affect a community of thousands. Not everyone can be involved all of the time and a combination of methods will be necessary to ensure the most effective involvement of the greatest number.

One-way channels

The community newsletter was one of the earliest manifestations of community action. In the early days it meant the laborious churning of the duplicator, or painstaking cutting and pasting for the printer. In these days of desktop publishing it is easy to produce good quality leaflets. They are, however, a one-way channel of communication. They can deliver news, but they can't collect views. Nevertheless, they can be valuable at certain stages of a project. Initially they can advertise the beginning of the project, alerting people and setting in train the participation process. In practice this has been the main use of leaflets, simply because the energy and time is not usually available to keep on producing them, But they could also be used to report progress at various stages and could be particularly valuable in broadcasting design options and agreed solutions.

Whereas newsletters are an effective way of channelling information to users, the most common method of collecting comprehensive information is the questionnaire. Scientific surveys are the preserve of sociologists rather than building designers. Generally, resources do not allow detailed exercises, although it has happened. In the Swinbrook development, for example, the GLC carried out a large-scale scientific interview survey. More usually a questionnaire survey is a relatively low-key exercise. Forms are sent out or delivered to residents, who are left to complete and return them. Response is entirely voluntary and usually well short of 100 per cent. Questionnaires are useful in collecting information at the beginning of a project. In an estate project, for instance, they may be used to collect information on family sizes, numbers of children by age groups, car ownership, and so on. They can also be used, perhaps less reliably, to collect opinions on key problems of the desirability of various options for improvement. The weakness of questionnaires is that, again, they are a one-way channel. They collect information but do not dispense it.

One way of generating an interchange of information is to mount an exhibition. Drawings of proposals can be displayed at a local meeting-place over a period of time. Users can inspect them at their own convenience and record their comments. Ideally, the designers will be on hand to explain and discuss. Information can be dispensed and responses collected. The drawback with exhibitions (as with questionnaires) is that response is entirely on an individual basis, that does not allow interchange of ideas between participants. Interpretation of the individual responses is left entirely in the hands of the professionals.

166

The decision-making hierarchy

Exchanging and debating ideas are essential if users are to take part in the decision-making process. This can only be done at meetings. The general meeting is often thought of as the epitome of public participation. Everyone affected can be invited, can give their views, exchange ideas and reach a conclusion. In fact, the meeting is a flawed instrument. First, a limit must be placed on those invited. In a planning issue it may be a street or a group of streets – a judgement of those affected that entirely rests with the professionals. In an estate project, the whole estate may be invited, but not those living nearby who may also have an interest. Secondly, the number attending is almost always relatively small. Public meetings rarely attract more than 50 people. On an estate, only 10–15 per cent of residents may be present, for a local planning issue even fewer. Only in small projects are relatively high levels of representation likely to be reached. Thirdly, large meetings are a poor forum for discussion. Many people lack the confidence to speak at such meetings. For those who do speak, it is not possible to have a worthwhile exchange of ideas or discussion of options. The value of public meetings is, realistically, limited to imparting information and obtaining general approval or disapproval of proposals.

A small group of 10–15 people, or fewer, is by far the most useful forum for creative and detailed discussion. With a small group the problems of communication are many fewer. Most people feel confident in small meetings and it becomes possible to discuss ideas in detail and exchange views. The problem is to make such groups representative. They may be elected by a public meeting or appointed as representatives of streets or blocks or of particular interest groups. A representative group may already exist, such as a tenants association or a local forum. Even if established on a representative basis, the group will not remain democratic unless its members regularly report back to their "constituency". In participatory projects involving relatively large numbers of users, detailed discussion is almost always, delegated to a small group. A co-operative will elect a design committee. A community centre management committee will do the same. Periodically the design committee will report back to the larger group for discussion and approval.

Some of the more detailed decisions can reserved for personal choice. On an individual basis the design professional can have a one-to-one relationship with the user. This is closest to the traditional relationship between architect and client. On most projects, however, it will be strictly limited in scope. Most decisions must be made on some sort of collective basis. Some may be delegated to individual choice, but the parameters must be set by collective decisions. On most housing projects internal decoration and colours of materials are left to individual choice. This may extend to kitchen layouts, heating design, and even to choices that affect internal planning or the external appearance. In a community project, some of the detailed decision may be delegated to particular users or user groups. The extent of individual choice is a key decision that will affect the final form of any project.

For most projects it is, in fact, impossible to achieve perfect user participation. No one method can create a perfect decision-making dialogue and all the techniques outlined have their limitations. Most successful projects use a combination of techniques that help to counterbalance the various shortcomings. On a typical housing project the following combination might be used. A newsletter might inform residents about the onset of a project and call a public meeting. This might discuss general objectives and elect a committee of block representatives. The committee would agree the format of a questionnaire and assist in its distribution and collection. It would participate in the formulation of options and report these back to a public meeting or by a newsletter or exhibition. The final design would also be approved by a public meeting. The committee would then oversee implementation and set the parameters for individual choice. While no technique, on its own, offers a perfect form of participation, used together they can be highly effective.

Hands-on participation

In most design participation, people have been involved primarily through informed discussion. Some techniques have been developed that give users more active involvement in the design process. In Sweden, the architect Johannes Olivegren has developed a technique using a series of seven steps through which participants are led. He has used this in small housing projects in which participants use drawings and models to collectively generate and evaluate alternative site layouts and house designs.[7] In America, Christopher Alexander developed a "pattern language" – a collection of 253 "patterns" defining a hierarchy from regional planning to the characteristics of a room. By selecting from these patterns, users can define the basis of a design.[8] Alexander applied his ideas in schemes such as the Mexicali project, in northern Mexico, where a group of low-income families used the language to design and build their own housing.[9] In Europe, laboratories have been set up where full size models of buildings can be assembled. These are mostly used for testing material and components, or for research. But they can be used by groups of users from housing co-operatives or workplaces to test out design ideas.[10]

Planning for real

In Britain there has been more limited use of hands-on participation, but a range of techniques has been developed from the work of Tony Gibson. During the 1970s, Gibson was involved in several community campaigns. In 1977 he worked with a local group in the Glasgow district of Dalmarnock, one of the most deprived areas of western Scotland, where the threat of a motorway and disputes between the authorities had created planning blight. The Dalmarnock Action Group had organized a neighbourhood survey of housing, health, schools, crime, public utilities, industry, welfare, shopping and leisure facilities. They demanded a say in priorities for improvement.

Gibson describes the participation exercise that followed:

> Two of us contrived a crude scale model of Dalmarnock – half a mile square shown as a 6ft by 8ft three-D layout. It covered five tables in a church hall in the middle of the area it represented. One evening, when the model was complete, four separate groups of residents (mums, elderly, youth and Action Committee members) came in to use the model in order to set out their own ideas fore Dalmarnock's immediate future. Along one wall there were 37 packets of cutout shapes, each to scale, and easily recognizable as zebra crossings, adventure playgrounds, rubbish collection areas, community huts, new housing – just about anything that could be useful to the community. To begin with each

168

group operated on their own. making their own selection from the packets, signing each cutout on the back and placing it where they saw fit, if necessary flagging existing buildings for demolition or conversion. After about an hour, groups began to negotiate with each other where they found themselves competing for the same derelict building of patch of waste ground, or doubling up in the facilities they proposed to provide. Sometimes they literally took scissors and trimmed the cutout areas in order to reach a sensible compromise. Every conflict was settled between the groups concerned without the need to anyone else to step in as arbitrator. At the end of the evening everyone came together and decided, again without fuss, on a list of priorities".[11]

Gibson's idealistic promotion of "planning for real" suggests it is a one-step cure-all – a kit game, like Monopoly™, which people can play to plan their neighbourhoods on their own. Although it has become a widely used technique, it is normally part of a broader exercise in consultation and discussion. Using the same basics – the crude model, the options cards – Michael Parkes developed his own version in his work for Planning Aid for London and CLAWS. He subsequently used it in consultation exercises, the largest of which was the community plan for the Kings Cross Railway Land. In preparing the community brief "planning for real" was a major component. A huge model was built and transported to public exhibitions in five locations (Fig. 7.5). Visitors were invited to participate individually selecting and placing option cards. Computation of the results helped to generate ideas and test support for various options. But in preparing the plan, the exercise was just part of a wider process of surveys, consultation with local groups, the findings of issues-based workshops, and independent technical advice provided by the School of Town Planning at University College London. Elsewhere "planning for real" exercises have been used on large housing estates to generate discussion of problems and options for improvement.

Figure 7.5
"Planning for real" used in developing short-term uses for the Kings Cross Railway land. A huge rough model was mounted on tables at various venues. Participants were given cards representing problems and possible improvements and were able to walk through the model, placing the cards.

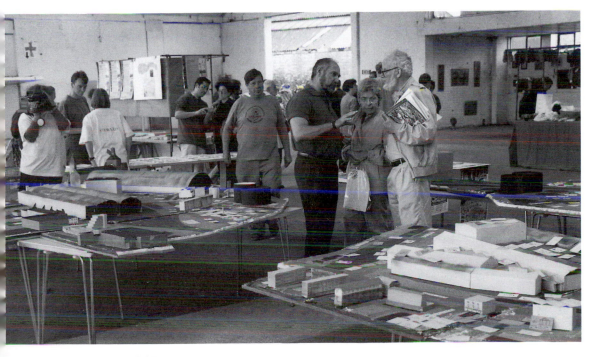

Design games

Design games developed as an offshoot of the type of debate generated in the Dalmarnock exercise. A design game specifically geared to landscape schemes has been developed by CLAWS. A baseboard of the site is prepared showing the site blank and the surrounding development drawn in. Flat "pieces" are then prepared of the various elements that could go on the site: different pieces of play equipment, a hard ball games area, a tennis court, meadows, cars with turning circles, paths, a BMX track, and so on. The pieces are made in flat card to scale and are coloured up in a representational manner. The pieces can have price tags so that people can work to budgets. In the game the landscape architect controls the board, and the participants suggest and discuss the placing of the pieces. Conflicts can be argued through and resolved. Several arrangements are tried, modified and adjusted until a preferred option emerges which has consensus support of the meeting. A sketch scheme is drawn up from the final version which goes back to a further meeting.

A variation of the game can be used for developing a site with new buildings. Here the base model would be prepared with the surrounding buildings modelled in card. Basic materials would be taken to the meeting: pens, paper, scissors, some blocks of balsa wood. The leader generates a discussion among the participants on the parameters of the development: size and type of buildings, road access, and so on. Options for development are then discussed and the "pieces" prepared. These could include options for road sizes and geometry drawn on paper and placed on the baseboard and building blocks made from card boxes or cut from polystyrene slabs. In early versions of the game, ready-made boxes such as matchboxes or cornflakes packets were used. The pieces are then assembled, and variations are tried and discussed until a consensus emerges.

Designers vs users

Over more than 20 years, a variety of techniques have been developed that have helped to demystify the design and decision-making process, and to involve users in planning issues, in designs for new and modernized housing, in improvements to estates and the development of community facilities. User groups have ranged from small co-ops and self-help groups, through tenants organizations of various sizes, to consortia and action groups representing entire neighbourhoods. Not all techniques are suitable for every circumstance, and the most successful projects have used a variety of different combinations. Nor has it all been sweetness and light. Considerable conflict has often been generated by tension between users and designers pitched together into complex issues and uncharted areas. The path was forged by planners, architects and other building designers committed to participation. Others have been forced into the process by the policies of their employers or their clients, or by concerted community campaigns.

There has been, and there continues to be, considerable resistance to user participation amongst design professionals. Some, perhaps as a result of experience, are genuinely fearful of attending consultation meetings, anticipating verbal, or even physical, assault and public humiliation. Others argue that it is not a useful process because those who become involved are not representative but are using the process to promote their

170

personal or sectional interests. At root, what many designers fear is that user participation is a means of undermining their expertise and removing their authority. Influenced by these reservations, many seek to maintain rigidly the separate roles of client and professional. Or they may play along with participation but remain secretly contemptuous of the users they come into contact with, constantly seeking to undermine the process and impose their own preferred solutions.

The first thing that designers must understand is that user participation grew out of community action. This was a protest movement against what "they" were doing – "they" the council, "they" the developers, "they" the architects. It is, perhaps, unsurprising that an "us and them" mentality often still characterizes the participation process. "It doesn't matter what we say, they will take no notice" is a comment often heard at public meetings. Designers have to bridge this gulf of hostility and earn the trust of users. First, by verbal persuasion and assurances that participation will be an open partnership, but more importantly by tangible demonstration that users' views have been addressed as the scheme develops. Hostility is often a result of a breakdown of this trust. But there may be other reasons. For many people unused to public speaking, generating anger in themselves is the only way to gain the courage to speak out. Those involved in participation must understand this basic psychology and accept that a certain amount of "rough & tumble" is par for the course. They must learn to handle it and turn it in a positive direction, either by arguing through the concerns or giving them wholehearted consideration in the development of the scheme.

The question of representation must be balanced against the advantages to be gained by participation. If participation informs and improves the design process, then the involvement of just one user would be better than leaving it to the professionals. Nevertheless, personal or sectional interests are inevitable and it is important to make the process as representative as possible. The various methods by which people can be involved all have their limitations and can present a distorted picture. Although no one process will ensure representation, a combination of techniques can ensure a wide input. A multi-faceted participation process will help to define and isolate a vocal but unrepresentative minority who may be able to dominate a particular forum. There are occasions, in all sorts of circumstances when progress through co-operation is disrupted by an individual or small group with an axe to grind. In such circumstances, confrontation may be the only means of ensuring the good of the greater number. Community designers must learn to recognize sectional and self-interested groups and individuals, and put their views into perspective through the wider participation process.

It is perhaps not surprising that many designers fear participation will undermine their powers. One rather extreme school of thought has it that the pure form of participatory democracy means users taking control of the design process reducing the professional to a mere cipher. This is not what happens in practice. Rather, participation enriches the design process, by better information and wider discussion. The designer retains substantial powers through the exercise of design skills and experience and through the power to interpret the information and views gained from participation. Competent designers have nothing to fear from participation. It is often the less confident who are the most fearful, but even they should recognize that wider discussion will bring strength to their schemes rather than humiliation through exposure of their weaknesses. Successful participation requires a genuine commitment on the part of designers to work with users. "I have spent seven years training to be a designer and

171

they think they know better" is often said by architects, not just about users but about conventional clients. To some extent this is sheer arrogance. Most people could not design an armchair or a motor car, but they know how to use one, and know when it works well and is pleasing to the eye. Architects must learn to sell their designs and not just impose them. But there is a deeper problem. Users often make snap judgements based on taste or prejudice. For participation to be successful, users need to understand that design is a complex process involving difficult choices and resolving multiple contradictions. The designer will not instil such understanding by hiding behind professional expertise or subverting the participation process. Far better to have a full and open discussion about design problems. In this way, users come to understand and value the skill of the designer, and schemes developed through open discussion are usually better than those conceived in the secrecy of the office. Committed designers find that participation is not a trial to be endured but an enjoyable experience that makes real what would otherwise be a purely technical exercise.

Participation does mean that decision-making is shared and this transfers some power to the users. But this also has an advantage for the designers. Sharing in the decision-making process ends the "us and them" syndrome. If users take part in the decisions, they also bear some of the responsibility for the successes and the failures. At the end of the day they cannot turn around and blame the architects for design faults. This aspect of user participation is often not understood. Usually it is presented as a way of giving users more rights. That it also gives them new responsibilities is one of the reasons for the success of the process, not just at design stage but in the longer term.

Tests of success

There are those who regard participation as an inefficient and time-consuming approach to design, and question whether it really achieves anything at all. To dismiss it as inefficient is, on one level, like saying dictatorship is more efficient than democracy. Participation can be justified purely on the grounds that people have a right to greater control over their environment. Democracy is a difficult process and considerable effort needs to be put into better communication and wider discussion and argument. It is a more time-consuming process. Designers need to spend time talking to users collectively and individually, and this time has to be paid for. Experience suggests, though, that participation does not necessarily lengthen the design period. It may be more intense, but it can usually be accomplished within a timescale similar to conventional development.

But it is not just a question of democratic rights. Those who argue that user involvement is inefficient are taking a short-sighted view which considers only the development process and not of the quality of the product and its long-term use. If participation can produce better designs, if it can produce buildings that are more suited to the needs of their users, then it can truly be described as more efficient. Whether it does do this is a matter of judgement. It can be argued that schemes presented as successes of participation are simply the result of the skill of their designers. Design skill is undoubtedly important and without it successful schemes are not possible. The key is whether these skills are put at the disposal of the users and directed to their benefit. There are two main claims made for design participation. First, that it produces more appropriate solutions and greater satisfaction for the users. Secondly, that satisfaction generates greater commitment and the schemes produced will be better managed and maintained, and will better stand the test of time.

Some tests have been made to measure satisfaction. Questionnaire surveys on Tufnell Park Estate in Islington showed that before improvements started only 43 per cent of tenants wanted to stay on the estate. After completion of the first phase more than 77 per cent were keen to stay. Surveys on other estate improvements have shown similar results. In 1985 Tom Woolley completed a major research study.[12] He used questionnaire surveys to measure the satisfaction of residents of new housing schemes. Three new build co-ops, where the members had participated in the designs, were compared with similar schemes produced by local authorities without participation. He found that satisfaction was higher in the co-ops, although generally only marginally so. Only in the Weller Street scheme was satisfaction significantly higher, and this he attributed to the achievement of the project rather than the design itself. In fact, comparing like with like is a very narrow measure of satisfaction. The achievement of the project may well be far greater than simply to produce an alternative design.

The key question is: What would have happened otherwise? Without the initiative of forming a co-operative, and the participation that followed, the Weller Street residents would probably have become council tenants in three-storey blocks of flats. Without the participatory campaign mounted by the residents, the Swinbrook area might well have been redeveloped as a warren of "streets-in-the sky"; indeed such a fate did befall a neighbouring site. Without effective participation many older estates might well have been treated with minimal repairs and improvements. Without the organization and participation in their own projects, many users of community facilities would probably have nothing at all. All the evidence suggests that participation has been a key to producing developments better fitted for their purpose than would otherwise be the case.

It is also arguable that involving users in decision-making gives them a sense of proprietorship that leads them to look after the buildings they use. More appropriate solutions, valued by their users, should last longer. Over the years the buildings should suffer less from neglect, poor maintenance and misuse. Certainly, many of the projects in which participation was a key component seem to have stood up well over the years. Many of them have now been complete for some time. The pioneering participation project, the first phase of Byker, was completed 18 years ago and it still provides a well maintained environment of remarkably good quality. Whether this is result of better design and the proprietorship generated by participation, or to other factors, is impossible to demonstrate. But there are now sufficient participatory schemes of good quality that *have* stood the test of time that the case must be at least partly proved.

If it is to achieve its full potential, participatory design has to pass one final test: professional approval. The design professions have a poor record on judging what constitutes success. Projects that were widely praised in the 1960s by architectural journals, and distinguished with design awards, have often proved unpopular with users and have developed real problems in the longer term. If user participation is to achieve widespread acceptance, then its products must be recognized by designers as models to be emulated and from which lessons can be drawn. There are now many architects, planners, surveyors and landscape designers with some experience and understanding of participation. The majority of professionals, though, have only the haziest awareness of both the process and the product of user involvement. If user participation is to become

173

more widespread, it remains to convince the professions that adopting its principles and practice – a fresh approach to building design – is a means to more successful ends.

References

1. Sherry Arnstein, "A ladder of citizen participation in the USA", *Journal of the Town Planning Institute* (April 1971), 176. First published in *Journal of the American Institute of Planners* (July 1969)

2. Colin Ward, *Tenants take over* (London: Architectural Press, 1974), 63.

3. Nigel Cross, "Participation", *The Architects' Journal* (20 January 1982), 76.

4. Alison Ravetz, *Remaking cities – contradictions of the recent urban environment* (London: Croom Helm, 1980), 293.

5. Robert Cowan, "Meat and gravy – Martlett Court, Westminster", *The Architects' Journal* (29 April 1987), 28.

6. Arnuf Löchinger, *Herman Herzberger* (The Hague: Nederland Arch-Edition, 1987), 36 [description of Studentenhuis Amsterdam].

7. Johannes Olivegren, "How a little community is born – Klostermuren, Göteborg, Sweden", in *The scope of social architecture*, Richard Hatch (ed.) (New York: Van Nostrand Reinhold 1984), 135.

8. Christopher Alexander et al., *A pattern language* (Oxford: Oxford University Press, 1977).

9. Christopher Alexander et al., *The production of houses* (Oxford: Oxford University Press, 1985).

10. Tom Woolley, "1:1 and face to face", *The Architects' Journal* (29 April 1987), 22.

11. Tony Gibson, *People power – community work groups in action* (Harmondsworth: Penguin 1979),118. The concept was further developed in *The Planning for Real Report* by Tony Gibson & Mark Dorfman, commissioned by the DoE (Nottingham University 1981).

12. Tom Woolley, *Community architecture: an evaluation of the case for user participation in architectural design* (PhD thesis, Oxford Polytechnic, 1985). Summarized in Ruth Owens, "Participation panacea", *The Architects' Journal* (11 June 1986), 24.

CASE STUDY
Besant Court: decentralization in action

By the mid-1980s, Islington had decentral-ized many of its staff into 24 new offices, each serving a neighbourhood of 6,000–7,000 people. The main purpose of these local offices was to bring housing manage-ment, repairs and personal social services within easy reach of the people who used them. But they also had a part to play in development. An Improvement Officer was based in each neighbourhood office, whose role was to identify possible schemes, work up briefs and establish local priorities. Better technical back-up was provided when the Architects Department was re-organized into eight area teams, each dedicated to a small group of neighbourhoods. The new

set-up offered a more flexible and sensitive approach than the old system, where devel-opment programmes and priorities were contrived by the management hierarchy working from the Town Hall. At its best, central programming worked well. But it could be a hit and miss affair.

Besant Court had been a victim of such flawed targeting. First included in the pro-gramme for improving post war estates, it was then omitted without local consultation. Meanwhile, other estates in no worse condi-tion had had major improvements. In 1985 the Besant Tenants Association, with the support of their new Neighbourhood Office. lobbied the Housing Committee. The flats

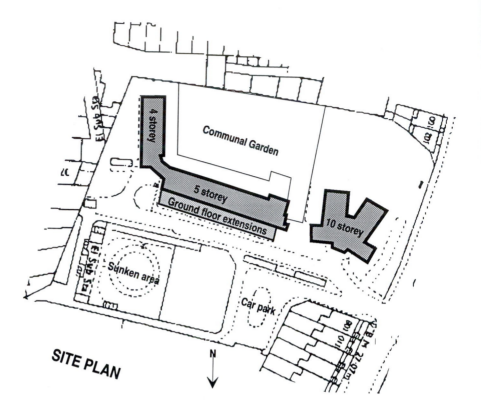

SITE PLAN

N

were damp, draughty and difficult to heat, they claimed, and the outside areas were "a real mess". They accused the council of neglect and delay in dealing with the problems of their estate. The lobby succeeded and, in fact, the delay worked to their advantage. Whereas, earlier, they might have received only package improvements based on a standard shopping list, by 1986 the climate had changed. A new funding formula had increased the money available for such work and, most importantly, the new decentralized structure was better geared to working closely with tenants to examine all the possible options for improvement.

Built in the early 1950s, Besant Court was an odd development. Two lower blocks of four and five storeys, mostly family maisonettes were linked together in an L shape. Alongside was a small tower block – ten storeys containing 40 tiny flats. Behind the blocks was a generous but underused green

space. In front, a disorganized car park shared with an adjoining estate and a large semi-derelict sunken area. No simple formula could provide a ready answer for such a heterogeneous mixture, and the search for solutions proved complex and controversial. Participation began, as usual, with a questionnaire to collect information about the age structure and family mix of the tenants and to seek their views on the problems and priorities for improvement in their homes and the surrounding environment. Simultaneously a building committee was set up, which all the tenants were invited to join. Discussion established that the maisonettes on the estate were generally well liked and provided good potential for improvement. The flats were the real problem. They were all small and some were seriously overcrowded. Many had severe condensation problems. Those in the tower block were reached by a tiny lift that often broke down.

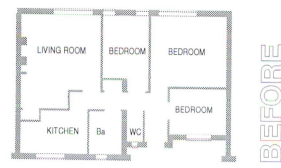

EXISTING 3 BEDROOM FLAT

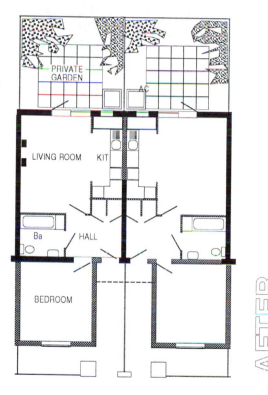

ONE-BEDROOM DISABILITY FLATS

The ground floor originally contained poorly planned family flats – undersized and suffering severe condensation problems. By extending the ground floor, each original flat was converted to two disability flats.

The low blocks presented the greatest potential for improvement. The 23 maisonettes provided reasonable space standards and, with new kitchens, bathrooms and fabric improvements, could be made into good housing. The tenants were keen to return to them after improvement work. The flats on the ground floor were a more difficult problem – undersize and poorly planned. They could re-modelled but perhaps there was a better solution. Space on the ground is at a premium and two options were discussed. The flats could be combined with housing above to make large family maisonettes. Alternatively, the ground space could be given over to the elderly and disabled. With new extensions and replanning small flats could be created with level access and private gardens. The options were discussed by the building committee at some length. The solution that emerged was to create one family maisonette by combining three bed-sitting-room flats. Seven disability flats could then be developed in the remainder of the ground floor, giving an opportunity for some of the elderly marooned in the tower block to move into new accessible homes. As well as re-planning, substantial improvements were carried out to solve the technical problems. The warped and twisted metal windows were replaced to cut out draughts; better insulation was provided to eliminate condensation; the leaking flat roof was covered over and insulated by a new pitched roof.

The improvements agreed for the lower blocks set a high standard. Applying such standards to the tower block created a major problem. In addition to internal and fabric improvements, the tall block needed a new lift to make it into decent housing. The extent of external walls made it difficult to insulate and there were problems in raising fire safety to modern standards. The cost of all this proved enormous – well beyond what was available under the funding formula. Feasibility studies showed that a similar-size new development of three and four storeys could be built on the same land, providing better housing – and at *less* cost. Seven alternatives were considered, including converting the tower to other uses. In the end it boiled down to two options – to demolish and start again or to improve the block to lower standards, which meant it would continue to provide substandard housing. The choice was so controversial that the Improvement Officer conducted extensive discussions and organized a ballot among the tenants to

The five-storey block before and after modernization. Improvements included a new roof, improved insulation, new windows and intercom security to the upper floors.

The communal garden to the lower blocks, secured against intruders and accessible only to tenants in the blocks. Adjoining the building are private gardens for the disability flats and lower maisonettes.

ensure the widest possible participation in such a key decision. For his pains he was threatened with disciplinary action by the management hierarchy for having the temerity to discuss such radical options with tenants. Eventually the controversy was referred to the Housing Committee. The council, bowing to local demands, agreed to the redevelopment option, although demoli-

tion was deferred until sufficient funds became available for rebuilding.

With the future of both blocks apparently settled, the external green space was divided between the two blocks. Part of it was landscaped as a secure communal garden for the lower blocks. The remainder was set aside for the new development. The car park was re-organized and re-paved. This left the

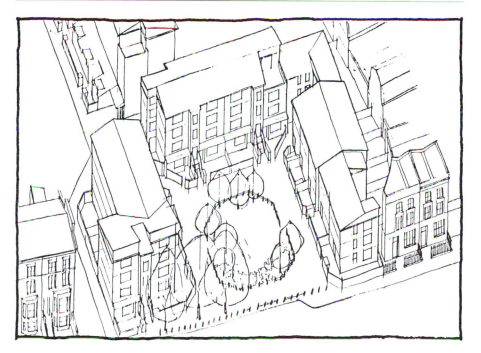

Sketch of the feasibility study that showed that the tower block site could be redeveloped at less cost than modernization

sunken area. The neighbourhood under-5's worker was in touch with a local playgroup that operated in insecure and inadequate premises. She also had access to funding for social services projects. A new nursery might provide a perfect use for the derelict but secure area next to Besant Court. To

Bowing to the tenants demands, the council agreed to demolish the tower block in 1988. Ever since, it has proved impossible to fund the re-development and the block has continued in use as poor standard accommodation for the homeless.

the officers it seemed and ideal opportunity. But among the tenants it created controversy. Although many of the younger tenants liked the idea of a nursery, a small group lobbied vigorously against it, claiming it would be noisy and would bring in a stream of outsiders threatening the security of the estate. In the face of such outspoken opposition the idea was quietly dropped.

Decentralization brought new powers and greater influence to local communities, powers that, in the case of Besant Court, were used to both positive and negative ends. Decentralization helped to prioritize their estate for major improvement. The tenants were then able to take part in wide-ranging discussion on the options for their immediate environment and they participated in every detail of the design of the improvements to their homes. Without such participation the development of the disability flats might not have taken place. The option of demolishing the tower block might well not have been discussed, much less agreed. More negatively they were parochial and protective about their surroundings to the point of excluding a project as innocuous as a children's play group.

In the longer run there have been positive

179

A young visitor explores the St Judes Playgroup's new nursery.

and negative effects of these decisions. More than six years after the decision was taken, the tower block had still not been demolished. Filled, ever since, with unhappy homeless people, it has progressively degenerated. It still stands as a festering symbol of government cuts in the capital funding available to local authorities and of the housing crisis that has been the result. For the St Judes Playgroup, denied their new nursery at Besant, there was a happier outcome. Through the work of the Neighbourhood Office and the architects' Area Team, a disused basement, originally built as a communal laundry, was found on a nearby estate. In 1992 it was renovated and converted for the playgroup and re-opened as the Walnut Tree Nursery.

PART THREE

Theory, debate and prospect

CHAPTER 8

The Ivory Tower

EDUCATING BUILDING DESIGNERS

The twentieth century has seen a relentless growth of professionalism. New specialisms establish their territory. build a mystique around their expertise and fence it around with restrictive practices. The building industry is no exception. In building design, architecture is the oldest profession – its Institute was founded in 1834. Despite the establishment of the new profession, during the nineteenth century most buildings were designed by their builders. Relatively few were the work of architects, being mainly prestige buildings in urban centres or commissions for the rich. Generally these architects took a synoptic view designing exterior and interior, structure and services, site planning and landscape and co-operating with building craftsmen in the details of construction. Sometimes specialists were employed to design gardens or – in the case of William Morris – interiors. But these were not separate professions and such organizations as the craft Guilds sought an integrated approach to design. The efforts of philanthropists and reformers to redress the problems of the cities gave architects new opportunities to work on projects with a social purpose, among them the model towns. The new expertise in the planning of settlements began the fragmentation of the professions. In 1909 W. H. Lever – founder of Port Sunlight – endowed the first Town Planning School at Liverpool University with Patrick Abercrombie and Stanley Adshead as its full-time tutors. In 1914 a new professional body was formed: the Town Planning Institute.[1]

The rise of the Welfare State gave new patronage and employment to architects and town planners. At the height of its power, the public sector became the major generator of building development, design and maintenance. As the numbers employed in building design increased, its practice began to mirror the specialist fragmentation that had come to characterize local government. New specialisms split off and became separate professions – landscape architects, interior designers, services and structural designers, quantity surveyors and, most recently, building surveyors. Each, in turn, established its own Institute and its own programme of education and training. When community action challenged the power of the Welfare State, it also challenged the world of this army of specialist professions who had, by then, clearly staked out their territory and were constantly vying with each other to protect their vested interests. Community architecture sought to break down the barriers of professionalism and to re-integrate design and development in the interests of building users. The strongest barrier to this process is the professional attitudes built up by specialist education and, in particular, the mystique surrounding the process of design.

The principles of community architecture

The term "community architecture" suggests simply an alternative form of architectural practice. That it is, and it poses a powerful challenge to the professional attitudes of architects. But it is also much more, stepping well outside the bounds of conventional architectural practice, embracing new skills and knowledge from a much wider sphere. From the wide variety of projects and activities that fall under the umbrella of community architecture, nine principles can be distilled that help to define its nature

1. *User participation* Despite its commitment to improve conditions in the deprived inner cities, social architecture failed because it imposed solutions based on presumptions about people's needs. Community architecture shared this social commitment but sought more relevant and sustainable solutions by actively involving people in shaping their own environment. It sought to empower those who had previously only been statistics in the briefs of architects and planners. The participation of building users in the design and development process became its cardinal principle. The involvement of groups of ordinary people – untutored in the language of design and development – meant the evolution of new methods and techniques. The requirements of this new approach has had far-reaching implications that mark out community architecture as crucially different from conventional professional practice and which generated new priorities in urban development.

2. *User needs* Taking account of the needs of users has become a crucial component in design. The importance of safety, security and accessibility emerged from participation as key concerns, particularly for the more vulnerable – women, children, the elderly, the disabled; safety from dangerous materials or components; protection against accidents; the security of people, both in their homes and the public environment, against crime and assault; access and safety for the disabled. Some of these matters can be covered by regulation and many are. But regulation is not a substitute for proper design consideration. Security is not just a matter of locks and bars, or better lighting, or providing video cameras. Properly considered it can affect the whole design and layout of buildings so that more spaces become secure, and public areas are better used and subject to the surveillance of residents and passers-by. Accessibility is not just a matter of tacking ramps onto existing designs. Properly considered it can focus the whole design approach, not just opening buildings to the disabled, but making them safer and easier for everyone to use.

3. *Urbanism* Understanding user needs requires an appreciation of the wider urban context, both social and physical, an understanding of inequality and deprivation; of the dynamics of social organizations and networks, whether these are based on class, culture, locality or communities of interest. Creating an appropriate built environment requires appreciation of the mores of the people of the area – their aspirations, their problems, their concerns. Responding properly to the surrounding physical fabric requires knowledge of the history of local development, the scale of buildings and the prevailing style and materials. Those practising community architecture need both a general knowledge of urban sociology and

183

history, and a particular understanding of this context in the communities in which they work.

4. *Co-operation*   Co-operatives became the prevailing form of organization in self-help and community groups and in many of the technical organizations set up to serve them. Co-operation with users in design and development partnership became the overriding principle of community architecture, But in the best practice, co-operation spread into the design team itself and into the relationship between designers and builders. Co-operation is not always sweetness and light. Often, strong passions are aroused. It is a process of arguing through concerns and options in an open, honest and equal manner. Solutions are not imposed by invoking authority or expertise, but are reached through democratic debate. Designs produced by this method are often better as a result of a thorough exploration and discussion of the issues. But it is not easily achieved. Many feel their status in the hierarchy or their professional expertise is threatened by such a process, and it does not fit well with the prevailing culture of individualism and competition.

5. *Multiple skills*   In the practice of community architecture, many architects had to develop new knowledge and new skills. Understanding of the social and planning context was just the beginning. Many working with community groups had to learn to understand the art of political lobbying, the process of acquiring buildings and sites, the sources and procedures in getting funding. They had to learn new methods of communication and the techniques of participation. Those in community technical aid had to learn self-servicing: typing, accounts, records. Those in design and build, and working with self-build groups, had to understand and convey the skills of building and to design in a manner appropriate to the skills of their user groups. It was all a long way from the traditional image of the architect spending a professional life seated at the drawing board, never dirtying their hands with prosaic or mundane tasks.

6. *Integrated design*   The growth in professionalism had led to each specialism to focus its interest on a narrow range of the process of design and development. Architects thought only in terms of new buildings, quantity surveyors understood only the costs of new construction. Building surveyors concerned themselves only with repair and renovations. To any particular problem each brought a preconception of the solution. In design, the various professions each focused on a different part of the project – the structure, the services, the interior, the external environment – often without due consideration of their interrelationship. The new climate, of which community architecture was the core, required consideration of a wide variety of options, free of preconceptions, consideration that the existing specialisms were ill equipped to provide. It also meant taking a broad overview where context, initiation, design and construction are considered as an integrated process rather than delegated to separate professional areas.

7. *Building re-use*   Much of the focus of community action was on saving communities from being dispersed by redevelopment. Very often this meant saving the existing houses and converting them to modern standards. What began with

housing spread to other buildings, and community groups in the new voluntary sector commonly found a home in an old building reclaimed for new uses. The effective and imaginative adaptation of old buildings became a key element of community architecture, one that fitted well the Green agenda of conservation and recycling, and with the public concern with the preservation of the familiar urban environment. But building re-use is a novel area of design for which none of the established professions is adequately trained. Those who developed the skill, whether architects or surveyors, have had to learn by experience. Given greater recognition and understanding, the skill of building re-use could be applied to more buildings with better effect.

8. *Modest scale*   Many community projects were done on a shoe-string budgets and often involved self-build. Of necessity they involved modest adaptations to existing buildings or small new developments. But in a movement that began as a rejection of large-scale redevelopment, modesty was also a virtue. "Small is beautiful" became a keynote of community architecture. Generally it is large developments and large-scale buildings that cause most disruption and excite public controversy. Small buildings and modest adaptations, even if they are not well designed, blend into the existing urban fabric, causing far less intrusion and disruption than large-scale new developments.

9. *Quality before innovation*   In a movement that focuses on the involvement of users and on meeting their needs, the highest priority is given to making buildings that work well and are pleasing to those who occupy them. Yet in the prevailing ethos it is the new idea, the startling design concept, on which praise and attention is lavished. Utility and commodity are often secondary considerations. If architects gave a higher priority to producing buildings that work, rather than to attention-seeking eye-catching innovations, they would deserve to receive greater public appreciation and support.

In many respects, these principles go beyond the conventional perception of community architecture. Yet they all developed from the change in climate created by community action and from which community architecture evolved. If some of the principles have filtered into general practice, that is all to the good. Such principles should be the yardstick of good practice for all building design. But they are still far from accepted by the educational machine that shapes the minds of the coming generations of designers.

The thrust of architectural education

The education of architects is at the centre of prevailing attitudes towards building design. This is partly because architecture is the original discipline, the core from which the other professions developed. It is also because architects consider themselves the leaders of the design team and are trained to believe they have an overarching view of all aspects of design. In many respects, architecture is a technical, scientific subject. Part of the education process is devoted to formal lectures in structural design, environmental science and construction. Technical training has become increasingly theoretical and would be improved if students were given more hands-on instruction in building skills – something that used to be quite common. The real problem, though, is that the importance of technical training has diminished and it has become a minor part of the education process. The predominant component of architectural education is studio work.

Architectural students are estimated to spend 70 per cent of their time in the studio. There they work on projects set by their tutors, through which they are supposed to learn the skill of design by practical experience. The pattern of studio training varies to some degree from school to school, but the basic form is common. In their first year, students are asked to design simple structures with projects such as "a room of my own" or "a shelter for four seasons". They next move on the small buildings – a nursery, a doctor's surgery, "a house for an artist". By the third year they can attempt projects of considerable complexity – a fire station, a school, a small housing development. In the final two years they move on to ever larger and more complex projects, which might involve the comprehensive redevelopment of a block of urban buildings for mixed uses. Or it might be a massive public building – a transport interchange, a national library, an arts complex or museum.[2]

All these projects involve designs for new buildings. Refurbishment never seems to be set as project work. Hardly ever is building re-use considered as a realistic option. For most projects there is a distinct air of unreality. Many projects are set in greenfield sites where there is no imperative to consider designing in the context of an urban environment. Often there is not a real site at all. Even if there is, it is used as the basis of a paper exercise and the students never get to see it. Rarely do students have the opportunity to talk to a real client, let alone someone who might use their building. Much project work is not only unreal, it is also approached on a narrow design basis – the design of the envelopes of new buildings. The planning context is not considered, the surrounding environment is given scant attention. Very often the uses, the interiors and the services are a secondary consideration to the drive to create exciting spaces and forms. A profession that claims an over-arching comprehension of design is ill served by such a narrow unrealistic approach. The result is that most architects think landscape design is just a matter of scheduling a few plants and that planners are put on Earth solely to frustrate their grand designs.

Throughout the studio programme there is a heavy emphasis on individuality. Almost always, each student is left to develop a personal solution to the problem set. To some extent this is necessary so that progress and achievement can be assessed. But it is also a central purpose to develop in each student a personal philosophy of design and a confidence in their individual ability to master complex creative problems. This process is cultivated by "the crit". At the end of each project all the schemes are put up on the wall and criticized by a panel of lecturers. This process is usually entirely negative, emphasizing the shortcomings of each scheme, Because it comes at the end of the project, students are forced to try to defend what they have done, rather than benefit from the observations by incorporating them in an improved design. Tom Woolley comments "Crits can be notoriously unfair and destructive . . . While some argue that the bruising and battering of crits is good preparation for life, they often suppress creativity, producing fear of failure and humiliation." Surviving the crit means that ". . . architectural design is a very personal and subjective process whereby the designers tend to be very possessive and defensive about their designs or the methods used to achieve them."[3] Success in education depends on each architectural student developing strong confidence in their own ideas and their own work, confidence that often borders on arrogance. It is small wonder that people trained by such methods so often find it impossible to work co-operatively in teams or to open the design process to creative discussion.

The architect as artist

Underlying the unreality and individuality of architectural education is the notion that architecture is an art, an art akin to sculpture. One problem with this is that the creative process of high art is almost impossible to define. In pursuing the art of architecture, the schools resort to lofty but vague proclamations. Bath School of Architecture claims ". . . there is a synergy between architecture and the techniques for achieving it, as there is between man and architectural space. Architecture draws in equal measure upon the arts and the sciences, the holistic characteristics of the task must always dominate and the "zen" of design become second nature to the mature architect". The Brighton school declares "It is our common belief that dreams are enriched, not compromised, by their engagement with reality; that the spirit and the flesh must be, in the profoundest sense, one."[4] High ideals, but given the predominance of studio projects over technical instruction, the arts tend to hold sway over the sciences. All too often it is the spiritualist dreams that take precedence over commodity, function and the needs of building users.

The pursuit of the art of architecture has been characterized not by tolerant exploration of alternative approaches but by entrenched battles over stylistic correctness in which, if they can, the winners take all. In the past these were serious and deeply felt debates between well developed schools of thought. The great debate of the Victorian era took place when the entrenched classical tradition was challenged by the Gothic revival and the Arts and Crafts movement with its wide-ranging philosophy embracing design, construction and social progress. Next, it was the turn of modernism to challenge established orthodoxy. Whatever its shortcomings, modernism was a widespread movement that took 50 years to reach fruition and it encompassed art, science and social purpose. In the 1950s the battleground entered education where modernists struggled against the traditional schools still teaching the principles of classical architecture.

With the triumph of the modernist movement in the 1960s, almost all student schemes were modernist, and experiment with other approaches was positively discouraged. Students graduated not knowing the simple basics of traditional construction, such as how to design pitched roofs. With the demise of modernism the schools have lurched rapidly in different directions in search of a new stylistic correctness. In the 1970s it was the vernacular revival and rationalized tradition that became the predominant academic style. In the 1980s it was high tech – developed from the technological and systematic legacy of modernism – and postmodernism – a combination of obsessive pattern-making and pragmatic classical revival. The latest fad is deconstruction, where the elements of a building are assembled in apparently random fashion. Described by one critic as "architecture which looks like train crashes", deconstruction is almost entirely a paper style, with very few projects actually built. Nevertheless, it is currently in favour in the schools and will soon be inflicted on an unsuspecting public, should their students ever get the chance to build anything.

187

The fickle experimentation with art and style has, over the past 20 years, made architecture as ephemeral as fashion design. These latest styles lack an underlying philosophy. They lack social purpose and this has been a grave disservice to the objective of making buildings user friendly. From the perspective of architecture as art, the views of users are not sought and their needs are inadequately considered. It is not clients that are sought, but "patrons" – sponsors of the architect/artist. Such self-absorption ignores some very important facts: first, that those who commission buildings want, first and foremost, a building that works well and fits the purpose for which they want to use it; secondly, that buildings last a long time and cannot be discarded like an old coat gone out of fashion; and finally, that people can choose the clothes they wear and the art objects they buy. They cannot, generally, choose the buildings that surround them or the environment in which they live and work. Regaining public confidence in building design perhaps requires a challenge to the very notion that architecture is an art and that the purpose of education is to produce architect/artists to whom the "zen" of design is "second nature".

Criticisms from the profession

Practising architects frequently complain about the impracticality of school graduates once they get into the professional office. Roderick Gradidge recently called for the re-institution of pupillage and in-practice training in preference to academic study.[5] His call re-echoes a controversy of more than 100 years ago when Norman Shaw resigned from the RIBA in defence of architecture as a craft learned by practice.[6] Gradidge's view was supported by Quinlan Terry, who commented "The average product of the schools is virtually unemployable. I interview many and, with a few exceptions, they are unable to draw or construct; they are arrogant, talkative and very expensive".[7] It is possible that the views of such leading classicists is coloured by the failure of the schools to service the needs of their own adopted style. But similar complaints are commonly heard among employers who encompass a broad range of stylistic interest and professional practice.

A most penetrating critique on the failure of education has come from Brian Avery, a practising architect who, on occasional visits to schools, has been disturbed by what he finds. Noting that the demands on students to master grandiose projects not only generates a high failure rate but engenders unrealistic expectations in those who succeed, he attacked the notion of architecture as art. "The difficulty with art, or more accurately modern art, is that it has no structure capable of useful academic evaluation until after the event, because the artist is thought of as a free spirit directed by inner drives and motivations and his work is often the more praised, the more it appears anarchic and subversive of current mores. The artist-architect is thus profoundly unprofessional." He goes on to observe that, despite the high profile given to a handful of leading architects, 99 per cent of the profession will never achieve the high-flown ambition nurtured by their educational experience: ". . . few will ever have the opportunity to design and this only for a fraction of their time." Most will spend their time carrying out "small works and refurbishment, the mainstay of 80 per cent of our practices but the very work which the schools so patently ignore."[8]

The failure of education to meet the needs of general practice can have serious consequences. Some years ago, a young architect was asked to design the fitting our of a new shop, as his first commission. He had the idea of using industrial palettes suspended on cables to give the impression of "floating" shelves. The work was completed and the day before the official opening the shelves were loaded for display. Under strain, the fixings to one stack of shelves came adrift and the whole lot collapsed, smashing several hundred pounds worth of art pottery. The architect was not to know. Educated only in the design of new buildings, all his training told him solid floors were made of reinforced concrete. He had no knowledge of "hollow pot" or "filler joist" construction from which pre-war commercial buildings were commonly constructed and which have very limited capacity to support suspended loads. But his client was left with the clear impression that, although architects might have good ideas, they were useless at practical problems.

There is no doubt that this young architect was talented. Undismayed by this initial setback, his supreme confidence in his own ability led him to international success as a designer. Most are not so lucky. Emerging from five years' hard graft, having demonstrated their ability to design the equivalent of Sydney Opera House, the requirements of general practice bring them down to Earth with a bump. Society provides few opportunities to design grandiose new buildings. If young architects entering practice are to succeed, they need to learn from scratch the rudiments of traditional construction and work to existing buildings, not to mention conducting surveys, specification writing, estimating and a host of interpersonal skills. All of these things are crucial to the great majority of general practice but are barely mentioned in their long, but other-worldly, academic training

The community agenda

In the practice of community architecture, many of the key principles overlap with the requirements of good general practice. Just as academic education has passed over the skills required for general practice, it has similarly ignored the community agenda. Rod Hackney has criticized architectural education in terms very similar to those of Brian Avery. At one time Hackney considered setting up his own programme, providing practical experience and academic training in equal measures. On completion of three years, trainees would graduate with a Certificate in Community Architecture, which Hackney considers would have more practical value than a degree from an architectural school.[9] It would be true to the spirit of community architecture to set up alternative organizations outside the establishment. But such enterprises are enormously difficult and most effort has been devoted to trying to influence the content of the architectural courses.

In 1992 the RIBA Community Architecture Group set up an Education Subgroup under the leadership of Bob Fowles from the Cardiff School of Architecture. This group has tried to establish links between schools and community architecture practices in an attempt to incorporate participatory design into student syllabuses. The initiative also has the active support of the Association of Community Technical Aid Centres. Part of the aim is to persuade schools to provide introductory course on community architecture and to encourage the teaching of participation techniques. Its main objective, though, is to generate more "live" projects. Many have seen the promotion of live projects as a means of bringing realism to the academic world and at the same time creating supportive links in the local community.

Instead of working to fantasy briefs and imaginary sites in their studio projects, students would be put in touch with a community group wanting to improve its premises

189

or build new; or with a tenants' association looking for comprehensive improvement to their estate. From the local group the students would get a real brief and a real site or buildings on which to base their designs. They are put in touch with ordinary building users, who have an opportunity to influence the designs and to comment critically on the finished product. The process has mutual benefits. For the students there is the much-needed context of the reality of an urban site and an opportunity to hear the views of building users, and come to understand their needs and concerns. For the community groups, who usually lack the resources to pay an architect, the students are a free resource and the designs they produce can be used to promote and seek funding for their projects.

The concept is not without pitfalls, and in the rarefied atmosphere of the schools the intrusion of reality can easily be deflected. In 1986 students at the Architectural Association worked on a project for the improvement of the Castlemilk estate in Glasgow. Quite why a London school should choose a community project in Glasgow is unclear, especially with so many deprived areas on its doorstep. The choice would have involved an expensive field trip, and the opportunity for the students to understand the area and the concerns of its residents must have been strictly limited. Using what information they could gather, two groups of students worked up alternative ideas for the improvement. The first group decided to demolish the estate and designed replacement housing. The second group opted for refurbishment, but the adaptations they proposed were so elaborate and far reaching that it would actually have been cheaper to redevelop. Tenants' representatives, ferried to London for the crit, expressed bewilderment and disappointment at the result, which did nothing to address their real problems and took them no further forwards in their efforts to improve their environment.

Nevertheless, properly conceived and supervised, the live project is a useful vehicle for bringing students face to face with reality and providing support for community groups. The concept is by no means new. It was used by the American CDCs in the 1960s and the Assist unit at Strathclyde was a notable success. A survey in 1977 showed several schools with some community involvement, but only five of the 38 schools carried out "community design" live projects and these were generally the smaller, more independent schools. It was noted, with regret, that "Large schools in metropolitan centres with severe environmental and social problems were generally among the least active".[10] The metropolitan schools were missing a real opportunity to develop community links and to use the surrounding physical and social environment as a positive input into the education of their students. Unfortunately the situation was no better 15 years later. Still, only a handful of schools carried out live community projects, notably Hull and Cardiff. Elsewhere, community architecture was tentatively promoted, notes Bob Fowles ". . . [by] an enthusiastic individual tutor in a generally unsupportive environment."[11]

After more than 20 years' practice of community architecture it is disappointing, and somewhat mystifying, that the educational establishment is still so unsupportive. Some blame the class base. Most architectural students are drawn from privileged upper middle-class families. Such people generally have little understanding, and less interest, in social issues, and they commonly propel their children towards careers in the creative arts and media. Feminists might offer an alternative explanation. The architectural profession is 91 per cent male[12] and is far more male dominated than most other professions. It is possible that male interests in technical problems and in

190

self-aggrandizement by building large structures might be leavened by the more feminine virtues of caring, service and sociability. One of the key problems is the narrow perspective of the educational establishment. Many lecturers have spent years in the system. Some, through nepotistic preferment, have graduated straight into teaching in their old schools. They perpetuate established values and appoint fellows in their own image. Most are wedded to the cause of Art and have little comprehension of the real world of practice. To this educational elite, closeted in their permanent ivory towers, community architecture is a peripheral interest. Besides, it is dull, mundane, and is well known to be "anti–design". In fact, user participation has far-reaching implications for design and might be more appreciated if these were better understood.

Design and community architecture

Community architecture is essentially small scale. Small new buildings or modest adaptations of old ones do not offer the excitement of grand new public buildings. But they are the real world of practice. They respond to popular needs and command public support. For this reason alone community architecture deserves greater attention. The idea that it is "anti–design" stems partly from the discredited notion that the architect's design skills are usurped by user control, partly from the concentration on process. The process of involving users in design is key to community architecture. Generally, its merits have been promoted almost exclusively in these terms. So important are the attitudes and techniques of user participation – so radically different from convention – that the concentration on process has been both necessary and understandable. So complete has been this concentration that it has left little room for discussion of the implications for design theory.

Where it is discussed, it is quickly passed over. Nick Wates and Charles Knevitt state simply that community architecture is "Unselfconscious about style. Any style may be adopted as appropriate. Most likely to be 'contextual', 'regional' (place specific) with concern for identity. Loose and sometimes exuberant. Often highly decorative, using local artists".[13] "Any style" begs the question of what styles are "appropriate". Some are more user friendly than others. The deepest and most fundamental division in the debates about architectural style are between the "formal" and the "informal". Formal styles are based on rules of design and the use of materials, and fundamental concepts of form, design and approach. Informal styles, although generally based around an underlying philosophy, have a much freer approach to planning, the design of space, and the use of elements of construction. Formalism subjugates user needs to the rigidities of style. Informal approaches allow the predominance of function and the expression of user preferences in design.

The conflict between formal and informal styles is a controversy that runs deep. In the nineteenth century it was at the root of the battle between classical and Gothic. Classical architecture developed over centuries into the most formal of all styles. Its rules of axis and symmetry governed both urban design and the planning of buildings, and resulted in such rigidities as staircases needlessly duplicated either side of a central axis, and rooms of equal size balanced around a central space regardless of function. Its rules of proportion governed the design of facades, so that windows were designed to

191

fit a pattern rather than to provide light, air or views out where they were needed. The three "orders" governed the design of details and the use of materials, and imposed a universal conformity that suppressed local traditions. Its rigid rules made it the supreme expression of order, and in the nineteenth century it was the predominant style of public and government buildings in both Europe and the USA. It symbolized the authority of the state and the regulation provided by government. It is no co-incidence that, in the twentieth century, it became the favoured style of both Hitler and Stalin.

The Victorian critic John Ruskin thought classical architecture was the "architecture of slavery". He and Pugin praised and promoted the variety and the relative informality of Gothic architecture and ornament. There was also a nationalist element. Classical architecture was considered a foreign imposition, unsympathetic to English tradition; unsuited in its form and materials to the British climate.[14] It was this line of thought that led to the foundation of the Arts and Crafts movement. In general, Arts and Crafts architects avoided the symmetry and rigidity of the classical plan-making utility, and function the generator of building layout. In their use of materials and design elements, they were eclectic, drawing on the range of traditional elements of vernacular architecture.

In the twentieth century it was modernism that challenged for supremacy. Despite its bitter opposition to classicism, it was in fact drawn from the same roots, harking back to the simplicity of ancient Greek architecture and seeking the fundamentalism of "pure forms". Mainstream modernism also developed the same preoccupations, the overall shape determined by a pure concept rather than derived from function, rigid rules determining the use of materials and building elements, order derived from mechanization and repetition. In its turn, modernism was also criticized for its alien nature and unsuitability for the British environment. Its successors, high tech and post-modernism drawing, as they do, on the modernist and classical legacy are similarly constrained by a formalist approach to design.

Given that most established styles are hidebound by formalist preconceptions, most are not, in fact, appropriate to community architecture, which places a premium on function and user preference. It is unsurprising that, in the main, community architecture revived the principles of the Arts and Crafts movement. As in that movement, buildings have been planned in an informal manner relating the their function; the existing environment has been respected with buildings designed or improved in a "contextual" manner. Like the Arts and Crafts architects, community architecture has been willing to draw pragmatically on a wide range of design elements. Theoretically these can be selected from any style, but generally the elements of design have been taken from traditional influences.

Architecture as a craft

The theory of style and preconception are central to the perception of architecture as an art. The shape of the building is determined by the "concept" – buildings conceived as boxes or tubes; a cathedral conceived as a "crown of thorns"; house elevations designed as faces. Perhaps the most banal example is the NatWest tower in the City of London, the plan of which was apparently derived from the bank's logo. Concepts are placed before use and they often constrain or deny the functional requirements of a building. In reorientating design for the benefit of users, it is perhaps more useful to regard architecture as a craft. Resolving a multitude of functional, environmental and regulatory requirements are a difficult enough task without aspiring to be an artist as well. Released from the pretension of being an artist, the architect is free to concentrate on the essential craft-skill of design. But freedom has its penalties as well. Without the certainties of the rules of style and the simplicity of the concept approach, design become a more demanding and, in some ways, more difficult process.

The essential approach of community architecture is that. through communication with users, the functional requirements of a building can be determined with some accuracy and in considerable detail. The designer is expected to understand the regulations and to command the skills to design in response to the environment: the demands of orientation, weather proofing and energy conservation, and a sympathetic response to the surrounding buildings. The designer must also understand the requirements of structural stability and sound construction. Resolving this multitude of requirements, without formality or preconception, is essentially a problem-solving exercise. Periodically, the evolving design, must be put forward for evaluation by the users to ensure it is working to their requirements: a multi-stage process of criticism, feedback and analysis from which the final solution evolves. In the process of problem solving, there will inevitably be some decisions that are arbitrary or peripheral. It is perfectly reasonable that the users themselves should take such decisions. As a result, elements of the finished building will be an expression of their choice and identity. Far from being anti-design, user participation frees up the design process and, properly applied, results in more appropriate buildings, more sensitively designed, and expressing a greater diversity of personal taste and cultural identity.

Participation without users

The practice of community architecture in Britain has centred on the development of new relationships with users and involving them in the design process. It is of peripheral interest, it is commonly argued, because for most building projects the future users are not known and cannot be identified. There are several counters to this objection. First, community architecture grew out of popular rejection of large-scale projects. Part of its aim is to encourage smaller-scale developments centred on user demands and needs and carried out with their participation. Secondly, even if the users cannot be identified, it is often possible to identify a similar organization or interest group to participate in the project – much as the local pensioners group was involved in the Palace Gates sheltered housing scheme. Thirdly, participation has now become the norm in the British planning system. Local residents are routinely invited to comment on planning applications, and this has given communities greater influence in their local environment. There is now considerable experience of neighbourhood planning, and its wider practice could positively involve local people in the overall nature and form of new developments.

Finally, more contact with users and greater awareness of their needs will generate a user-orientated approach to the design of new buildings, even where the users are not directly involved. User-orientated design has been a minority interest in British architecture. In continental Europe, where social architecture developed differently, it has acquired a more central role in mainstream architecture. Northern Europe was

193

the birthplace of the modernist movement. In its early days, modernism generated a great deal of discussion and produced a range of different ideas. The mainstream developed around the formalism of the International style and it was the mainstream that prospered in Britain. A minority stream, which was more socially orientated and more informal, developed around the ideas of Bruno Taut and others in the radical atmosphere of 1920s Berlin. It is to this stream that the approach of Ralph Erskine belongs, with its emphasis on the importance of local culture, environment and user participation in building design. It also generated two other lines of development, which place the interests of users at the focus of building design without seeking their active participation.

"The New Building"

"The New Building" was a term coined by Hugo Häring, who was at the centre of the early modernist debates and was a determined opponent of the International style and the ideas of Le Corbusier and Mies van de Rohe. Häring believed that the shape of a building should be completely derived from the various functions it has to perform. Form should be allowed to grow in response to function, instead of being imposed through formalist geometry and stylistic rules. Häring died in the late 1930s with very few buildings to his credit, but his ideas were developed by his close colleague Hans Sharoun. Sharoun was prolific and highly successful. During the 1920s and early 1930s, he built several social projects: schools, housing and public buildings. After the war he became one of West Germany's leading architects and was responsible for the design of the Berlin Philharmonic Hall and the massive State Library.

Sharoun's approach to each building project was to analyze, in the greatest possible detail, the functional requirements – whether those of use, environment or construction. In the process of design he sought to resolve and satisfy these functional requirements as precisely as possible and with the least possible formality. This results in organic planning and the creation of spaces of enormous complexity and variety. In the use of materials and building elements he was eclectic, using both traditional and modernist construction.[15] Despite his status in Germany, Sharoun is undervalued in Britain, partly because his pragmatic approach did not produce a consistent and recognizable "style", partly because his work cannot be effectively represented by illustrations, but must be experienced to be appreciated. Greater study of his work and his methods would offers, an important contribution to the cause of designing buildings for the benefit of use.

"Structuralism"

The minority modernist stream also developed through the work of the Dutch architect Aldo van Eyck and the journal *Forum*. It was from these roots that John Habraken developed the ideas expressed in *Supports* and which formed the basis of the work of SAR. Habraken's original idea was that only serviced shells would be built – *structure* – which would later be fitted out and completed by the users – *infil* (see Ch. 3). The architect Herman Hertzberger developed this basic idea somewhat differently. Hertzberger's buildings are complete, rather than half-finished shells, but they are designed in such a way that the spaces within them can be adapted and used in several different ways in accordance with the needs and choices of their occupants. The term "structuralism" was later borrowed from ideas developed in anthropology and literature to describe an adaptable architecture, which provided a basic formal structure that was open to a variety of interpretations by its users.[16]

This approach is most clearly demonstrated in Hertzberger's Diagoon houses (1971) and his most celebrated building: the Centraal Beheer complex at Apeldoorn (1972). The Diagoon houses are, on the face of it, a modernist development of one- and two-storey terraced houses. But the design allows horizontal and vertical subdivision in a variety of ways. Some spaces can be external or enclosed as part of the interior giving a degree of "extendibility" to meet changing needs.[17] Centraal Beheer is a massive office complex. It is designed on a "tartan" grid to create a basic structure, which gives overall order to the building and provides all parts with services, light, air and access. The grid creates many relatively small spaces, which can be used in various ways, adapted and re-adapted to suit the developing needs of a large organization.[18] Hertzberger's approach has been described as participatory. It does not, as in community architecture, involve the users in the design process before construction. It is *post hoc* participation, allowing the users to modify and adapt the completed buildings to suit their taste and requirements.

The aim of creating adaptable buildings may seem superficially similar to the standard modernist approach to speculative commercial buildings, where large open serviced floor-spaces were created to allow flexible partitioning in a variety of ways. This simply creates standardized monotony where, even when subdivided, all the spaces are almost exactly the same. Hertzberger's approach is to create spaces that vary in scale, shape and size and in their relationship with each other, so that users are offered variety and genuine choice. Like Sharoun, Hertzberger is eclectic in his use of materials and building methods, selecting those most appropriate to any particular project. The approach of both architects, each, in their different ways, making use and function the prime objects of design, precludes formalist dogma and the development of a personal recognizable style,

An integrated approach to education

The current system of professional education is based on narrow perceptions that largely ignore the primacy of utility and social service and the approaches necessary to achieve these aims. The system produces architects who are drawn from an exclusive social base, whose primary motivation is their desire to fulfil themselves by the creation of large new buildings that reflect their personal philosophy of design. Through the five long years they have spent learning their art, they have been trained to consider themselves superior to others who are untrained in design. What is true of architects is hardly less true of landscape architects and interior designers. Although these professions are less male dominated, their training inculcates similarly grandiose ambitions and an exclusive view of their expertise in their chosen field of design. To these design elites, planners, engineers and surveyors who are untrained in the art of design, have no worthwhile contribution to make; still less Joe Public, who has even less comprehension of the heady world of artistic creation.

These narrow and fragmenting preoccupations, the self-regarding arrogance of the design professions, is inimical to the principles of community architecture. These emphasize openness, co-operation, and the integration of a wide range of skills in the interests of users and the wider community. In many ways, the services offered by community architecture are similar to those offered by many small, locally based private practices. True, private practices work for relatively wealthy individuals who can afford to pay, rather than groups of the relatively poor who can't. There is also less emphasis on participation in the design process. But in the concentration on small projects, on work to existing buildings, on traditional construction and, above all, on satisfying user requirements, there is a marked similarity. Education has not only failed community architecture, it has failed to provide for the predominant concerns of professional practice. In producing graduates who are ill equipped to practice it has neither served the interests of the profession nor those of the public.

Brian Avery proposes reversing the priorities of education, putting practice before theory, pragmatism before art: "A degree course in general practice could qualify us all, after an apprenticeship in practice, to administer a contract run a practice and to design and detail small works and refurbishments simply, economically and well".[19] Indeed it could, and, if the architectural profession does not move rapidly and determinedly in such a direction, it will find itself outflanked and made redundant by competition. Such general-practice skills are the stock in trade of building surveyors. Their training provides them with skills in repair and maintenance, contract management, basic services and structural design and, on top of that, estimating and valuation skills. They are not trained in building design, but many have acquired, through experience, the necessary competence to produce good design solutions for small works and refurbishment projects. Neither are they trained in participation techniques or social issues, but, in this, they are no more handicapped than the great majority of architectural graduates.

Avery's proposed course would serve many of the needs of community architecture. But ideally a redesigned degree course should be orientated to integrating the design professions by providing a common foundation. It should certainly be dedicated to good general practice on the lines Avery suggests. It should also include the basics of sociology, urban history, town planning, landscape, interior design and the techniques of participation. Graduates would be fit to enter small-scale practice, whether as community architects or working for private clients. Or they could become professional clients in estate management, bringing to that sphere greater understanding of the design process. Those wishing to specialize could go on to postgraduate courses in town planning, conservation, engineering or in the design of large and complex projects. A degree in architecture revamped in such a manner would be seen as providing training of eminently practical value, rather than as a stepping stone to specialization of an increasingly complex and largely irrelevant nature.

Moving in such a direction requires not just a broader attitude towards design but a more liberal view of the role and interrelationship of the building industry professions. Such a view is wholly contrary to the increasing specialization through which the professions have defined and protected their separate roles. Integration, and the co-operation it requires, flies in the face of the entrenched attitudes of the professions and the narrow perceptions that divide them from within. If it happens at all, it will not come about without conflict. Community action was contentious because it challenged established attitudes and, for the same reasons, community architecture has had to struggle for recognition. That struggle, and the controversy surrounding it, is essentially political in the broadest sense.

196

References

1. Peter Bate, "Town planning education – as it was then", *The Planner* (April 1993), 25.
2. Information and examples substantiated by an education special issue of *The Architects' Journal* (20 March 1991).
3. Tom Woolley, "Why studio?", *The Architects' Journal* (20 March 1991), 46.
4. Quoted from information material issued in 1993 by the University of Bath School of Architecture and Engineering and by Brighton Polytechnic School of Architecture and Interior Design
5. Roderick Gradidge, "Pupils or students: for pupillage?", *The Architects' Journal* (15 December 1990), 26.
6. Peter Davey, *Architecture of the arts and crafts movement – the search for Earthly Paradise* (London: The Architectural Press, 1980).
7. Letter from Quinlan Terry, *The Architects' Journal* (12 December 1990), 22.
8. Brian Avery, "Deeply flawed", *Building Design* (26 June 1992), 18.
9. Nick Wates, "The Hackney phenomenon", *The Architects' Journal* (20 February 1985), 47.
10. John Hurley & Gerry Metcalfe, "Appropriate education", *The Architects' Journal* (19 October 1977), 762.
11. Bob Fowles, "Where are the people?", *Building Design* (10 April 1992), 18.
12. Annual Report 1992/93 Architects' Registration Council of the United Kingdom
13. Nick Wates & Charles Knevitt, *Community architecture* (London: Penguin, 1987), 25.
14. For an illuminating discussion of this debate, see Peter Blundell Jones, *Hans Sharoun – a monograph* (London: Gordon Fraser, 1978), 87ff.
15. Ibid.
16. Arnuf Luchinger, *Herman Herzberger* (The Hague: Nederland Arch-Edition, 1987), 9.
17. Ibid., p. 72 ff. See also Richard Hatch (ed.), *The scope of social architecture* (New York: Van Nostrand Reinhold, 1984),12 ff.
18. Ibid., 87 ff.
19. Brian Avery, op. cit.

CASE STUDY
Lambeth Community Care Centre: a new-build health centre

The National Health Service was another powerful bureaucracy set up by the Welfare State. Unlike local government, its structure did not even possess the semblance of democratic accountability at community level. Most development decisions were taken on a strategic level, generally governed by technical and managerial objectives. It was to redress the imbalance created by a very centralized structure that Community Health Councils were set up during the 1970s. Lambeth's CHC proved to be exceptionally vigorous in its role of protector of the community interest. When, in 1975, the NHS proposed the closure of the local hospital, the CHC mounted an energetic local campaign, not to prevent the closure but to put something better in its place. Local residents and health workers (GPs, district nurses and the like) were mobilized into an action group to plan a new type of health facility that would act as bridge between general practice and the large modern hospital.

The Community Care Centre was conceived much like the rural cottage hospitals. It would provide out-patient treatment of a more specialized nature that GPs could offer. At the same time it would provide beds for those needing short periods of care but who were not in need of major surgery or expensive treatment. And it would provide these services within easy reach of patients' homes. The Lambeth Centre was not intended to be a one-off project. The Action Committee was fired by the ideal of creating a new type of building that would be widely replicated – a model for a new, decentralized Health Service. Such an idea was deeply threatening to the pyramid of power within the NHS. The management hierarchy became strongly opposed to the new venture and refused to finance it. This might well have killed the project stone dead, but the support of the local Council was obtained and a successful application was made for funding under the Urban Partnership Programme.

Financial backing was achieved only after several years of promotion and lobbying. During this time, the Action Committee had developed a detailed brief for their new centre that evolved over a long series of open meetings and intensive discussion. At the end they had a comprehensive schedule of accommodation and the image of a building that would be more domestic in character than a conventional hospital and which would avoid compartmentation into separate specialisms. Armed with a detailed concept, and the money to build it, they began to look for an architect. They wanted a practice that would be sympathetic to their democratic ideals and was itself small enough not to be divided into specialist departments. They settled on Ted Cullinan's practice, which had been founded on the principles of

co-operation and democratic management.

Once a site had been selected and secured, the architects began to meet with the project team of 15 GPs, local representatives, nurses, therapists and an NHS works officer and administrator. At first the meetings were all talk, as the designers sought to take in the collective view of their many-headed client. In September 1981 the architects produced their first plan. This was for a two-storey building with a flat roof that would fill the street frontage and allow a large south-facing garden behind. It was a very formal concept, symmetrically planned around the axis of the main entrance and staircase. It was not met with applause. The project team strongly criticized the separation of functions, which they blamed on the rigid symmetry, They did not like the separate zoning and the long narrow corridors it produced. Corridors, they felt should be wide and open, encouraging loitering and the sociability of chance meetings. To his credit, Ted Cullinan took all this on board. At the end of the meeting he re-drew the plan on a much more informal basis.

That sketch, the architect's reply to just criticism, became the basis of the second scheme. This time the project team responded more warmly and the main principles were agreed. Over the next 2½ months a series of individual meetings were organized with the health specialists to assess their detailed requirements and to refine the scheme to meet their needs. A key change resulted from the meetings with the NHS works officer. He objected to flat roofs

The first scheme – a formal symmetrical plan based on standard concepts of zoning and specialization – was firmly rejected by the user group.

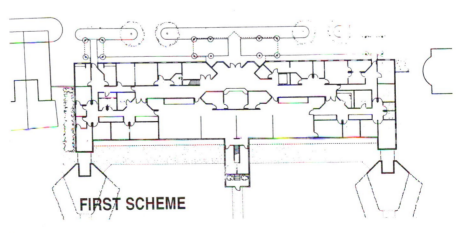

FIRST SCHEME

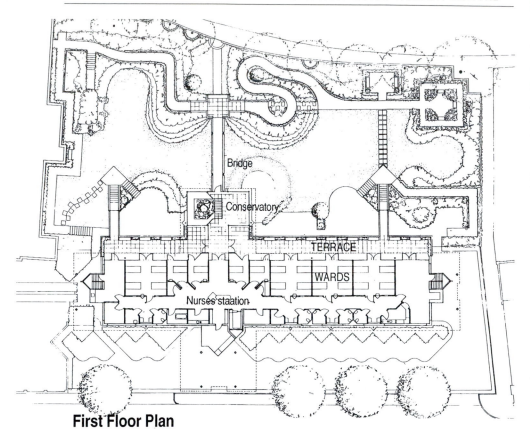

First Floor Plan

In the final scheme, wards for in-patients are concentrated on the first floor. The ground floor contains day-rooms, offices, rooms for physio- and occupational therapy, and for chiropodist, dentist, hairdresser, speech therapist and social workers

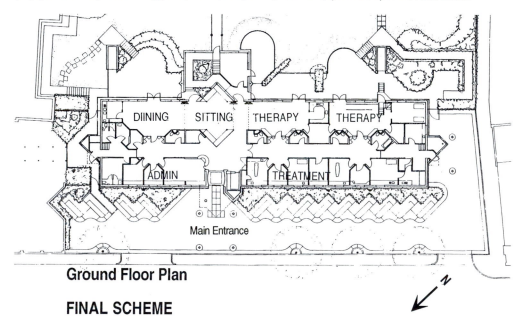

Ground Floor Plan

FINAL SCHEME

200

Main entrance. The arrival of ambulances and patients can be observed from the window to the nurses' office on the first floor – nick-named "the crow's nest".

down to the door handles and the light fittings, was discussed with the project team. It seems clear that throughout this process the clients' role was that of customer and critic, whereas the design initiative was always with the architects. The client team knew what spaces they wanted and how they should work, but the final form of the building is the result of the architects' response to these demands and their resolution in the detailed design, construction and materials. Only in the layout of the garden did the clients appear to have clear design ideas of their own. Several were keen gardeners and were not impressed with the flat lawns the architects first proposed. Paradoxically, although they had criticized the rigid symmetry of the first building proposal, they liked the idea of a formal garden. The landscape design finally agreed was a compromise, with an informal path snaking through a series of formal elements.

At the end of the day the key question is: Does the building work better? Was all the argument and extra work worthwhile? Jules Lubbock sought the views of staff and patients: ". . . the building not only assists therapy but is therapeutic in its own right. Its beauty and intricacy teases one to explore and encourages patients to walk and become independent. . . . The building also supports patients. There is none of the depersonalization of waiting in dreary corridors. . . . People talked of 'feeling safe here' . . . Staff find the place makes stressful work more relaxing. They appreciate how different it is from most health buildings with their windowless rooms and fluorescent light. The staff have views from their offices on to the internal [corridor], the garden and the street outside. They are not departmentalized – hence patients are not depersonalized – and they cannot hide behind their desks . . . . So is it a dream come true? Almost. There are a few teething problems but they are so trivial I refuse to mention them."[1]

Eight years on, the building still looked good and worked well, although a storage problem was developing, particularly with the mountain of paper files demanded by NHS bureaucracy. Sadly, it remains a one-off project, although one that has attracted

on maintenance grounds. At the same time, it became evident that good cross ventilation would greatly improve environmental quality. These concerns stimulated a new roof design based on double pitches that provide high-level lighting and ventilation to the wards on the upper floor. Over a period of seven months the design evolved through three further schemes. this was partly because of cost problems, but essentially it was a result of the dialogue between the user/clients and the designers. In response to criticism, the architects revised their proposals and developed new ideas to resolve the users' requirements that were being defined in greater and greater detail. Each revised scheme was subjected to further criticism from the user group – and further revision – until a solution was eventually reached with which everyone was satisfied.

Design participation was not restricted to the overall scheme. Over the course of design development, practically every detail,

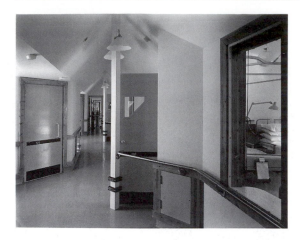

The client group wanted wide corridors that would encourage chance meetings and give the centre a sociable atmosphere.

widespread interest and admiration. It is to hoped it will eventually be emulated in other urban communities.

The Lambeth Community Care Centre is a vivid illustration of the potential of participatory design and of how it can produce results that are quite different from the conventional design process. Normally, the architect would be given an accommodation schedule and a technical brief and would go away and produce a design. In the conven-

tional process, design would probably have stopped at stage one. Cullinan's initial proposal based on formality and preconception would, with minor modification, have become the final design. The influence of user-clients generated a radically different approach to the layout of the whole building. Their detailed criticism and demands also stimulated the architects into producing new ideas, and new approaches to solve the problems defined, which enriched the final

The Wards face south-west, overlooking the garden and adjoining a terrace where patients can sit out in fine weather.

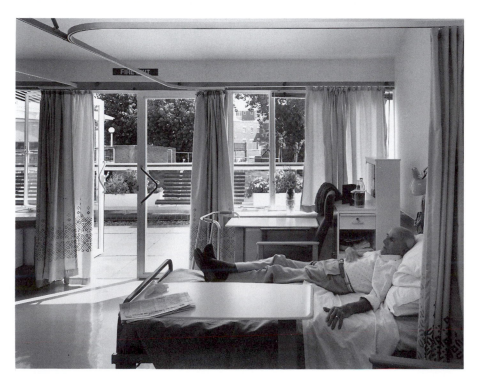

At the back of the building, a conservatory links the wards with a bridge that leads to the raised garden. For the ground floor rooms there are outdoor patios linked by steps to the garden above.

solution as the process of discussion and refinement progressed. Of course, all this extra discussion cost time and money but, in the cause of producing a building better fitted for its purpose, it was a price well worth paying. The finished project is not just a model of participatory design but a striking demonstration that community architecture is not limited to small-scale and relatively simple design problems. Its principles can also be applied, with great success, to relatively large new buildings of considerable technical complexity.

References

1. Jules Lubbock, "A patient revolution", *The Architects' Journal* (16 October 1985), 63 ff. See also Jules Lubbock, "Place of healing", *New Statesman* (1 November 1985), 36–7.

CHAPTER 9

Left, Right and Centre

THE POLITICS OF COMMUNITY ARCHITECTURE

Community architecture has attracted support from all parts of the political spectrum. Politicians from the Conservative, Labour and Liberal Parties – when in power at local level – have supported and promoted various community-based initiatives. As a result community architecture is sometimes presented as a universal panacea, transcending politics and party. At the same time, it has encountered almost equally widespread resistance from the professional and local government establishment, and from entrenched political attitudes. This apparent paradox can be explained only by a recognition that the political nature of community politics, and the architecture it spawned, lies outside the traditional divide between Left and Right. For too long, the world was polarized between the ideological certainties of capitalism and communism, free market and State, individual and society. A political world divided so, could recognize only black and white, "us" and "them". Any alternative, any attempt at neutrality, was dismissed from the one side as "neo-capitalist" or from the other as "crypto-communist".

Co-operation has long since excited such controversy and, in the ideological squeeze, condemnation from both sides. Community architecture offered a range of co-operative endeavour covering a broad spectrum from self-build at one end to the egalitarian collective at the other. Such a spectrum, when interpreted from the perspective of political orthodoxy, offered elements that could appeal to almost any ideological hue. Equally, when it threatened vested interests, a peg could always be found on which to hang a denunciation. For a time, during the 1980s, the interpretation of community architecture in conventional political terms created controversy and division within the movement. Now, in the more open atmosphere that follows the end of the Cold War, it may be possible to reassess its political significance. The differences between the various strands of community architecture offer endless nourishment for dispute. But if the similarities are emphasized, it can be recognized as a distinctive and broad-ranging movement that has much to offer in the never-ending search for urban solutions.

The third way

The ideological divide that has characterized much of this century has its roots, like much else, in the nineteenth century. It was from an analysis of early industrialization in Britain that Smith and Ricardo drew their theory of the market economy, and

Marx and Engels created their radically different model. Whereas Adam Smith sought social justice through the mechanism of perfect competition, Karl Marx saw equity only in the planned economy. In co-operation Robert Owen saw a third possibility. While promoting the social merits of co-operation, though, nothing in the writings of Owen or William Morris could elevate it into a macroeconomic model. Lacking a grand design of political economy, co-operation was squeezed in the clash of the Titans – Marxism versus The Market – and was reduced to a political undercurrent. By the mid-twentieth century, however, both grand designs had failed to deliver the promised land, and disillusionment had set in.

In Eastern Europe, the failings of the Marxist model were only too evident. Communism delivered good education, health provision and public services. But public order and a high degree of fairness were achieved at the cost of political repression, the loss of economic liberty and the right to local self-determination. The struggle for these rights was at the heart of the Prague Spring of 1968. For their pains, Alexander Dubcek and his fellow rebels were dismissed, by Marxist orthodoxy, as "counter-revolutionaries" and "capitalist-roaders", and were forcibly removed from power. In truth, it was not capitalism they had sought, but a third way that combined the equity of socialism with the liberty of locally based political and economic democracy. Although it failed, the Prague Spring began the search for "the third way" – an alternative to the extremes that characterized the prevailing ideologies.

Meanwhile, in the West of the late 1960s, there was considerable disillusion with The Market. Capitalism was, then, at its most successful. It had produced high growth and low unemployment. Yet it had failed to deliver "perfect competition" and the social equity and "consumer sovereignty" it promised. Instead it had produced gross inequalities and failed to provide for the worst-off in society. It was this failure that had led, in the advanced Western economies, to social provision from the public purse. The Welfare State was itself organized on a bureaucratic model that was not dissimilar to the State socialism of eastern Europe, although with the nominal sanction of democracy. Disillusion with remote and insensitive large organizations was matched by a distaste for the morality of capitalism, which emphasized greed, individualism and cut-throat competition. Ideologically, what was offered was a choice between the self-seeking individual and "the group". In the Welfare State "the group" meant society as whole, with universal egalitarian benefits delivered paternalistically from the centre. But perhaps "the group" could be more than the individual but less than a whole nation – a community small enough to be self-identified and democratically managed. It was this aim that led many into community action.

The mainstream

Community action was a popular response to the destructive impact on urban communities of the combined efforts of the social State and the powerful demands of private capital. Those involved sought alternatives to the old order. Organizationally, they revived the co-operative model, on a small scale, and breathed new life into an old form. Politically they were motivated by a perceived failure of the democratic system. At that time national government alternated between the two large parties: Conservatives, generally perceived as representing the interest of large-scale capital; Labour, the party of the large trade unions, which had developed in reactive response to growth of large private companies. Both parties supported the powerful organs of the Welfare State, although perhaps for different reasons. "Democracy" was conceived solely in terms of elections. The active participation of the average citizen was restricted to the right to place a cross on a piece of paper every few years.

Once elected, government made the decisions, whether at national or local level. This restricted concept of democracy has been described as "elective dictatorship" by no less a person than the Conservative Lord Chancellor, Lord Hailsham. The remoteness of the elective dictatorship put government in hock to powerful vested interests. Denied an active voice, the interests and views of ordinary citizens were ignored, both in the places where they worked and the communities in which they lived. What community action sought, what it demanded in its campaigns, was a more active part in the relatively local and small-scale decisions that affected everyday life. As Peter Hain put it in 1976, "Advocates of community politics seek to create a participatory democracy – one based on a series of self-managed communities through which people can control the decisions which affect them: Power would be exercised from the bottom upwards and resources would be co-operatively owned. Ideologically, participatory democrats wish to use the egalitarianism of socialism to underpin a libertarian ethos that rejects all forms of hierarchical organization".[1]

It was a radical approach and its burgeoning success was to create considerable strains in the body politic. The activists, although sharing a common analysis, were by no means united in their political goals. The mainstream was a loose coalition that included liberals, libertarian socialists, anarchists and others. Some saw the development of participatory democracy as strengthening the effectiveness and purpose of government: decentralizing decision-making, directing resources to areas of greatest need and ensuring that money was spent in accordance with community need. Others sought to establish community organizations as self-governing co-operatives independent of the State structure. On a national or regional level these groups might organize on a "syndicalist" basis, creating umbrella organizations to co-ordinate information, training and advice for all their locally based member groups. No matter how strong the desire for independence, however, most groups remained dependent on State funding to a greater or lesser degree, particularly for the large-scale resources they needed for capital projects

The Marxist perspective

Within the community movement the influence of Marxists was quite strong, particularly in the early years. In their view of the urban process, Marxists drew heavily on the detailed analysis developed by Manuel Castells.[2] In Castells' view urban growth and development is all governed by the needs of capitalism. The key urban process is "the reproduction of labour power". The purpose of cities is to provide labour that capital can exploit to maximize its profits. Cities must reproduce labour not just in the literal sense of forming an environment for breeding. They must provide labour with the correct level of skills, education, health and aptitude. They must provide transport systems to bring labour to the workplace. They must also ensure social control and reasonable harmony by providing entertainments, diversions and safety valves to neutralize protests. Certain things capitalism cannot provide, but they are, nonetheless, necessary to maintain the system. Here the State must step in to provide housing, health, education and transport for the poor. The State acts on behalf of capital and it makes provision at the minimum necessary level.

This view of the State takes no account of the long tradition in Britain that had fought to make the State a benevolent provider of a high standard of social provision. Nonetheless, British Marxists adopted Castells' critique. For them community action was part of a class struggle and their degree of involvement had to be carefully gauged:

> "Community organising can establish groups which negate their own attacks on the State either by making good the State's failure to provide resources (by providing their own playgroups, community centres and so on) or by making bureaucracy more efficient as when they clarify some need through action which the State could never do (by campaigns for maintenance on estates, parent/teacher organizations etc.)".[3]

For Marxists, the key function of community action was to raise the political consciousness of the participants and, by seeking alliances with other community and trade union groups, to advance the workers' cause.

Independent socialist Jim Radford, veteran campaigner on squatting and homelessness, found the participation of Marxist groups negative and obstructive. They were ". . . profoundly conservative in their determination to avoid accepting responsibility for anything other than their frequent manifestos."[4] Where they were actively involved, Marxists made demanding preconditions, insisting that the groups they supported had authentic working-class credentials and refusing to do anything that would foster the power or prestige of the State. At the same time they consistently failed to define any real alternative to the more positive strategy for community development pursued by mainstream activists. Although the analysis of Marxists was strong and exerted considerable influence, their prescription was weak.

The Right approach

Almost from the start, Conservatives had actively supported some community campaigns. Although the growth of local authority power had been succoured by Conservative governments, many Conservatives now took a different view of the large urban authorities which were largely controlled by their political opponents. Their view of the local State was in contra-position to that of the Marxists. Far from being an instrument of capitalism, urban local government was the very epitome of bureaucratic and paternalistic socialism. Any campaign that would blunt State interference, improve individual choice and the freedom of the market, was worthy of their support. On the positive side they were nourished by notions that stemmed from Victorian values. In his famous tract, *Self help*, Samuel Smiles wrote, in 1859 "Help from without is often enfeebling in its effects, but help from within invariably invigorates. Whatever is done for men or classes, to a certain extent, takes away the stimulus and necessity of doing it for themselves; and when men are subjected to over-guidance and over-government, the inevitable tendency is to render them comparatively helpless".[5]

For Smiles, self-help was almost entirely a matter of individual self-improvement. In many ways, the concept of people co-operating in a community initiative was contrary to the concept of individual responsibility, self-reliance and self-promotion that was the cornerstone of Conservative values. Nevertheless, self-help groups came to be seen as a worthy cause, creating independent organizations, and building facilities by their own efforts, freeing themselves from the baleful influence of the social State. At one and the same time they were perceived as a means of reducing the power of local government and, by providing for themselves, reducing the call on the public purse and the drain on national and local taxation.

Party lines

The explosion of activity that characterized the search for the third way invoked unlikely and uneasy alliances. It brought together strange bedfellows who, by the definitions of conventional politics, were ideologically irreconcilable. The lessons they drew from their forays into the arena of community politics were to have a considerable impact on the political establishment. Among the conventional parties, the Liberals provided the easiest target. During the 1960s the Liberal Party was the shell of a once-great governing party with minimal representation both at local and national level. In the politics of protest, which blossomed in the late 1960s, the Young Liberals had become a prominent and radical force. Their ideas clashed sharply with the coalition of small business and middle-class conscience which had sustained the party in the wilderness. For a time there was considerable conflict, but out of it emerged a new commitment to "community politics" which the party saw as a route to power at local level and a platform for national revival.

The Labour Party presented a tougher proposition. During much of the 1960s and 1970s it was the party of government. Its power rested on the support of the trade unions and the organs of the Welfare State that it had done so much to create. Many urban local authorities were under the control of Labour councillors in near perpetuity. Often these were the very authorities that had done so much damage to communities in the inner cities. Many of them were dominated by leading councillors who were prepared to exercise the powers conferred on them by election in the dictatorial manner of a private fiefdom. Yet the Labour party also contained a strong strain of non-conformism. It had long been allied with the old Co-operative movement and its political wing, the Co-operative Party, was affiliated within the party structure. During the 1970s this strain was joined by a new breed of local activist radicalized by community action. Power in the Labour Party became a target simply because the Party was itself the key to control at local level. In various parts of the country a struggle ensued between the entrenched Labour traditionalists and the new forces that sought to transform local government. Participatory democracy was central to this new force, but it based its appeal on a "rainbow coalition" of ethnic, cultural and special interest groups. It was the demands of these groups that gave rise to equal opportunities policies, some aspects of which were eagerly seized on by the popular press and dubbed "loony left", masking and trivializing the very real, and popular, changes that were taking place in the structure and exercise of local government power.

The play of the forces unleashed in the Liberal and Labour Parties by community action had some bizarre results, particularly in Liverpool. Formation of the Liverpool co-ops had had the active support of the Co-operative Party in the person of Harold Campbell, a leading member. Many of the members of the new co-ops were also members of the Labour party. At the same time, Liverpool was a major focus of the Liberals' new emphasis on community politics, a focus so successful they were able to gain control of the City Corporation. Once in power they put policy into practice in an extreme way, seeking to abandon the Corporation's provision of public housing entirely in favour of the development of housing co-ops. Meanwhile, conflict in the Liverpool Labour Party assumed the traditional struggle between right and left. In 1983 the Militant Tendency seized control of the Labour Party and with it the City Council. In a stark reversal of policy, Militant sought to destroy the co-ops and replace them with a massive programme of council housing. In the popular press Militant were tarred with the same brush as the "loony" Left. In point of fact they were the exact opposite. Militant were a hard-line Marxist group seeking to control the organs of the State, and exercise power, on behalf of the working class. To them, participatory democracy was an anathema. The strange conflict in Liverpool was extreme and largely negative, yet it is a perfect illustration of how the forces unleashed by community action created cross-currents that transcended the boundaries of traditional politics and defied the application of familiar labels.

Meanwhile, changes were taking place in the Conservative Party. By no stretch of the imagination can these changes be attributed to community action, but they were nonetheless radical. Under the leadership of Margaret Thatcher, the Conservatives abandoned the consensus of the centre ground in favour of a new emphasis on market forces. Whereas traditional Conservatives had supported the role of local authorities, the Thatcher Government saw them as a barrier to economic reform. The budgets of the large urban authorities became a particular target. They were perceived to consume too much of national income. Not only did they spend too much, they spent it inefficiently. One of the first acts of the new government was to devise a new funding formula that diverted central government funds from inner-city councils to rural and suburban authorities. This was soon followed by "capping", a restriction that deprived councils of their long-established right to determine the level of local taxation. This concerted attack on urban local government was, no doubt, assisted by the poor light that community action had cast on it. At the same time there was no sympathy for the reforms that activists sought to impose.

The conflict between community-orientated reform and government priority came to a head in the battle over the Greater London Council. The GLC was a large authority with a budget exceeding that of many nation States. Its support, after 1981, for community initiatives was just part of its policy platform. Sponsorship of community arts, popular music festivals and, in particular, its policy of cheap public transport were generating widespread public support despite sniping by the tabloid press. Too much support: in the view of the government the GLC was creating a popular alternative to its own policies for local government. It had to be destroyed. The GLC was abolished, leaving London the only world capital without its own government. The Thatcher Government created a new agenda in which local government was forced to retrench and re-examine its role. It was this new agenda that community architecture now had to address.

Friends in high places

With such diverse political parentage it was, perhaps, inevitable that different views of community architecture should develop. The divisions that characterized the late

1970s were to continue. In the architectural profession the proportion choosing to remain outside the RIBA rose steadily. By 1983 it had reached 20 per cent – a non-conformist proportion which has remained constant ever since.[6] Most of these architects worked in local government or in the expanding field of community technical aid. In the public sector, some were pursing the reforms that would provide better community service and ensure the participation of tenants and user groups in development projects. Those in technical aid were seeking a wider integration of building design beyond the narrow perceptions of a single professional interest. Within the RIBA – facing a relative decline in its membership – a minority sought to maintain an interest in the growing field of community architecture. They faced a continual struggle against an establishment that viewed community architecture as small-scale work demeaning the function of architects and challenging the traditional role of professional expertise.[7] The claims of community architecture received an unexpected boost from a turn of events that turned the inner cities from a target of expenditure cuts to the focus of major problems.

The Scarman Report

In the spring and summer of 1981 a series of violent and destructive riots swept through deprived inner urban areas. In Brixton and Southall (both in London), Toxteth (Liverpool), Moss Side (Manchester), and in several places in the West Midlands, young people, many of them from ethnic minorities, fought running battles with police, looting and burning on a large scale. While the Prime Minister dismissed the rioters as "criminals", the Home Secretary appointed a distinguished judge to investigate the "disorders" in Brixton. Lord Scarman might have focused solely on the issue of law and order, but he chose to interpret his brief much more widely. His report had much to say on the policing of inner urban areas, but it also looked closely at the implications for social policy. He found that little had changed since the *Inner area studies* a decade earlier. Brixton contained abnormal proportions of the low-paid and low-income families; high proportions of the elderly, of the very young, and of single parent families; a high incidence of mental illness and a concentration of the mentally and physically handicapped. Worse, ethnic minorities were disproportionately affected by these indices of deprivation.

Recognizing a link between social deprivation and crime, Scarman concluded: "The common strands in many of the major disorders . . . are to be found in shared social conditions, in economic insecurity and perceived deprivation, in enforced idleness because of unemployment, and in the hostility of at least a section of young people to the police." Although social conditions did not provide an excuse for disorder, arson and riot or the "grave criminal offences" that had occurred: "Sympathy for and understanding of, the plight of young black people . . . are good reason for political, social and economic aid, and for co-ordinated effort by government to provide it."[8]

Scarman chastised government for its failure to tackle inner-city decline over 30 years and highlighted the reluctance of the private sector – banks, building societies and private companies – to invest in urban regeneration. He called for projects to develop employment, social facilities and nursery education; for greater community participation in planning, in the provision of local services and in the development and management of housing and community projects; and for encouragement for the work of voluntary organizations.

210

Lord Scarman's report was largely ignored by the government, which had consistently refused to recognize the link between deprivation and crime. In any case, it was concerned with cutting urban expenditure, not with heeding calls for more. Nevertheless, at that time local authority budgets were still comparatively large and unfettered. Scarman's conclusions were influential with many urban authorities and there followed a period in which the aims of community architecture received much more recognition and support. There was more widespread experiment with decentralization of local government structures. More councils began to address the problems of their housing estates and to involve the tenants in their resolution. There was greater recognition and support for the new voluntary sector and the work of community technical aid. In Lord Scarman, the community movement found a major establishment figure who supported its claims. Three years later, support was to come from an even more exalted source in an intervention which, if not divine, at least came from the highest family in the land.

Enter the Prince

In May 1984 the RIBA organized a banquet at Hampton Court Palace to celebrate its 150th anniversary. The Prince of Wales was known to be interested in architecture and was invited to give a keynote speech. As the pillars of the architectural establishment enjoyed their sumptuous meal, they could have had little inkling of what was to come. Prince Charles promptly bit the hand that had fed him so lavishly with a wide-ranging attack on modern architecture. His speech is best known for its dismissal of the proposed National Gallery Extension as "a monstrous carbuncle on the face of a much loved and elegant friend" and much of it was devoted to criticism of the design of major public buildings. But he also criticized the way architects and planners had ". . . ignored the feelings and wishes of the mass of ordinary people" and destroyed extended family patterns and community life by insensitive housing redevelopment. He praised the development of community architecture and singled out Rod Hackney and Ted Cullinan as exemplars of the new approach.

The Prince of Wales's speech caused great consternation. Elaborate defences were mounted. Some sought to dismiss the Prince as an untutored amateur dabbling in deep waters. Others sought to deflect responsibility. The housing disasters of the 1960s were the fault of planners, councils, the funding system – anyone but the architects. Prince Charles has since written:

> It wasn't the local councillors, or the developers, who had read Le Corbusier and other apostles of modernism, and then persuaded reluctant architects to adopt "progressive" ideas. Architects deliberately staged a revolution within their own organization and their own system of education. It was the "great architects" of this period who convinced everyone that the world would be safe in their hands. Their descendants still retain prestige, and a kind of glamour among their peers; they set the style, control the curriculum, and have commanding positions in the Royal Institute of British Architects, the Royal Fine Arts Commission, and the Royal Academy. It is they who keep a tight grip on architectural education and who are the heroes of a largely sycophantic architectural press, and the focus of much uncritical attention from the media in general.[9]

211

This passage neatly sums up most of what is wrong with the established approach to building design. With the clear-sightedness of an outside observer, Prince Charles was able to give voice to a widespread public concern with the quality of the built environment. His support for community architecture is undoubtedly genuine and he has frequently lobbied for a more sensitive approach to development. But it is part of a wider interest in architecture. In his oft-expressed preference for the classical style, he seems unaware of the contradiction between its formality and the satisfaction of user needs. At the same time he has argued for a revival of interest in all the traditions of architecture, including the humble domestic: ". . . it is the responsibility of us all to ensure that the vernacular traditions of building continue to nourish us in our treatment of old buildings, and our designs for new ones."[9]

The selling of community architecture

The Prince of Wales' attack on the establishment in 1984 gave the proponents of community architecture in the RIBA a unique opportunity to promote their cause. Over the following months the Prince was ushered around a range of projects that were promoted as models of community architecture to the attendance of a great deal of publicity. This publicity campaign reached its peak in 1986. Buoyed by the gathering momentum of public promotion, Rod Hackney mounted a challenge to the establishment candidate for the presidency of the RIBA. In the autumn of that year he visited all the major party conferences to advocate community architecture as an extra-political approach to the continuing urban problems. The year culminated in the Building Communities Conference. Billed as the "First International Conference on Community Architecture, Planning and Design" it was presided over by Rod Hackney, on the verge of his election victory; chaired by Lord Scarman and addressed by the Prince of Wales, Michael Heseltine and senior government ministers.

Writing contemporaneously, Nick Wates and Charles Knevitt were almost ecstatic:

> A new era has been opened up in which the creativity of professionals can once again be directed towards enhancing the lives of the population as a whole. No-one will ever know whether this sea change could ever have been possible without the assistance and influence of the Prince of Wales . . . his recent outspoken and continuing support for community architecture has been one of the most welcome and remarkable events of the 1980s.[11]

Those who claim to witness a "sea change" are, almost always, courting disaster. In retrospect the Building Communities Conference may have been the point at which the campaign lost its way. Flattered by the attentions of its new friends in high places, it tried too hard to court the establishment and lost the confidence of many ordinary mortals who should have been the bedrock of its support. The conference organizers had persuaded a property company, Regalian, to sponsor and substantially finance the proceedings. Regalian had been in partnership with Wandsworth Council – flagship of the radical Right – buying up cheaply blocks of flats from which the tenants had been removed. The old flats were then renovated and sold on the private market. It was all part of Wandsworth's efforts to shed its social housing responsibilities and engineer the gentrification of the borough. If this was community architecture, many did not want to know. The conference was boycotted by many established community groups and experienced activists and by the national housing charity, Shelter. However, once the pact with Mammon had been forged, others began to join in. Architectural practices with the most tenuous links with user groups became "community architects" overnight. Other developers began to clothe themselves in the now fashionable garb of community architecture.

Their motives were well illustrated by the contest over the Bishopsgate Goods Yard. The 10 acre site was owned by British Rail, whose prime concern was to get the best financial return from its development. The Tower Hamlets Environment Trust wanted to see community involvement and wrote to all four interested developers. Only one supported the idea. London and Edinburgh Trust were developers for the neighbouring Spitalfields market and were anxious to expand their interest. They called in Hunt Thompson to organize a Community Planning Weekend. In all, three "planning for real" sessions were held but, despite widespread publicity, only a handful of local people attended each one. Those who did attend were presented with a virtual *fait accompli*, with most of the site earmarked for commercial offices and housing. Nevertheless, the facade of community participation was sufficient to ensure success. London and Edinburgh Trust became developers for the site and Hunt Thompson were appointed as master planners.[12]

The sponsorship of the Prince of Wales and the publicity generated by Rod Hackney's term as RIBA president did much to promote the idea of community architecture and implant it in the public mind. They did not intend that it should be exploited for commercial gain, nor did they support such exploitation. Nevertheless, as the bandwagon began to roll, the freeloaders jumped on board. And many others jumped off. Many with long experience in user participation and community action were profoundly alienated by the tenor of the RIBA's campaign, by its concentration on a few leading personalities and the promotion of the work of RIBA members. Those in local government, striving to reform community service, were left out in the cold. Public sector projects, it seemed, could be "community architecture" provided they were designed by private firms of architects. Those in community technical aid resented the sidelining of their efforts and the exclusive promotion of the work of architects in contradiction to their aim to re-integrate the design professions. Many in the new voluntary sector rejected the mantle of commercialism and the re-casting of their efforts as "community enterprise"[13] in a naked appeal to the political spirit of the times.

Tom Woolley had been a long-time advocate of community technical aid and a leading representative of the architects who were outside the RIBA. Woolley had written extensively on community architecture, but now repudiated the mantle. "Community architecture", he wrote in 1989, "is a term which has been promoted by the Royal Institute of British Architects to convince the public that it is concerned with the needs of low income groups and the 'Inner City' ".[14] Many shared his disillusionment, the feeling that the work of a whole movement had been hijacked in the interests of just one section of it. But the selling of community architecture might just have been worth the price, had it succeeded. For a time it seemed that it might.

The impact of public policy

In the early hours of 12 June 1987, at the very moment of her third electoral triumph, Margaret Thatcher stood on the steps of Conservative Central Office and declared "No one must slack . . . there is work to be done. We must do something about these inner cities" After eight years in power, had she finally noticed? Forced to venture forth in the cause of the hustings, had she suddenly become aware of the parlous state of much of urban Britain? Had she heard the message of community architecture? If so, it could be significant. In the elective dictatorship she headed, Mrs Thatcher was, by then, totally dominant. She was close to being an absolute ruler. On her word could turn a major policy initiative. A Cabinet subgroup was set up on urban policy but, Rod Hackney recorded, ". . . it was evident that Thatcher was reluctant to channel more money into deprived areas and that, by her absence even at the group's first meeting, she clearly couldn't invest the required energy, enthusiasm and commitment to make things work."[15] The unsolicited promise, so publicly given, was quickly consigned to the dustbin of history.

In the year that followed, the inner cities and the cause of community architecture were to suffer severely from the impact of general policy. First, the 1988 Budget with massive tax handouts for the rich. Few of them lived in deprived urban areas and the tax cuts served to increase the spending power of the most wealthy ex-urban areas. Next, the Poll Tax, in reality another tax break for the wealthy, although it was presented as making local government more accountable. What it actually did was make local authority finance almost unworkable, particularly for those inner-city councils whose concentrations of low-income residents were hardest hit by the tax. Until 1988 many inner urban authorities had evaded the successive attempts to cut and restrict their spending by ingenious schemes of creative accountancy. Now the game was up, creativity was exhausted, and the cuts began in earnest.

The impact on housing

Significant changes were brought about by the 1988 Housing Act. Ostensibly this simply changed the basis for funding Housing Association developments. Previously, developments had received 95 per cent grant aid. Now a much smaller proportion – generally 67 per cent – was grant aided. The reminder had to be raised on the money markets, and the Act required that rents were set at a level sufficient to repay the loan. This had far-reaching implications. In order to keep rents down to a reasonable level, Housing Associations were forced to cut costs and standards to the bone. Design work had to be minimized and costs were cut by competitive tendering and "design and build" package deals. More difficult projects were prohibitively expensive. This meant an end to the rehabilitation that had redeemed so much of the inner cities. It meant an end to developments organized by housing co-operatives. An end to the provision of social facilities which had helped to humanize new estates. Most new estates built under the new regime are mean, repetitive and designed to poor space standards. High rents mean that many estates are predominantly occupied by claimants whose rent is paid by housing benefit. In introducing the new Act, the government increased funding to Housing Associations and, effectively, made them the sole providers of social housing. In 1988, local authorities were still producing more new houses than Housing Associations. By 1993 they were producing none at all, yet were still required to house the growing army of homeless.[16]

It was in 1988, too, that the government began to restrict local authority flexibility in dealing with its existing housing. Housing Action Trusts (HATs)were introduced. Deprived estates were promised massive funding if they opted out of local authority control. Initially HATs were spectacularly unsuccessful, as estate after estate voted to remain in council tenancy. Only much later, when the government was forced to relax this rule, did some HATs get under way. Frustrated by the rejection of this initiative, Ministers increasingly centralized control over funds for housing improvement. More and more of the diminishing capital available was channelled into Estate Action. The Department of the Environment made the rules, they selected and approved the schemes, they controlled the purse strings. Under this regimen, lavish sums were targeted on problem estates with a high public profile and into schemes that were often questionable in their effectiveness. Meanwhile, smaller problem estates and the general maintenance and improvement of the stock was starved of the necessary finance.

As the spending power of local authorities was cut and squeezed, their services were subject to an expanding regime of privatization through "compulsory competitive tendering", a measure first introduced in 1980 but extended to "white collar" services by the 1988 Local Government Act. Centrally directed funds, such as Estate Action, have increasingly been subjected to the market "discipline" of competitive tendering which is mostly about costs and little concerned with the quality of service. Such was vividly demonstrated in 1993 by the controversy of the Angell Town Estate Action scheme in Lambeth. A small private practice, Burrell Foley Fisher had spent years working with tenants and had completed a highly praised pilot scheme. They were obliged to tender for the feasibility for the complete scheme and were supplanted by Hunt Thompson with a tender of £0.00. The nil bid was a "loss leader" designed to secure the lucrative contract for the substantive phases. Cheap it was, but for the tenants the impact was summed up by the RIBA Community Architecture Group:

> If Angell Town is a community project, the community will have to spend extra time briefing new architects, who in turn will spend time being briefed and learning about a situation with which others were already familiar. This is hardly efficient. It appears there will be a high price to pay for "free" architecture . . .[17]

Overall, the impact of government policy on housing was dramatic. Between 1979 and 1992 government spending on housing fell from £12.5 billion to £5.5 billion in real terms,[18] Much of the capital budget that remains has been diverted to housing associations. Most of the rest is locked into centrally directed programmes. Local authorities are left with barely sufficient capital to maintain their existing stock and none for new housing or for radical improvements to existing estates. From 1996 their housing management services and the design services of the architects' departments will be privatized by compulsory competitive tendering. The destruction of the "social State" has been wrought, not in pursuit of community service and democratic control, but out of obsessive obeisance to the dogma of the "free market".

The impact on community initiatives

While the antipathy of the Conservatives to local government was undisguised, their attitude to the work of self-help groups and the new voluntary sector has been equivocal. On visits to self-build schemes and housing co-operatives, ministers have been unstinting in their praise for voluntary initiatives. Their vocal support has been hardly less generous for the many groups running training and employment projects for the disadvantaged; or for those providing services for children, for the elderly, for the handicapped in self-managed community centres. Perhaps they were misled by the reinterpretation of this work as "community enterprise" into believing that these initiatives were entirely self-sustaining. To some extent, these groups did depend on voluntary work, on fund-raising appeals to charitable trusts and, to a very limited extent, to commercial sponsorship. For the most part, though, they depended on support and funding from the State.

The government has given scant support to community self-build. New-build schemes have minimal funding, while rehabilitation has been severely restricted by the curtailment of improvement grants. The introduction of market principles to the provision of social housing, has made the propagation of housing co-operatives virtually impossible. Worst of all, through increasingly draconian cuts in local government funding it has cut off the lifeblood to community groups. As councils have been forced to cut their revenue budgets, so the grants to many voluntary organizations have been reduced or eliminated. There is certainly no money to fund new projects. While revenue cuts made it much more difficult for community organizations to operate, restrictions on capital spending have similarly curtailed building projects. For the development of their facilities, many groups were funded by capital grants made through Urban Partnership, 75 per cent funded by central government. In 1993 the Partnership programme was abolished.

Such capital as remained available was initially channelled into City Challenge. Under this scheme, councils were invited to generate a partnership with local business and community organizations. They then bid against each other for a share of a crock of gold. The winners received substantial capital funding for the regeneration of run-down urban areas, funding that had to be managed by an independent City Challenge Company. The initial round of City Challenge was highly focused. All the available funding was channelled into certain restricted areas, leaving unmet the equally pressing needs of areas not favoured by selection. This shortcoming, at least, was recognized by government. From April 1994, partnerships have been able to bid for a more generally available Single Regeneration Budget administered by Regional offices integrating several government departments.

The idea of partnership may be not without merit; it has barely begun to operate, let alone realize anything on the ground. Yet, once again, the rules are centrally conceived, the beneficiaries centrally selected, the funding centrally controlled. Even at its inception, the organization of the Single Regeneration Budget was criticized for disregarding the needs of voluntary organizations[19] and, above all, for re-enforcing central government control.[20] Its very concept is the antithesis of local democracy – of the bottom-up approach advocated by community action and supported by the Scarman Report – where communities would be able to identify and prioritize their own needs and manage the funding necessary to address them.

Is community architecture dead?

From the pinnacle of its high public profile, community architecture faded quickly from the headlines. In 1989, Max Hutchinson succeeded Rod Hackney as president of the RIBA. "Community architecture is dead. It was not simply killed; it was over-killed. It was a PR exercise masquerading as a crusade . . ." wrote the new president. "For a while community architecture was capital's plaything. Money had quit industry and the Welfare State and was amusing itself with minor entertainments. Money discovered community architecture, rescued it from the gutter and glamorized it. And then tired of it."[21] Community architecture had been eclipsed, he claimed, in a developer-led boom. In one sense he was right, the "new era" never dawned, the "sea change" never took place. Victory was claimed with the battle barely joined. In Hutchinson the RIBA found a true symbol of 1980s values and a defender of the modernist establishment. With his election, the advocates of the elite function of design regained control, and architects were encouraged to market their special skills in a bid for their share of the spoils in the new property boom. Community architecture was put on the back burner, safely tucked away and sidelined as a minority pursuit.

In the event, the boom that Max Hutchinson and many others had proclaimed proved short-lived. Within two years, the building industry, as a whole, was plunged into its deepest-ever recession. By 1993, 50 per cent of architects were unemployed or so underemployed as to make no difference. The profession was ill served by its adoption of market values, and ethical standards seemed to descend into the gutter as architects scrambled to secure the little work that remained. In the catatonic state of the building industry it was commercial architecture that looked dead. Inevitably, community architecture suffered too, party as a result of public expenditure cuts that reduced investment in the social fabric to an all-time low; partly from the dogmatic and ruthless application of market principles and the relentless centralization of decision-making and control. It must have become evident, even to those who once thought otherwise, that it had nothing to gain from a government whose zeal has long-since turned from stimulating reform to the unfettered exercise of power and ideological monomania.

Hutchinson was not just wrong about the boom and in his enthusiastic promotion of market values. He was wrong in basing his interpretation of community architecture entirely on the RIBA initiatives. It was never the sole preserve of the RIBA. It proponents are to be found in equal, if not greater, numbers outside the RIBA and outside the architectural profession itself. It was the weakness of the RIBA-led campaign of the 1980s that it failed to mobilize the hundreds in community technical aid and in local government who were equally intent on developing participatory democracy, equally concerned to involve users in design and development decisions. Had it done so, community architecture could never have been portrayed as "capital's plaything" or its essentially small-scale nature been characterized as "the gutter" of architectural practice. It could have been recognized for what it is: a new and more democratic approach to the realization of social architecture. For 50 years, the design professions have depended on public spending on the social estate for a major part of their work. Public investment, as a whole, has generally provided the majority of employment, commerce the minority. Had this been recognized, more effort could have been put into vigorous opposition to the relentless cutbacks in public spending.

More emphasis could have been placed on the common values of the various

217

strands of community architecture, rather than on the divisions – values that could have helped to define a distinctive social purpose for the design professions. Over more than 20 years, the various approaches to community architecture have established a solid body of practice and theory based on co-operation rather than competition; on participatory democracy and on decentralization. To be against competition does not deny choice. It favours choice in the quality of service rather than the narrow and spurious choice based on price alone. To be in favour of co-operation and participation does not negate the contribution of specialist skills and experience. It generates constructive debate based on openness, honesty and the positive involvement of all those concerned. To be in favour of decentralization is not to deny the essential co-ordinating function of central and local government. It emphasizes local control over local decisions creating a more pluralist, more varied concept of democracy which actively involves people in the decisions that directly affect them.

Community action was both anti-State and anti-market, In promoting a third way, it incurred the opposition of supporters of the social State and was impeded by a political and economic structure geared to the promotion of market values. With the notion of bureaucratic and centralized provision through the social State under attack and disintegrating, there was a headlong rush to embrace market values. Now, the market itself has been found wanting. The definition of an alternative concept of social organization has become highly desirable. Some have regarded the "third way" as a fantasy. It has never succeeded in defining a complete answer, an all-embracing solution to political and economic organization. But it does exist, in part, in co-operation and participation and in the promotion of collective egalitarian community values. Community architecture may be dormant, but it is not dead. Properly promoted, its revival could do much to stimulate the development of alternative values. For the inner cities still characterized by social disintegration and physical decay, the revival of community values has never been more urgent.

References

1. Peter Hain (ed.), "Introduction: the future of community politics", in *Community politics* (London: John Calder, 1976), 24.
2. Manuel Castells, *The urban question* (London: Edward Arnold, 1977). First published in French (1972).
3. John Cowley, Adah Kaye, Marjorie Mayo, Mike Thompson, "Community or class struggle?" (Stage 1 1977), 15.
4. Jim Radford 3. The Community movement in op. cit. Peter Hain (ed.) p 74
5. Samuel Smiles *Self-help* (London: John Murray, 1879; 1st edn 1859)
6. Annual Reports 1979–1992 Architects' Registration Council of the United Kingdom show the numbers of architects outside the RIBA rising from 16% (4,381) in 1979 to 20% (5,583) in 1983; by 1992 the figure was 22% (6,906).
7. Jim Sneddon & Ian Finlay, "A turbulent decade", *Building Design* (21 November 1986), 20–23.
8. *The Brixton disorders, 10–13 April 1981*. Report of an inquiry by the Rt Hon. Lord Scarman OBE (London: HMSO 1981 Cmnd 8427), 14.
9. HRH The Prince of Wales, *A vision of Britain – a personal view of architecture* (London: Doubleday, 1989), 9.

10. HRH The Prince of Wales – foreword to *Village buildings of Britain,* Matthew Rice (London: Little, Brown, 1992).

11. Nick Wates & Charles Knevitt, *Community architecture* (London: Penguin, 1987), 157.

12. Maxwell Hutchinson, *The Prince of Wales: right or wrong? An architect replies* (London: Faber & Faber, 1989), 121–3.

13. Charles Knevitt (ed.), *Community enterprise* (London: The Times 1986).

14. T. A. Woolley, "Design participation today" (Unpublished paper, Architects' Registration Council of the United Kingdom, September 1989).

15. Rod Hackney, *The good, the bad and the ugly* (London: Frederick Muller, 1990), 155.

16. Lecture by David Parkes (RIBA Housing Group) and Lynn Moseley (Circle 33 Housing Association), 3 June 1993. Similar conclusions supported by research by Molly Warrington of Cambridge University, reported in *The Guardian* (7 January 1994).

17. Letter from Richard Fielden of the Community Architecture Group to *The Architects' Journal* (28 July 1993), 11.

18. *The Guardian* (12 March 1992); figures in real terms at 1990–91 prices.

19. Leader in *The Guardian* (4 April 1994).

20. Report of AMA Conference, *Planning Week* (31 March 1994), 3.

21. Maxwell Hutchinson, op. cit., 119, 145.

CASE STUDY
Broadwater Farm:
a large problem estate

Until 1966 Broadwater Farm was just that – low-lying and waterlogged agricultural land. The farm was surrounded by low-scale late nineteenth-century housing, but had never been developed because of its high water table. The brave new world of 1960s housing design provided the answer – streets in the sky. Over the next seven years, a huge estate of slab and tower blocks was built amid the modest two- and three-storey terraces. It was as if a little bit of New York had landed in a Victorian suburb. All the blocks on the new estate were linked together by continuous pedestrian access decks at first-floor level. The ground level, considered unsuita- ble for housing, was given over to the bleak- ness of a massive car park. At first it seemed a success. The scheme won a government award for good housing, and people on the waiting list were keen to move into the 1,063 newly built homes. It was not to last. The social facilities originally proposed – shops, a pub, doctor's and dental surgeries – were cut out as the money ran short. The tenants were marooned in a relatively iso- lated area, entirely without services. The heavy panel industrialized system from which the estate was constructed began to leak and cockroaches infested the voids within the structure. The open access system, as in so

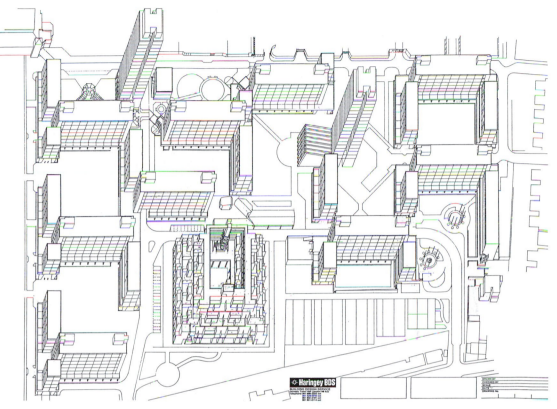

The new estate of tower and slab blocks created an environment wholly alien to the Victorian terraced street surrounding it.

The blocks are linked together with continuous pedestrian decks raised above ground level.

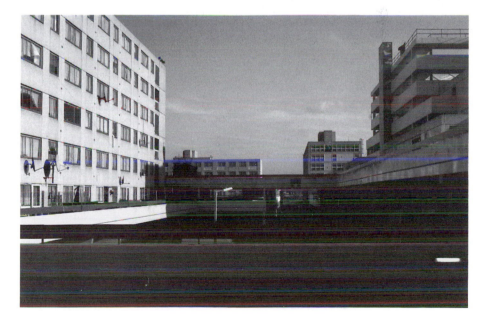

221

Land adjoining the estate – now a public park – is till subject to persistent flooding

many estates, was prey to vandalism crime and abuse.

The estate became hard to let. Increasingly, the only families who would take up offers of accommodation were the most desperate – those in the worst accommodation, the unemployed, single-parent households – many were from the ethnic minority communities of recent migrants. Some of these families had serious social problems and, as every housing manager knows, one problem family can make life hell for dozens of neighbours. The estate became a focus of drug abuse and drug-related crime and the object of increasing attention from the police. One night in October 1985 the police raided a flat in a drugs "bust". During the raid the tenant, Mrs Cynthia Jarret, died. There followed two days of riot, arson and running battles with the police, in the course

of which a young constable, Keith Blakelock was brutally murdered. In the aftermath, the attention of the nation was focused on the estate and its problems.[1]

From within the estate, initiatives began to address two key problems – youth unemployment and the absence of social facilities. In 1983 an Association had been set up to try to provide youth facilities. It now began a new venture. With the help of local building contractors, a company was set up – Broadwater Youth Association Co-op Ltd – to train and employ young people on construction projects. The co-op began by designing and building public gardens on the estate. As it developed skills and confidence it progressed to take on Council contracts for painting, maintenance and repair work. Another initiative was to raise money from Urban Partnership to build 21 enterprise

New workshops in unused space beneath the walkways. Designed by the Area Team, built by the Youth Association Co-op. They provide managed workspace for residents to start businesses generating employment and at the same time providing new services for the estate

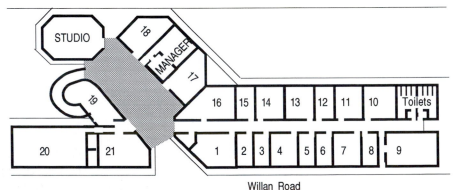

Willan Road

PLAN OF WORKSHOPS

222

workshops. These were designed into the bleak unused space beneath the access decks. The workshops were built by the youth co-op. By 1993 half of them were occupied by a variety of manufacturing uses and businesses providing local services – video hire, take away food, a mini-cab service, an off-licence. Money was also raised for a play centre and a large new community centre that have been built on land adjoining the estate.

Meanwhile, Haringey Council was developing plans for the revitalization of the estate. As part of its decentralization programme, architectural and housing teams were established in a temporary building in the centre of Broadwater Farm. A Strategy Group was formed comprising representatives from each block and from community organizations – Senior Citizens, the Youth Association, the Residents Association, ecumenical groups and others. The group developed a scheme to break down the estate into manageable units. The high-level walkways would be demolished. The entrance to each block would be controlled by a "concierge" who would be able to monitor lifts, corridors and other strategic points through closed circuit television cameras. Each block

would be given a distinctive identity with replacement windows and new cladding. The ground level would be improved with new paving and landscaping, and secured with better lighting.

In 1989, the government agreed to a pilot scheme to two of the blocks funded under the Estate Action Programme. In developing the details of the scheme, tenants of the blocks were invited to meetings to discuss types of windows, external insulation, colours of material and the design of the new entrances and landscaping. Work on the two blocks was completed in 1993 and the Department of the Environment decided to commit £33 million to extend the scheme throughout the estate. At the same time the Regional Health Authority committed funding for a new health centre. Implementation of the scheme will rectify the insecurity of the original design and will replace the monolithic uniformity with a varied and more attractive environment. The estate will be provided with a range of social facilities that should have been there from the start. Through their detailed involvement in the scheme, the tenants seem to have developed confidence in the improvements. There are fewer transfer requests, and some tenants

Improvements to the two blocks in the pilot scheme included new windows, re-cladding and landscaping, transforming their appearance.

New entrances have been built so that each block is now entered separately through a single lobby controlled by a concierge and monitored by video cameras.

who have left the estate are seeking to return.

There is no doubt that the controversy and widespread discussion generated by the riots helped to focus attention on the estate's problems. Broadwater Farm is not unique, though. Similar schemes have been developed, under the Estate Action Programme, on other large estates with comparable problems but less dramatic public profiles. The question is – will they work? There have been repeated attempts to secure large housing blocks. Generally, electronically controlled entrances break down very quickly through vandalism and abuse. The development of magnetic locks provided a technical improvement, less prone to malicious damage. But the latest attempts are heavily dependent on camera surveillance and the presence of the concierges. Although many tenants appreciate the security provided by the new systems, some resent the extent to which their lives are under observation by hidden eyes. There is a fine line between creating a protected environment and the danger of producing supervised incarceration. Above all, the new systems are reliant on effective management and maintenance, the costs of which are con-

siderable. It is an open question whether the running costs will continue to be found by authorities whose budgets are under greater and greater pressure.

Even if the systems can be made to work, it is still questionable whether they are good value for money. £40 million has been committed to Broadwater Farm. For that sort of money, more than half the estate could have been rebuilt as low-scale housing. Demolition is considered under the Option Appraisal procedure of the Estate Action Programme. But it is doubtful if it is a realistic choice. Under government policy, any redevelopment would have to be carried out by a Housing Association. This makes it unattractive to many local authorities whose stock, already diminished by "right-to-buy" sales, is under increasing pressure from homelessness. For the tenants, demolition would create a world of great uncertainty that most would rather not enter. Above all, the funds are centrally directed by a government that seems intent in putting all the housing eggs into a few high profile and problematic baskets. Money might be better spent on smaller-scale, less dramatic improvements in other parts of the social estate. Given a free hand with such lavish funds, it is a fair bet that Haringey Council and the local community would not have opted to sink them all into one estate.

The key question with large 1960s estates, such as Broadwater Farm, is whether they can provide good housing for families. Are high-rise flats an appropriate environment for bringing up children? No matter how beautiful the environment, no matter how secure the common parts, no matter how much money and care are lavished in maintaining the complex electronic systems – the answer is probably no. Children would be much better housed on the ground. Continuing social problems may well cause the decision-makers to regret the capital invested in attempting to redeem such housing. It might well be better to demolish and rebuild at least in part. What remained of the high rise could be successfully converted to sheltered accommodation for the elderly; to housing for students, single people or the childless; or simply for those who genuinely chose to live there

References
1. Rod Hackney, *The good, the bad and the ugly* (London: Frederick Muller, 1990), 129–35; and reports in *The Observer* (14 November 1993).

CHAPTER 10

The urban imperative

REDEEMING THE INNER CITIES

It is 150 years since the problems of Britain's cities first began to arouse public concern. For another half a century they continued to grow and fester, before serious attempts were made to address urban squalor. Regulation and social architecture – philanthropic housing, schools, social facilities – brought some relief. But the greatest efforts went into decentralization – the flight from the hated cities, which robbed them of the better off and most enterprising people. With the growth of the suburbs and dormitory towns, and the relocation of many working people into vast peripheral estates, the Victorian city became "inner city" – concentrations of the worst housing and the poorest people. The post-war drive of urban planning and housing policies attempted to solve the problem once and for all. But it ended in the housing disasters of the 1960s and created more problems than it solved. Much of the inner city areas has been redeemed by the public and private rehabilitation of the 1970s and 1980s, and by the renovation of the social estate. But serious, and perhaps intensifying, problems remain, a seemingly perpetual hangover from the ill considered urban industrialization of the past.

Some of these problems are physical, demanding investment in social housing, places of employment, education, training and recreation. To a large extent, though, they are social and economic, and no solution can be found that does not redress intensive poverty and unemployment. Part of the answer is public investment. The commitment of central and local government is as necessary as ever. But the best efforts of paternalistic government have failed in the past. They would be no more successful now. The engagement of local people is essential: their consent and support for the nature and quality of development, and the active commitment of their energy and skills in addressing the problems of their own neighbourhoods. The community movement has pointed the way, and community architecture is the mirror of its achievements. Overall, the impact has been small, but it could be much greater. Given greater recognition, given much more organizational and financial support, community architecture could provide the key to the redemption of the inner cities.

The Wasteland

In the early 1990s, much was still wrong with the state of urban Britain, as a few snapshots will indicate.

226

Figure 10.1
The Gorbals, 1993.

Glasgow

In Govan, the Taransey Street area (the tenement rehab pioneered by Assist) still thrives and still provides good housing. But it stands like a message that came too late. Gone, now, are so many of the similar tenements, considered unfit for human habitation. Along the Clyde nearby, all that remains are empty and derelict sites. In the Gorbals, once Britain's most notorious slum, almost all the tenement housing was demolished during the 1960s. In their turn, many of the huge new blocks of flats that replaced them deteriorated into slums. Now they, too, have been demolished and much of the Gorbals is a vast, empty sea of rubble awaiting the next attempt at building Utopia (Fig. 10.1).

Liverpool, Toxteth

Every tenth house or flat seems to be empty and tinned-up. Quite a few have been burned out. Here and there, small empty sites mark what once were houses and are now "adventure playgrounds" for the local children (Fig. 10.2). A public park is closed down and overgrown. The Granby Street area, partially reclaimed by the SNAP initiative, is now affected by the blight. Poorly dressed groups huddle around the fortified shops that stand on each street corner. The Liverpool Housing Trust has abandoned 20 houses in the area because of persistent vandalism and break-ins.[1] In stark contrast, the successful housing co-ops, whether new build or rehab, stand like oases in a desert of dereliction and run-down blocks of walk-up flats.

227

Figure 10.2
Toxteth, Liverpool.

North Shields

In the city centre of North Shields, derelict industrial buildings and sites cleared for temporary car parks line the banks of the once-busy Tyne. Little over a mile from the centre lies the Meadowell Estate, sometimes dubbed "the worst estate in Britain". It was the scene of riots in 1991, when teenagers burned their own youth centre which had recently closed because of local government cuts. Four hundred of its 1,700 houses have been abandoned. Some of them stand like skeletons picked bare by scavengers (Fig. 10.3). Yet here there are no tower blocks, no "streets in the sky", on which to pin the blame. These are straightforward two-storey "council houses" laid out as a cottage estate, poorly built and poorly maintained certainly, but of a basic and adequate type. Poverty is the problem. Grinding poverty and endemic unemployment.[2]

Sheffield

Playwrite David Hare describes a visit to Sheffield during the 1992 election campaign:

> "I walk out into the streets which lead off from the Arena. This was once the manufacturing heartland of Britain, where the steel industry grew and prospered. Now there are only small redbrick parades of shops and desolate, crumbling factories. As I walk past the little doomed windows I look at the lard cakes, the fish and chips, the chip sandwiches. Eventually even the crumbling buildings give way to a huge piece of wasteland, pockmarked with a pitch black sump of

Figure 10.3
*Meadowell – houses
picked bare like skeletons.*

small groups of vagrants are huddling around fires. For a second, Sheffield looks like Benares."[3]

Manchester, Moss Side

Writer Gordon Burn recorded the gang culture of the drugs trade in the Moss Side area of inner Manchester.

> Driving round the Chesham Hill area and Moss Side at night, two things area noticeable: the prostitutes whose pale legs are picking up the headlights in the street running off the main artery; and the telephone boxes that stand proud and unmolested in the darkness and dereliction. Both, it turns out, are crucial to the local economy and jealously protected by men with lifestyles to maintain. "More phone boxes round here than private phones" [his informant] points out "an' none of them get smashed up". Junkies depend on them to call up dealers on the estate on their Vodaphones . . .[4]

Nottingham

Nottingham was identified in 1993 as the most dangerous area in Britain for violent assaults. Reporter Lesley Gerard surveyed the city's streets at night.

> 2.30 am. Arthur, a retired miner, and his wife Joan moved into St Anne's council estate, dubbed Crack City, from Arnold, to be near their married daughter. They are walking the almost deserted streets with their dog. "Twocking" (taking cars without consent) and other car crimes are rife. But Arthur is reassuring. "our square isn't too bad at the moment because some the local crooks are in prison. Round the corner its worse". 3.30 am. A hollow-eyed prostitute is picked up by a taxi on the outskirts of the town centre. Half an hour after turning her trick she is dropped in Radford Road. She disappears into an alleyway, buys her drugs and goes home."[5]

Central London

In Central London the single homeless huddle in doorways wrapped in thin blankets, intoning repeated pleas to passers-by for "spare change". Behind the South Bank Arts Centre, dozens sleep in discarded boxes and makeshift shelters in the capital's "cardboard city"; 2,800 are estimated to sleep rough in London. Many have been discharged from mental hospitals under the government's "Care in the Community" policy. The destitutes sleeping rough in London are most visible to the media, but in Britain's other cities another 5,600 are thought to share a similar plight.[6]

London, Bethnal Green

Bethnal Green in London's East End is home to a substantial Asian community and the scene of some vicious racial attacks. Amid the streets of Victorian cottages, now redeemed by the middle classes, is the Delta Estate (Fig. 10.4). It is a typical 1930s tenement, but has never been modernized. Its low standard, run-down flats are now mostly occupied by Bengali families. As always, the poorest people − those with least choice − get the worst housing. The Delta Estate could make very good housing, but an application for Estate Action funding was turned down by a government more interested in pouring money into more high-profile problems.

Figure 10.4
Bethnal Green − those with least choice get the worst housing.

London Docklands

London's Docklands have been the flagship of the government approach to urban regeneration. During the 1980s, millions of pounds were poured into spanking new offices and private housing, and almost nothing into transport, communal facilities or social housing. In Wapping, Tobacco Dock has been converted to shops dedicated to luxury trade, where you can buy a BMW but not a loaf of bread. Behind it, cheek by jowl with comfortable new private houses, stands Corbett House (Fig. 10.5) – another run-down 1930s estate – whose tenants endure third-rate conditions amid the surrounding opulence.

London, Newington Green

In London's Newington Green, an independent community centre operates from an old piano factory. Its premises are cramped, run down, poorly serviced, and have no disabled access. Yet, with over 1,000 users each week, it is one of the most successful social action centres in the country. Its users range from the very young to pensioners, a rainbow mixture of creeds and colours. Although independent, it is 70 per cent funded by local authorities. In 1992, cuts forced the closure of its youth club in an area of high unemployment among the young. And an application for Partnership funding to extend and improve its premises was turned down shortly before the programme was abolished.

Figure 10.5
Docklands – third rate housing amid modern opulence.

Images such as these say more than bald statistics. Yet the 1991 Census revealed a bleak picture. Many inner-city areas had very high levels of unemployment, sometimes over 40 per cent. Within these overall figures, unemployment amongst the young was often over 50 per cent. Alongside the workless there were higher than average levels of the permanently sick and disabled. There were high proportions of single parent families, which are generally the poorest of households. In many inner- city wards between 50 per cent and 65 per cent of children lived with lone parents.[7] At the same time, statistics showed that the gap between rich and poor had widened dramatically during the 1980s, with income levels of the poorest families falling by 14 per cent in real terms.[8] The number of families on income support trebled and, by 1993, almost 3 million children were living in poor families.[9] Add to all this the relentless increase in crime in general and in drug abuse and drug related crime in particular. In this depressing picture some see a "doom scenario" of permanent deprivation in the inner cities, leading to social disintegration and violent unrest.[10] Certainly, the situation is serious and needs to be addressed with some urgency. In the search for a more positive urban future, the lessons of the community movement and community architecture have much to offer

The social city

The small towns of Britain tend to have mixed communities, but the cities are divided, socially and physically, between the suburbs and the inner cities. The social division was created by urban conditions of the past and by planning policy – or sometimes by the lack of it. For most of the nineteenth century it was the aspiration of both rich and poor to escape from the squalor of the cities. For the rich, it was no problem. Everyone else had to wait longer. The building of the railways increasingly created satellite towns and suburbs, to which the middle classes could migrate and commute. From the 1920s onwards, the migratory tide became a flood, offering opportunities to all classes to enjoy the suburban idyll. The enjoyment of a house and garden became the English ideal, but for the great majority it was available only in the outer city and the urban fringe.

Some had little choice in the matter. The great peripheral estates were built by local authorities to relieve overcrowding, Most of the tenants there were more or less forced to move so that their substandard houses could be demolished. Many were unhappy to be separated from their friends and family, isolated in estates that were poorly serviced by transport and facilities and which offered few opportunities for employment. The continuing problems of the peripheral estates are a longstanding legacy of enforced decentralization through public policy. The great majority, though, were willing emigrants who actively sought release from the ills of the city. For many years, migration to the suburbs was an almost universal aspiration. Those who could afford to took the option. They were, almost invariably, the better off, those in regular and better paid employment, and the younger and more adventurous members of the community. Those who could not afford to go stayed behind, and they were predominantly the poor, the sick and the elderly. The housing the migrants left behind could generally be bought or rented cheaply, and the unloved inner cities became home to successive waves of immigrants.

So was made the social divide. The communities established in the suburbs became monocultural: almost exclusively ethnically English, almost all of working age and in relatively well paid employment. Many had common roots. City and suburb were linked. Most preferred not to move far, and the nearest suburban area became the destination. Many from north London aspired to Barnet or leafy Hertfordshire. The population of Essex largely originates in the migration of the upwardly mobile from London's East End. Whatever their origins, the inhabitants of these new settlements soon developed a patina of uniformity. Safe in their suburban havens, these communities of like individuals shared common values of personal self-improvement and the enjoyment of comfortable lifestyles. They saw themselves mirrored in their neighbours and they reinforced each others' taste and prejudices. For them the inner cities became places of dread – foreign places of alien culture, rife with vice and crime, where it was unsafe to walk the streets even in the brightness of day.

For many inner-city dwellers the suburban culture is narrow and mean, and they do no recognize their communities in the nightmare fantasies conjured in the suburban mind. From the start of the great migration, the inner cities developed increasing diversity. Migrants from other parts of Britain and from abroad brought with them their own history, their own culture, often their own language. Such foreignness initially clashed with the native culture and, to a degree, such conflict still persists. Generally, though, the migrant cultures have been absorbed into the richness of urban life. Diversity was increased when, during the 1960s, the middle classes rediscovered the inner cities. Good homes were, after all, to be had with the investment of a little capital. What was more, they were close to the centres of white collar employment. This, too, created conflict in the "gentrification" that resulted. But once that settled down, the invasion of the liberal middle classes brought considerable benefits to the inner cities. In the most successful urban areas there is great social and cultural variety. In any street in north London might be found a mix of middle class, working class and underclass; nuclear families, single parents and the unattached; owner-occupiers, public and private tenants and housing for the handicapped; ethnic origins from all over Europe and from the Caribbean, Asia and Africa. All this is reflected in the broad range of clubs, societies and community organizations, and in the wide variety of shops and restaurants that have prospered on the patronage of the better off.

This is the inner city at its best. But even in the successful areas there is considerable deprivation. Crime is an increasing problem. For most people, experience of its direct effects is relatively rare, although it is an ever-present background to daily life. Most are exercised by the fear of crime and inconvenienced by the side effects: the emanations of the burgeoning dog population, the constant nuisance of untended alarms. In the less successful areas the middle classes are missing and deprivation is more prevalent. Even in the most deprived areas, such as inner Liverpool, there is great cultural diversity. Rarely, in Britain, have cultural ghettos developed, still less the nightmare of crime-ridden, uniformly poor, black ghettos that seem to characterize many urban areas in the USA. In the inner cities of Britain, cultural diversity and the relative harmony are a strength that offers considerable potential for their regeneration.

Inner-city housing needs

The needs of the inner urban areas are many and various, but most of them are embraced by two overarching issues. The first of these is housing. Lack of adequate

233

housing is a key cause of poor health, family breakdown and social disintegration. Despite decades of social housing policy, there are still so many people without good homes. The thousands of rough-sleepers, the single homeless, are the most visible. On top, almost 150,000 households were accepted by local authorities as homeless in 1992. Nearly 8,000 of them were in "bed & breakfast" hotels; 62,000 more were in temporary accommodation. On top again, are the "hidden" homeless – households needing a home of their own but forced to share with others, and the elderly and disabled trapped in housing with inadequate access and services. 1.2 million people are thought to suffer the stress of hidden homelessness.[11] Most authorities agree that a social housing programme producing 100,000 new homes a year over a 6–7 year period is required to solve the problem of homelessness.[12] Of those who have homes, many are living in poor conditions. The English Household Condition Survey of 1991 estimated that 1.5 million homes – almost 8 per cent of occupied housing – were "unfit for human habitation", needing extensive repair or improvement.[13]

All these are national figures, but it is unquestionable that the bulk of the housing problems still lies in the inner cities. The present commitment of resources is both insufficient and misdirected. Public investment in housing needs to be more than twice the present level to address the problem within a reasonable timescale. Removing the dogmatic sanction on local authorities would help. Allowing them to use capital receipts to build new housing would do much to resolve the problem. As it is, Housing Associations are the sole providers and are building well under half the number of houses required. What is more, the restrictions of their funding regime mean that most of their developments must be in cheaper outer urban areas. In the inner cities lies both the need and the opportunity. The large swathes of unused and derelict land are obvious enough. But thousands of houses could be built in small infill sites. In 1979, two young architects surveyed small vacant plots in the London Borough of Newham. They concluded that there were enough sites to house 3,000–5,000 people in single-family houses.[14] Such is still the case and most inner urban areas have many small plots that could successfully provide new housing.

If and when the commitment to social housing is made, it must not be on the old model of paternalistic provision by local government. The new model of Housing Association monopoly is even worse: equally paternalistic, less subject to public accountability, and to much meaner standards. Community architecture has shown the way people can be involved in providing their own housing and, by being involved, produce new and rehabilitated homes that meet their needs and their wishes – homes far more likely to stand the test of time. Housing co-operatives should be revived both for new housing and modernizing old estates. The community movement has produced models for specialist housing associations for cultural minority groups and for those with special needs. Self-build associations could provide a significant contribution in developing small sites and rehabilitating run-down houses, and they would provide skill training and employment for themselves at the same time. Where the councils and the large housing associations do develop, they now have ample evidence of both the necessity and the benefits of encouraging the future users to participate in the design of their own homes.

Tackling the crime wave

The relentless rise in urban crime is the second overarching issue. Its causes are complex and there are no sure-fire or quick-fix solutions. Part of the answer must lie in improved education and social organization, and in increased access to employment. For most people, the link between crime and unemployment is obvious. It is enshrined in common-sense folklore: "the devil makes work for idle hands". Most crime is committed by teenagers, generally by young men. It can be no coincidence that this group has been severely affected by unemployment for many years, particularly in the inner cities.[15] It has become evident, too, that the hopelessness generated by unemployment and the propensity for crime is infecting much younger children. Social orientation also needs to be addressed and this goes to the root of child care and education needs. It is now well established amongst educationalists that pre-school education can dramatically affect children's prospects, particularly those from deprived backgrounds. In the inner cities, there is a desperate need for increased child care and pre-school education. This shows negatively in the high numbers of single parent households. It is demonstrated more positively by the large range of child-related groups and facilities created by the new voluntary sector. These facilities not only benefit the children, they free single parents to take up training and employment, which improves their own lives and those of their children.

When inner-city children reach school age, they get a much poorer deal than their suburban and ex-urban counterparts. The inner cities were amply provided with Victorian Board schools. Since then, the length of schooling has increased, but the inner urban population is now much smaller. The result is that many inner-city Victorian schools are still in use. On paper they are adequate, in practice they provide a poor environment for education. Many are in bad repair, with leaking roofs and antiquated services. Those that are not provide bleak classrooms set in a sea of featureless tarmac. Given investment, these schools could be renovated and re-serviced, their playgrounds could be greened up and given better facilities. Properly modernized, the Victorian schools could provide an environment better than new buildings and give the children pride in their surroundings and an incentive to learn. Out of school, many children have benefited from facilities generated by voluntary action – adventure playgrounds, city farms and the like – although these are now under increasing pressure from funding cuts. On a neighbourhood basis all these things could be tied together, with the community school providing a link between such social facilities and the formal education system.[16]

Beyond the school years, teenage crime would be diminished by generating more employment and training, creating more recreational and social facilities to keep young people off the streets and to give them a more positive focus of interest. Here again the new voluntary sector has spawned promising new ventures in the inner cities. It has provided community education and training, workshops for new enterprises and employment initiatives. It has provided youth centres and sports and recreation activities. It has done all this in makeshift and inadequate buildings and with minimal and decreasing financial support. Given more support and funding, such initiatives could and would achieve much more. Child care, education and community facilities are, like housing, an area of social provision that needs greatly increased public investment. It this commitment were made, it would not only improve the quality of urban life but could help to roll back the increasing wave of crime.

The neighbourhood resource centre

In the regeneration of the inner cities, few would question the need for large-scale funding from the public purse. What is in question is how this funding is to be directed, how it is to be managed. The cardinal lesson from community action was that social provision paternalistically supplied by the local state was not successful. The generation of large pyramidal hierarchies in urban local government created a remote and insensitive bureaucracy that became inimical to the interests of those it was supposed to serve. As a counterweight, the community movement created small-scale organizations. Internally these were democratic and co-operative, but they were often parochial in promoting and protecting the interests of their members. In themselves they did not provide an alternative to local government. The present government has built on its hostility to local authorities by side-lining them. Funds for new social housing are now centrally directed through the Housing Corporation. Funds for estate modernization are centrally directed through Estate Action and Housing Action Trusts. Funds for community development are centrally directed through City Challenge and the Single Regeneration Budget. This is not better than what went before. It is worse, because it denies the opportunity to local communities to determine democratically their own priorities and the options for realizing them.

There is an alternative. One of the most positive concepts to emerge from the community movement was the idea of neighbourhood: the recognition that people in urban communities identified with distinct geographical areas. This theory, and the experiments with neighbourhood organizations, led to the decentralization of local government structures into neighbourhood offices. Where these have operated, they have provided a degree of democratic participation and a counterweight to the bureaucracies. But the idea has never been sufficiently developed. The range of services provided in neighbourhoods has been very restricted. In planning and development, Neighbourhood Forums have had an advisory role. But they have rarely been given effective influence in the allocation of large-scale funding or in the preparation and implementation of development programmes. The idea of neighbourhood planning has emerged, but it has mainly been used as the basis of community campaigns.

If neighbourhood planning were incorporated into the statutory system, plans could be prepared with participation of local people, community groups and tenant organizations. These plans could measure the extent of local housing need, unemployment and crime. They could identify and quantify the need for improvements to housing, social facilities and transport. By locating vacant sites and other development opportunities, they could help to generate new housing, employment and community facilities. Neighbourhood plans could provide a mechanism through which a collective view could emerge on local needs and opportunities. If carried out on a widespread and comparable basis, they could provide the foundation on which local communities could bid for capital funding. Central capital spending would be distributed not on the whim of central government or even of the town hall hierarchy, but on the basis of plans determined from the bottom up. There would need to be co-ordination and extensive debate between conflicting claims. But at the end of the day, capital spending would be based on the requirements and priorities identified by communities themselves.

If local people should be involved in planning and capital allocation to their communities, so, equally, they should be involved in implementation. If the mistakes of the past are not to be repeated, they need to be able to participate in the design process and their energies need to be harnessed in the development and management of new housing and social facilities. This process could be facilitated, particularly in the most deprived communities, by the establishment of neighbourhood resource centres to serve areas ranging from 10,000 to 30,000 people. These could be based on the models that have now been well developed by community technical aid centres and by area technical teams in local government. They could provide planning and design services to assist the generation and initiation of new projects. They could provide financial, management and organizational advice to help local groups set up co-operatives, housing associations, self-managed community facilities and enterprises providing employment and training. Most funding would come from public sources, but the neighbourhood centres could also help to raise funding from philanthropic and commercial sources. They would even generate some entirely self-sustaining enterprises.

Neighbourhood resource centres would need statutory funding for their planning and advisory work. They could be part of local government or quasi-independent. Either way, they would need to be flexible in their organization and operation, free from the rules, conventions and procedures with which local authorities are hidebound. Their role would be to channel the central funds necessary for urban regeneration and to ensure that capital spending met the expressed needs of those who were to benefit and had their full support. From the perspective of the community movement, the answer to remote and insensitive local government is not to make decision-making even more remote, even less accountable; it is to break down the operation of local government into much smaller units, units accountable to local people and which would actively encourage their participation in the improvement and development of their own communities.

The image of the city

The evils of industrial urbanization enormously damaged the image of the city in Britain. Whereas the older, smaller cities – such as Brighton, Bath, York, Durham and Edinburgh – were much admired and lovingly preserved, the industrial cities were places of dread. The new industrial cities of Victorian Britain were besmirched by appalling housing conditions and terrible pollution, and they were rife with poverty, crime and disease. Although many of the older cities were spared this fate, the capital was not. Outside the western enclaves of the rich, London – the hub of the empire – was engulfed with small-scale industry and its attendant pollution and overcrowded slum housing. Such conditions devalued the idea of the city. It was a place not to be. Instead, the ideal became the small settlement that would combine the best of town and country: the Garden City. In its mass realization, it succeeded only in creating the worst of both – neither urban or rural – a soul-less monotonous sea of low-density suburban sprawl.

The industrial cities were devalued and disliked. Their fabric was poorly planned and poorly built. The urge to rebuild them was understandable and the abundant problems made much rebuilding essential. It was an issue that should have been addressed much earlier. If it had been, Britain's cities might well have been redeemed in a more positive image. If the architects and planners had drawn on the native urban

237

heritage – the squares and terraces of Georgian urbanity, the informal streets and spaces of medieval cities – the results could have been very different. Instead, when the time came, in the great post-war building boom, the re-builders drew on the alien and largely untried ideas of modernism. They destroyed the concept of the street, casting people to live and work in cities of towers. They separated pedestrians and vehicles, creating windswept and dangerous precincts and subways, driving great motorways through the urban fabric. The careless and wholesale destruction reaped the inevitable whirlwind of public rejection and protest.

The persistent myth

Much of the protest was reactive. Building on this reaction it was, perhaps, inevitable that some should revive the ideals of an earlier urban age. Early critics of high-rise housing, such as Nicholas Taylor, sought to resuscitate the ideals of the Garden City in counter-position.[17] The idea of recreating the inner city as low-density houses and gardens became a powerful strand in the community architecture movement and influenced many of its projects. It has continued to exert a strong influence. As recently as 1985, Colin Ward summed up this ideal:

> The once despised bylaw street of the late nineteenth century as well as the suburban street of the first half of the century, are well adapted to change to accommodate new patterns of living, Modern high-density housing, whether high or low [rise], is not. As the Victorian city, losing population continuously and industry disastrously, declines in importance, the chance arises for its adaptation as a low-density city, manageable by its inhabitants.[18]

In one sense such a reaction was understandable, given the manifest failure of the Modern urban image. In another sense it was regressive and contradicted the very notion of urbanity. It was rooted in the populist concept that "people want houses and gardens". Perhaps, given a free choice, most people would opt for a house and garden. But, other things being equal, they might also choose to be able to walk to work rather than commute long distances. They would probably elect to have a wide choice of entertainment, recreation and shopping facilities within easy reach. Such choices are available only in cities, where higher densities concentrate housing closer to employment centres, where the sheer numbers of people generate variety and choice, and where easy access through frequent and efficient public transport becomes possible.[19] For those who want them, there are houses and gardens a-plenty in the suburbs. Reducing the inner cities to low density is not the answer; a choice of suburbia for all is no choice.

It is the attraction of cities that they are not like suburbs. Socially, they are radically different. Their strength, too, is that they have a distinctive visual character, where streets and urban spaces are defined and enclosed by continuous terraces of buildings 3, 4 and more storeys high. Such character is most cherishable in the old cities admired by everyone. But it is there in the legacy of the Victorian inner city, even if its potential has not always been realized. To defend higher densities against the perpetual yearning for the Garden City is not to defend the towers and slabs, the excessive and insensitive developments of the 1960s and later. To seek an alternative image of the city it might be helpful to go back to where it all went wrong. During the 1930s the pressure to redress urban problems was at its height, and the search for solutions embraced more alternatives than the all-conquering principles of the International Style.

Urban idealism

The pre-war search for urban solutions was motivated by both negative and positive images. Planners were concerned with the negative impact of uncontrolled decentralization. Thomas Sharp's powerful critique of the suburbs is still largely valid. They are still socially divisive. They are still eating up open land that could more valuably be used for agriculture or recreation. They still banish the countryside for the city dweller. Above all, they are still wasteful and inefficient in their use of land and are highly expensive to service. It is the excessive ownership and use of motor cars (essential in the low-density suburbs) that has caused the decline of public transport and is choking the road network despite its endless expansion. In Sharp's day, the transport nightmare was still to come, but the disbenefits of suburbia were clear enough. But if decentralization was then creating a negative image, the degenerate state of the cities themselves was an even stronger negative.

From her travels in Europe, Elizabeth Denby brought back a more positive picture:

> . . . what combines to make the charm of a city, what makes some particular town linger in the mind? Its shapes, or smells, or sounds? Why is it agreeable or disagreeable? Why for instance do families from the surrounding countryside flock in hundreds into Prague or Brno on Sundays and summer evenings? Is it their new and exquisite central parks and swimming pools, their open air cafés, their dash and fun? Why do the French seem so comfortably at home in their towns? Is it the enchanting alleys of trees trained but not mutilated, the public gardens unguarded by a vestige of railing, the innumerable little street markets . . . the inexpensive little restaurants sheltered behind a box-grown hedge? Is it because women sit comfortably knitting, sewing, gossiping on chairs on the pavements, happy family groups drink coffee or wine in the cafés which in summer overflow on to the pavements . . . ? Although the courtyards, pitch-black passages and steep narrow stairways lead to homes which are undoubtedly both overcrowded and sanitarily deficient, there is no sense of constraint but a general and profound air of content in these towns.
>
> Where have we, one of the greatest nations in the world, gone wrong? What has happened to our wealthy cities to make them so hideous? For British industrial cities are in fact proverbial abroad for their excessive size, their wasted land, their lack of civic dignity and beauty and opportunities for enjoyment. Beauty with us is too often sacrificed to utilitarian ends and financial gain. Numbers, output, is our blinding passion. Money is spent on schemes which are slums before they leave the drawing board.[20]

Those words were written in the 1930s. But they might, almost equally well, have been written at the end of the 1960s after the aspirations of the Modern movement had wreaked havoc in Britain's cities. Both Thomas Sharp and Elizabeth Denby despised suburban sprawl and the industrial city with almost equal venom. They sought an urban ideal in the social, economic and aesthetic advantages of the high-density city. They admired the small-scale housing of early modernism, yet neither embraced the vision of "a city of towers". They believed the urban dream could be

239

realized in high-density developments of houses and small blocks of flats. Elizabeth Denby pointed to the low overall densities of most British cities, outside London, where the housing might be cramped and crowded, but enormous areas of land were derelict or under-used. Most cities, she considered, could be humanely rebuilt within their existing boundaries and still leave ample open space for leisure and recreation. There was simply no need for high buildings on a large scale:

> . . . are flats in fact necessary in England for rehousing ill housed families? Consider the density figures of an English town. If high flats with common services and common amenities were built for the childless, the unmarried, for anyone who wanted to live that way, ample space would remain within the existing borders of the cities for traffic and industry and for rehousing the workers and their families in cottages with small gardens, with allotments, with playing fields, restaurants and all the requirements of a civilized community. This does not mean, of course, that housing would sprawl at twelve cold and draughty, detached or semi-detached cottages to the acre, in estates banished to the periphery of town far from friends and work. Why not cut out the romantic sentimentalism, the pseudo-refinement of the early twentieth century as resolutely as the materialistic wastefulness of the nineteenth? Why not return for inspiration to the traditional English squares and terrace cottages with small gardens, built during the early nineteenth century at thirty and forty to the acre in the centre of town.[21]

Here, then, was an alternative route waiting to be taken, a route that was neither "garden city" nor "radiant city". If the views of such as Denby and Sharp had been heeded by the architects and planners of the post-war boom, then millions of pounds would not have been wasted thrusting families into high-rise housing or into isolated peripheral estates. Millions of pounds more would not now be spent on their re-modelling, trying to salvage some humanity from the follies of the 1960s. All our cities would, instead, be better places to live. Most people would be appropriately housed and would enjoy the pleasure of plentiful open space and the stimulation of a lively street life. With more people living better in the cities, fewer would have felt the need to migrate to the suburbs and satellites. Pressure would have been eased on the countryside and the urban fringe. City and country would have retained more of their distinctive character and society as a whole would have been the better for it.

The historic compromise

As it was, it fell to the community movement to challenge both the nature and form of wholesale redevelopment. While one strand of community architecture lapsed into "romantic sentimentalism" in trying to apply the principles of the Garden City to urban development, much effort was directed to a more appropriate urbanity. Much of the new housing generated by community action was in a humane and sustainable high-density form. Much of the new building respected the scale and context of the inner city. Key battles were fought to save areas of Victorian terraced housing. These battles led to the rehabilitation of large areas of three-, four- and five-storey terraces which were converted into a mixture of family housing and small flats. The same principles were later applied to renovate tenement blocks of four and five storeys, with family maisonettes on the ground and small flats above. These developments are neither low density nor high-rise, but something in between. In their nature they have returned to the historic concept of urbanity and, at the same time, they provide a model for successful future urban development.

Community architecture presents an incremental approach to urban renewal. As much as possible of the urban fabric is retained. Old buildings may need adapting and extending, but where they can be re-modelled for new uses they should. New buildings are possible on small sites, but they should respect the scale and character of their surroundings. Infill developments can intensify the use of the inner cities and, if sensitively designed, can reinforce the character of urban streets. Sometimes, redevelopment is essential and there are many areas of derelict land that need to be brought into use. Where large-scale new developments are necessary, their layout and design should be based on forms that have proved successful and sustainable. Such a low-key approach may not provide the excitement that architects are trained to crave. Neither, though, would it invite the failure and public distaste that constant experimentation with form and construction has wrought.[22]

Building democracy

The history of the various attempts to address urban problems has been paralleled by the development of political democracy and, to a large degree, there has been an interaction. At the time of their most rapid growth, the most rapid intensification of their problems, the cities were disenfranchised. The electoral franchise, in any case, covered a very small proportion of the population. Progressively, through the nineteenth century, the franchise was extended. As more and more people flocked to the industrial cities, so urban electoral representation increased. More representation meant more attention. So it was that, towards the end of the nineteenth century, the focus of central and local government was increasingly turned to addressing urban problems. By the end of the First World War, the cities were a power to be reckoned with, a power to be feared by government, which had to be seen to be positively seeking solutions to the continuing problems. In the event, the slump of the 1930s restricted spending power. Although considerable progress was made during this period, it was never enough.

The 1945 Labour Government, elected with a huge majority, owed its power base almost entirely to the industrial cities. It was no coincidence that the legislative machinery was put in place, the capital programmes scheduled, for the most determined assault yet on urban deprivation. For the following 20 years or more, the cities were at the height of their power. They received more attention and more investment, than ever before. But the State machine that was built to implement this programme grew too large, too unwieldy, and ran out of control. The individuals involved were, no doubt, sincere in their commitment to social improvement, but too many of them had little real understanding of urban communities. Some were carried away by the sheer scale of the exercise; wrong priorities were adopted, untried ideas were implemented too quickly and on too large a scale. Others were trapped by the weight of the bureaucratic machine. Nemesis was inevitable. It became clear that electoral power was not enough. What was needed was real democracy.

Community action was founded on the demand that urban communities should

241

have some say in the decisions that affected them. As it grew, it developed the principles of co-operation, of open debate, of participatory democracy. These became the cornerstones of community architecture. These ideas flourished in the pluralism of the 1970s, and for several years afterwards they continued to receive nourishment from some progressive urban local authorities. By the 1980s the energy of the community movement had pushed forward the frontiers of democracy. But by then the cities had lost their electoral dominance. The population of what were the Victorian cities had become a minority and by the early 1990s probably accounted for a third or less of the electorate. Marx's dictum was reversed. No longer was the country subjected to the rule of the towns. Now the cities are subjected to the rule of the suburbs, the satellites and the largely gentrified countryside.

This was the power base of the Thatcher Government. Thatcherism openly eschewed consensus. It had no time for pluralism, preferring the purity of an exclusive ideology. Debate and dissent were not tolerated, even with the Conservative Party itself. All that mattered was the ruthless exercise of elective dictatorship in the single-minded pursuit of market dominance. The Conservative Government had no electoral interest in the cities: very few of its MPs held urban seats. It was openly hostile to urban local authorities and it set in train their slow death by a thousand cuts. Its one-dimensional concept of democracy left no room for participation and had little understanding of its nature, its purpose, or its potential benefits. As the urban movement pushed forward the frontiers of democracy, the government was resolutely pushing them back. With each election victory for the extra-urban majority, the power of the cities grew weaker.

What imperative could impel an unsympathetic government to apply itself seriously to the problems of urban deprivation? There were some. The growth of homelessness, and its very visible manifestation on the city streets, should have been enough to shame the government that had brought it about. The growth of crime and drug abuse in the cities could so easily spill over into the more tranquil suburbs. Fear of crime might motivate the new purveyors of Victorian values, just as fear of disease had activated their predecessors. Violent and repeated urban disorder focused international attention on the problems of Britain's cities. That, at least, did bring some response. The community movement offered positive solutions to these problems. Sometimes lip-service was paid to their efforts, or a facade of "consultation" erected. But, in the practical impact of government policy, the real lessons were ignored. At best, they were misunderstood.

Perhaps the cities would fare better under an alternative government, one that was based on urban representation and a better understanding of the problems. That, however, is by no means sure. Certainly there are strands within the Labour Party and the Liberal Democrats that have sponsored co-operation, participatory democracy and decentralization. On the other hand, both parties have embraced the ideology of the market, although perhaps not to the exclusion of all else. More importantly, the prime objective of the Opposition is the achievement of central power. It is now a fact of social geography that no government can come to office on the strength of the urban power base alone. This means that a part, at least, of the suburban and ex-urban majority must be convinced of the case for redeeming the inner cities. The negative case is made in the need for pacification and the restoration of social order.

The positive case lies in the tremendous potential of the inner cities. There are opportunities for development that would free the pressure on other areas. Regenerating the inner urban economies would not only reduce the burden of the benefits budget and the social damage of unemployment, it would create a positive contribution to the national wealth. There is need for more investment in housing, education, training and employment. Properly directed, such investment would quickly repay itself in reduced crime and social costs. Community action has generated new forms, new structures through which the energies of people can be positively harnessed, through which they can participate in developing and managing their own facilities, and, through participation, they can increase their achievements, their skills and their social wellbeing. Community architecture, through the physical realization of such initiatives, has shown how the urban environment can be regenerated in a sensitive, democratic and sustainable way. Despite serious setbacks, these achievements remain a blueprint for the future, a model for a more enlightened age.

References

1. "Vandal gangs force out Housing Trust", *The Guardian* (5 October 1992).
2. "For rich read poor in 1993", *The Observer* (2 February 1993); and *An English estate* – a film directed by Hugh Kelly for *Critical Eye*, shown on Channel 4 on 22 October 1992
3. David Hare, "Chronicle of a defeat foretold", *The Guardian* (7 October 1993).
4. Gordon Burn, "A Moss Side story", *The Observer* (7 March 1993).
5. Lesley Gerard, "Tensions of a city looking over its shoulder" *The Observer* (9 January 1994).
6. "Shelter appeal for 'forgotten homeless' ", *The Guardian* (7 December 1993).
7. "No money, no jobs, no future, no point", *The Observer* (5 October 1993).
8. "Poorest families' income fell 14% under Thatcher", *The Guardian* (1 July 1993).
9. Figures drawn from government statistics by Frank Field MP, Chair of House of Commons Select Committee on Social Security; reported in *The Observer* (2 January 1994).
10. Report of address by Professor Brian Robson to Association of Metropolitan Authorities "Future of Cities" conference, *Planning Week* (30 September 1993), 11.
11. Figures provided by Shelter.
12. A figure quoted by Shelter, the RIBA Housing Group and the RICS.
13. Reported in *The Guardian* (10 September 1993).
14. Colin Ward, *When we build again - lets have housing that works!* (London: Pluto Press, 1985), 76; gives an account of the survey by Graham Bennet & Stuart Rutherford.
15. This view is supported by research by David Dickinson of Cambridge University, reported in *The Guardian* (7 January 1994).
16. As in St Paul's Community Education Project in Balsall Heath, Birmingham; see *Radical urban solutions – urban renaissance for city schools and communities*, Dick Atkinson (London: Cassell, 1994).
17. Nicholas Taylor, *The village in the city* (London: Temple Smith, 1973).
18. Colin Ward op. cit., 115.
19. Development of these arguments can be found in *Cities are good for us – the case for higher densities, friendly streets, local shops and public transport*, P. Harley Sherlock (London: Transport 2000, 1990); and *Reviving the city – towards sustainable urban development*, Tim Elkin & Duncan McLaren, with Meyer Hillman (London: Friends of the Earth, with the Policy Studies Institute, 1991).
20. Elizabeth Denby, *Europe rehoused* (London: George Allen & Unwin, 1938), 259-60.
21. Elizabeth Denby, ibid., 263-4.
22. Some recognition of this approach has now entered European public policy; see Commission of the European Communities Green Paper on the Urban Environment (Brussels: EUR 12902 EN 1990).

FURTHER READING

Full sources of information and corroboration are given in the notes at the end of each chapter. The following are recommended as particularly valuable or interesting reading for those wishing to explore the subject further. The texts are divided into three sections: historical and cultural background, participatory design, and organization and funding of community projects.

Historical and cultural background

John Burnett, *A social history of housing,* 1815–1985 Second edition (London: Routledge, 1986)   A key work on the organization and development of housing both urban and rural. Limited information on design. Particularly good on the 19th and early 20th century.

Stefan Muthesius *The English terraced house* (New Haven and London: Yale University Press 1982)   Probably the best book on the design of English urban housing. Lavishly illustrated with drawings and photographs.

Peter Davey *Architecture of the Arts and Crafts movement – the search for Earthly paradise* (London: Architectural Press, 1980)   There are many books on individual Arts and Craft architects. This seems to be the only contemporary book which recounts the history and origins of the movement as a whole. Well illustrated.

William Morris *News from nowhere* (1890) (London: Routledge & Kegan Paul, 1970) Morris's political creed encapsulated in fictional form- a model society visited in a dream. Idealistic, like all utopias, but still inspirational.

Robert Tressell, *The ragged-trousered philanthropists* [*c.* 1906] (London: Grafton, 1965) The personal account of a painter and decorator. Tressell's analysis of the way the system of competitive tendering destroys craft skills, quality of work and job satisfaction has never been more relevant.

George Orwell *The road to Wigan Pier* [1937] (London: Penguin, 1989)   Orwell's account, in the form of a journal, of his travels through the cities of the north of England in 1936. A vivid picture of urban life during the great depression.

Elizabeth Denby *Europe re-housed* (London: George Allen & Unwin, 1938)   Denby's record of her journey through Europe in the early 1930s. Long out of print but written with such optimism and infectious enthusiasm that it is well worth tracking down.

Peter Blundell Jones *Hans Sharoun – a monograph* (London: Gordon Fraser, 1978) Ostensibly a biography of Sharoun; on the way, Blundell Jones provides a penetrating analysis of most of the design and social issues that were at the centre of the debate in the modern movement.

Michael Young & Peter Wilmot, *Family and kinship in East London* [1957] (London: Penguin 1962)   Seminal work which first defined social networks in inner urban communities and drew attention to the damage caused by their destruction through redevelopment and decentralization.

245

Participatory design

Richard Hatch (ed.), *The scope of social architecture* (New York: Van Nostrand Reinhold, 1984)   A collection of case studies of participatory projects from the USA, Latin America, Britain and Europe; contains valuable accounts, of many seminal projects, by their architects and others; lacks general analysis and perspective.

Brian Anson, *I'll fight you for it! Behind the struggle for Covent Garden* (London: Jonathan Cape, 1981)   Though coloured by his personal perspective, Brian Anson's insider's account of the fight to preserve Covent Garden presents a vivid picture of the very real conflicts involved in a community campaign.

Nick Wates & Charles Knevitt, *Community architecture – how people are creating their own environment* (London: Penguin, 1987)   The first synoptic account of community architecture in Britain; focuses heavily on the role of the Prince of Wales and concentrates generally on the self-help aspects of the movement; few illustrations.

Rod Hackney, *The good, the bad and the ugly – cities in crisis* (London: Frederick Muller, 1990)   Hackney's autobiographical account of his role in community architecture together with his views on design, urban regeneration and public policy.

Jon Broome, *The Segal method* (*The Architects' Journal* special issue, 5 November 1986)   Short, well illustrated and accessible account of Walter Segal's simple and highly compelling method of self-build house construction; reprints available from the Walter Segal Self Build Trust, London.

Alan McDonald, *The Weller way* (London: Faber & Faber, 1986)   The story of the Weller Street co-operators in their journey from condemned back-to-backs to newly built homes; written like a novel with the humour and human interest of Coronation Street.

Matrix, *Making space – women and the manmade environment* (London: Pluto Press, 1984)   Essays by members of Matrix Feminist Co-operative on aspects of design and user participation from women's perspective; focuses on housing.

Jeremy Seabrook, *The idea of neighbourhood – what local politics should be about* (London: Pluto Press, 1984)   Not about design, but very much about the basics of participation. Seabrook's reportage about the experiences and issues that led to decentralization in Walsall makes fascinating reading.

Colin Ward, *When we build again – lets have housing that works!* (London: Pluto Press, 1985)   An entertaining account of various small scale participatory approaches to housing provision; mainly British-based, but includes coverage of Third World squatter movements; short, easy to read, but no pictures.

Organization and funding of community projects

Setting up and funding a community project is a daunting task for those with limited experience. There is no single "how to" book to ease the path, but there are several publications that can help with various aspects of organization and funding.

Four publications offer useful basic guides to setting up, organizing and managing community groups and voluntary organizations; between them they cover such matters as legal structure, employer's obligations, insurances, accounting, as well as a range

246

of management structures and procedures:

National directory of community technical aid (Liverpool: Association of Community Technical Aid Centres, semi-annual)   A directory of ACTAC members; lists, by region, community technical aid organizations, together with practices and individuals specializing in providing design and development services to community organizations.

Duncan Forbes, Ruth Hayes, Jacki Reason, *Voluntary but not amateur – a guide to the law for voluntary organizations and community groups* (London: Voluntary Service Council, 1990)

Christine Holloway & Shirley Ohb, *Getting organised – a handbook for non statutory organizations* (London: National Council for Voluntary Organisations, 1985)

Sandy Adrondak, *Just about managing* (London: London Voluntary Service Council, 1992)

John Edginton & Susan Bates, *Legal structures for voluntary organisations* (London: National Council for Voluntary Organisations, 1984)

Directory of grant-making trusts (Charities Aid Foundation, annual)   The comprehensive guide to all trusts operating in the UK. Information is given about each one together with some guidance on their area of interest. Nevertheless, the *Directory* is not classified, and ploughing through it can be time-consuming and not very productive. One of the selective guides may prove more fruitful.

A guide to the major trusts, vol. 1, Andrew Farrow & Luke FitzHerbert (eds), vol. 2, Michael Eastwood, David Casson, Paul Brown (eds) (London: Directory of Social Change, annual)   Although charitable trusts dispense about £600 million in grants each year, most of this (about £550 million) is given by the top 300 trusts. Volume 1 lists these 300 and gives information on their interests; volume 2 lists 700 trusts, which give about £25 million. All the other trusts not listed in these two publications generally give very small grants.

Environmental grants – a guide to grants for the environment from government, companies and charitable trusts, Stephen Woollet (ed.) (London: Directory of Social Change, published annually)   This covers all matters relating to the environment but may help with sources of funding for some categories of community architecture project. Directory of Social Change publishes other focused guides including those covering regional grants in London and the West Midlands

A guide to company giving, Michael Eastwood (ed.) (London Directory of Social Change, published annually)   Commercial companies are said to give up to 3,000 million annually though it often seems hard to harness this to community architecture projects.

The central government grants guide, Anne-Marie Doulton (ed.) (London Directory of Social Change, published annually)   Despite seemingly incessant cuts, Government Grants are still the biggest single source of funding for community projects. The rules are sometimes complicated and seem to be constantly changing. This guide, regularly updated, sets out the current position.

Finally, there are two other major sources not covered by the notes above. First, the Housing Corporation has in the past funded Housing Co-operatives, specialist community Housing Associations and Self-Build Associations. Funding has become more restricted since the 1988 Housing Act, but is still available for some community housing. A range of information on various aspects of housing development and management is available from the Housing Corporation. Secondly, the European Union offers Structural and Regional Aid. Funds may be available for community projects from the European Social Fund (ESF) and the European Regional Development Fund (ERDF). Finance from both funds is subject to matching funding from central or local government. Community organizations cannot access them directly, but may be able to do so through local authorities. The procedures are said to be daunting. Information is provided in the booklet *Finance from Europe*, which is available free of charge from the European Commission Information Office, London.

INDEX